All About Orchids

All About Orchids

Charles Marden Fitch

All photographs by the author
unless otherwise credited

DOUBLEDAY & COMPANY, INC.
GARDEN CITY, N.Y.

*To my friends around the world, who build upon
their orchid interest a love for all.*

Library of Congress Cataloging in Publication Data

Fitch, Charles Marden.
   All about orchids.

   Bibliography: p.
   Includes index.
   1. Orchid culture. 2. Orchids. I. Title.
SB409.F57   635.9'3415
ISBN: 0-385-15848-3
Library of Congress Catalog Card Number 80–1806

Design by Jeanette Portelli

Note: The typeface of the captions in this volume—Times Roman italic—has
been selected for legibility and design considerations. Genus and species names
are in Times Roman.

9 8 7 6 5 4 3 2 1

Acknowledgments

CONGRATULATIONS AND THANKS to orchidists who have sent their prize orchids to pose for my camera at American Orchid Society judgings. Thank you to photographic assistants Anthony Jacques, Christopher Quinn, and Gary Roach who have helped with the Awards photography. Special appreciation to Dr. O. Wesley Davidson, Professor Emeritus of Rutgers University, and Harry C. Burnett, Plant Pathologist with the Florida Department of Agriculture, for their assistance in providing the latest information about solving orchid problems.

Thank you to Charles R. Long, Director of the Library at the New York Botanical Garden, and his staff, for making available the Garden's extensive collection of rare orchid literature. Continuing gratitude to orchidists around the world for your willingness to share orchid information, and your warm hospitality during my explorations in your countries.

C.M.F.

Contents

ACKNOWLEDGMENTS *v*

INTRODUCTION *xi*

1. THE BEAUTY OF ORCHIDS *1*
Basic Structure *2*
Growth Styles *3*
Increased Popularity *6*

2. BEGINNING YOUR COLLECTION *8*
Size of Plants *9*
Commercial Sizes *11*
What Orchids Cost *11*
Orchid Names *13*
Intergeneric Hybrids *13*
Duplication of Orchids *15*
Catalog Translation *15*
Compact and Miniature Species *17*
Fragrant Species *18*

3. TEMPERATURE AND HUMIDITY *19*
Microclimates *20*
Temperature Range *20*
Humidity Control *23*
Air Circulation *25*
Prolonging Orchids in Bloom *26*

4. SUNLIGHT AND ARTIFICIAL LIGHT *27*
Light Intensity *28*
Practical Application for Different Species *29*

Diffusing the Sun *30*
Fluorescent Lamps *32*
Light Gardens *34*

5. CONTAINERS AND SUPPORTS *37*
Clay Pots *37*
Plastic Pots *40*
Foam Plastic Containers *41*
Baskets *42*
Hangers *43*
Wooden Containers *45*
Wooden Slabs and Branches *45*
Tree Fern Slabs and Poles *47*

6. POTTING MATERIALS AND METHODS *48*
Potting Media *49*
Basic Mixes *58*
Preparing the Potting Medium *59*
Repotting *60*
Care After Potting *64*

7. WATERING AND FERTILIZING *65*
General Rules for Watering *65*
Fertilizers *66*
Timed Release Chemicals *70*
Organic Fertilizers *71*

8. ORCHIDS IN A WINDOW GARDEN *72*
Humidity *72*
Window Shelves *73*
Hanging Containers *73*
Shade *74*
Supplemental Lighting Sources *75*

9. GREENHOUSE ORCHID GROWING *77*
Basic Styles of Greenhouses *77*
Shading *79*
Humidity *79*
Ventilation *80*
Heat Conservation *82*
Air Conditioning *83*

10. OUTDOOR ORCHID CULTURE   *84*

Climate   *85*
Watering   *86*
Benches and Racks   *86*
Lath Houses   *88*
Terrestrials   *88*
Epiphytes   *89*
Other Outdoor Concerns   *90*

11. THE SIX MOST POPULAR ORCHID GENERA   *92*

Cattleya   *92*
Cymbidium   *95*
Dendrobium   *100*
Paphiopedilum   *103*
Phalaenopsis   *107*
Vanda   *112*

12. ORCHID GENERA: *ACINETA* TO *ZYGOPETALUM*   *117*

13. PROPAGATION TECHNIQUES   *185*

Backbulb Growth   *185*
Division   *186*
Propagation by Offsets   *193*
Flower Stem Plantlets   *195*
Cloning   *196*
Seed Production   *197*
Seed Sowing   *204*

14. KEEPING YOUR ORCHIDS HEALTHY   *209*

Grooming   *209*
Pseudobulb Care   *214*
Training Stems   *215*
Diseases   *216*
Rots on New Growth   *220*
Fungicides and Bactericides   *221*
Bud Blast   *223*
Insects and Other Small Pests   *224*
Pest Control   *227*
Mice, Rats   *229*
Care of Orchids While You're Away   *229*

15. FUN WITH ORCHIDS *233*

Orchids as Cut Flowers *234*
Decorating with Orchids *239*
Orchid Societies *241*
American Orchid Society Judging *241*
Local Show Judging *244*
World Orchid Conferences *244*
Photographing Orchids *245*
Other Hobbies for Orchidists *249*

16. SOURCES OF ORCHIDS AND SUPPLIES *251*

Shipments from Abroad *251*
Shipping Methods *253*
Source List *254*

APPENDIX *261*

Changes in Nomenclature *261*
Advanced Orchid Photography *262*
Official Hybrid Registration *262*
Orchid Periodicals *264*

GLOSSARY OF BOTANICAL TERMS *265*

BIBLIOGRAPHY *269*

INDEX *271*

Introduction

ORCHIDS ARE the world's most highly developed and prestigious plants to grow and own. Since the nineteenth century tropical orchids have grown in popularity with knowledgeable gardeners around the world. In the twentieth century there has been an increasing interest in easy, reliable, inexpensive methods to grow orchids, and scientific advancements in orchid culture have encouraged hybridizers to create thousands of superior hybrids.

Due to modern culture techniques and space age propagation procedures, anyone can grow beautiful orchids right in his or her own home. Even people of moderate means can now afford a collection featuring the best tropical orchids from around the world. This book contains all the basic instructions you'll need to successfully grow these exotic plants in a window garden, sunporch, or greenhouse.

For more than twenty-five years I have studied orchids around the world, from subtropical Florida to Latin America, Asia, Africa, and the South Pacific. By growing thousands of orchids under varied conditions I have learned how culture techniques practiced in your own home should match each species' original habitat. Incorporated into this book are my findings on practical, successful techniques to grow orchids under a variety of conditions and environments.

1. The Beauty of Orchids

WHAT MAKES ORCHIDS so special? Why are they different from more usual tropical houseplants? Horticulturally orchids are fascinating to grow because plants vary greatly in terms of the color, size, and shape of flowers, leaves, growth, and even fragrance. More than twenty-five thousand species are officially recognized. Add to this naturally large family thousands of man-made hybrids created in numerous genera each year and you have some idea of how many orchids are available for your pleasure.

Cymbidium *Tiger Tail 'Talisman Cove', a yellow-green orchid with red-dotted white lip and upright spikes.*

Botanically orchids are different from other ornamental flowering plants by being highly advanced and specialized in their life-styles. Many popular orchids are epiphytes, adapted for life in trees or on mossy rocks. A few grow on the ground as terrestrials. All orchids have complex flowers, much more advanced than in other plant families.

The intricate design of orchid flowers gives them their charm. In a collection that includes the six most popular genera—*Cattleya, Cymbidium, Dendrobium, Paphiopedilum, Phalaenopsis,* and *Vanda* (see Chapter 11)—each genus has a different flower form. By studying contrasts in flower form, color variations, and changes in plant growth among different species, you can discover an overwhelming variety of fascinating orchids for a comprehensive collection.

BASIC STRUCTURE

Botanical classification of orchids is based on flowers having three petals and three sepals. In many genera these parts are highly modified to form the complex flowers so characteristic of the orchid family. Cattleyas, for example, have one petal that forms a large colored lip. Paphiopedilums, the "Lady Slippers," evolved until a petal became a pouch.

The important parts of a typical Cattleya *flower are: L, the lip; S, the sepals; P, the petals; and C, the column formed by the fused stamen and pistils.*

The reproductive parts of orchid flowers are different from other plant families. Orchid pollen grains are massed together, not free or fluffy like the powder found in other flowers. On each orchid plant the female reproductive parts are fused to the male pollen clump (pollinia) in a solid waxy organ called the *column*. Part of the column is a sticky stigma on which pollen grains sprout an ovary-penetrating tube to complete fertilization. The joining of sperm and egg, to produce orchid seed, depends upon a specific creature to pollinate each species.

Some night-fragrant white or light-colored orchids are pollinated by nocturnal moths when the insects visit flowers to suck nectar. Other orchids depend on bees, flies, or hummingbirds for pollination. Hybridizers produce variations in flower form, color, and size of a plant by transferring pollen from the anther of one plant to the stigma of another plant. (See Chapter 13, "Propagation Techniques.") Few orchids pollinate their own flowers, fortunately for us, since pollinated blooms quickly fade.

GROWTH STYLES

There are different potting and propagation methods for orchids, depending on their growth style.

In the case of *sympodial* orchids, each new growth develops from a bud at the base of the previous year's stem. The active new growth is called a *lead* and the bud from which it develops is called an *eye*. Cattleyas, brassavolas, dendrobiums, and cymbidiums are some of the popular orchids with a sympodial habit.

The other style of growth is called *monopodial*. Monopodial orchids, such as phalaenopsis and vandas, grow taller each year, producing flowers on mature plants from between the single stem and upper leaves. These orchids seldom branch, but some sprout offsets at the base (as seen in vandas and angraecums) or from flower spikes (as in phalaenopsis).

Besides the monopodial and sympodial variations, orchid species differ in rooting habits. Some orchids are ground-dwelling *terrestrials,* such as paphiopedilums, adapted to rooting in humus, moss, or well-drained soil on the ground. Such terrestrial species thrive in moisture-retaining potting mixtures of humus, peat moss, charcoal, sand, and similar ingredients.

Other orchids, such as cattleyas, are *epiphytes,* adapted to life on tree branches, rocks, or even fence posts in settled areas. Epiphytic orchids thrive when potted in mixtures of tree bark such as fir or redwood, often with the addition of coarse perlite, tree fern, or rough peat moss. Epiphytes also can grow on slabs of cork bark, tree fern logs, or even in baskets and pots with only gravel, lava rock, or charcoal, as long as they are fertilized regularly. All orchids in cultivation must receive bright light and mineral nutrition in some form. No orchid can survive on air and water alone, nor are orchids parasites, although the epiphytes usually do live upon other plants.

The division between terrestrial and epiphytic orchids is not always clear-cut. Even a single species may be found as an epiphyte in one moist region while in another microhabitat where moisture is scarce it may thrive as a terrestrial. Within a genus, such as *Cymbidium,* some species are commonly found as terrestrials, others as epiphytes. *Lithophytes* are orchids commonly found on rocks where they usually live in shallow accumulations of humus, but these same species may also be encountered as tree-dwelling epiphytes. Fortunately, the popular cultivated orchids adapt to various potting mixtures when other cultural factors are favorable.

Hardy epiphytic Shomburgkia *orchids dominate this tree branch in Nicaragua.*

FAVORITE ORCHID GENERA AND THEIR BASIC CHARACTERISTICS

Genus	Habit	Height	Flowers	Temperature Preference
Brassavola	epiphytic	6" to 2'	Night fragrant, white to yellow	Intermediate
Cattleya	epiphytic	6" to 3'	Small to large, white, lavender, yellow, blends	Intermediate to Warm
Cymbidium	terrestrial	12" to 3'	Sprays, all colors but blue	Cool to Intermediate
Dendrobium	epiphytic	2" to 4'	Sprays, lavender, yellow, white, and blends	Intermediate to Warm
Epidendrum	epiphytic, a few terrestrial	3" to 4'	Short to long sprays, white, red, yellow, green, brown, pink, and blends	Cool to Warm; most are Intermediate Preference
Laelia	epiphytic	4" to 3'	Short sprays, lavender, white with colored lip, red, orange, yellow	Cool to Warm; most are Intermediate Preference
Odontoglossum	epiphytic	6" to 3'	Arching sprays, white, yellow, brown	Cool to Intermediate
Oncidium	epiphytic	2" to 2'	Arching sprays, small, yellow, brown, pink, and blends	Intermediate; a few species are Cool Preference
Paphiopedilum	terrestrial	4" to 3'	Upright, Lady Slipper shape, white, yellow, brown, green, maroon, blends	Cool to Warm
Phalaenopsis	epiphytic	3" to 2'	Sprays, white, pink, yellow, peach, blends	Intermediate to Warm
Vanda	epiphytic, a few semi-terrestrial	1' to 4'	Upright to arching sprays, yellow, pink, blue, purple, brown, blends	Intermediate to Warm

INCREASED POPULARITY

Tropical orchids were first grown in greenhouses by wealthy European collectors, mainly Englishmen who began receiving new species from plant hunters around the end of the eighteenth century. Interest in exotic plants increased, prices soared, and although many gardeners gave the orchids too much heat and moisture, enough species survived to encourage further exploration.

Orchids as cut flowers are a multimillion-dollar crop for Thailand. This woman is packing freshly picked dendrobiums for air export around the world.

By the 1840s, thousands of showy orchids were being imported from South America and some from tropical Asia and Africa. These species at first went only to wealthy people who sponsored their own hackers or field orchid hunters. Fortunately a few knowledgeable gardeners discovered that many species did much better with less heat and confinement than had been used in the early days of orchid growing.

Gradually orchids became easier to obtain. Orchid auctions brought exorbitant prices for some unusual varieties but many species became common enough for people of moderate means to afford.

While the United States was engaged in the Civil War, Europeans were making progress in orchid culture. By the end of the nineteenth century several excellent English orchid books had been written, which encouraged orchid growing as a popular hobby and which caught the interest of some wealthy people in the United States. Since then, growing orchids as a hobby has become increasingly popular throughout this country.

Nonetheless, orchids are still regarded as unusual, prestigious plants to grow and own. They are not mass-marketed like African violets, foliage plants, or indoor succulents. No national company has yet developed a marketing plan to offer blooming orchids in supermarkets or garden centers all over the country. Gardeners who want to find orchids must do a little hunting and also search around for up-to-date information about growing methods. The results—exquisite orchid plants that you can grow at home—are definitely worth the effort.

2. Beginning Your Collection

WHERE DOES ONE buy the best orchids? Healthy well-grown orchids are offered by numerous mail-order nurseries and local growers around the world. In tropical countries orchids are sold at outdoors markets, from the backs of carts or trucks, and in garden centers. You can also locate excellent plants at private greenhouses where the owner sells a few orchids to help support a hobby. Some growers offer "plant-a-month" plans in which you can receive a ready-to-bloom orchid each month of the year.

If you live near a commercial nursery, go for a visit every month or two to consider an orchid you admire. Most professional orchid growers welcome visitors to their nursery and are prepared to ship plants to customers in many countries. By visiting local orchid growers, you'll have a chance to study firsthand different genera and new hybrids. After a year or two of buying plants in bloom, you'll have a custom-made collection that always has flowers.

Often botanical gardens have a collection of orchids; look over the flowering plants before making up your mind about what kinds you'd like to grow. Or, to observe an abundance of superior orchids, attend an orchid show. The American Orchid Society *Bulletin* and similar publications in other countries list orchid show dates. Some local societies hold regional shows once or twice a year.

By consulting Chapters 11 and 12 in this book (which provide detailed information about orchid genera and species) and by looking through catalogs offered by commercial growers, you can make a list of the orchid types you're interested in. The larger orchid catalogs often include a brief culture note regarding genera they offer, a helpful feature when you are trying to match the plants you'd like to grow with the amount of space, light, etc. in your home or greenhouse. For example, avoid buying selections marked as Cool Growers if they will be kept in a warm environment.

SIZE OF PLANTS

Before ordering orchid plants, you should study the growth habit of those plants with flowers you admire. Color photographs of flowers seldom give one any idea of the mature plant's size. Even well-written catalogs do not always provide plant size in the descriptions. Whereas people who live in the tropics can start an orchid collection with tall-growing vanda or dendrobium plants, those people who must keep orchids under cover in temperate climates usually select more moderately sized plants.

If you don't have unlimited space, it is wise to collect orchids whose height at maturity is under 3 feet. People with indoor light gardens will look for even shorter sorts. Many vandas and some of the strikingly beautiful dendrobiums that are very popular in the tropics reach 4 to 5 feet in height. Choose orchids appropriate to the space and conditions you have available.

Cattleya *Small World, a dwarf yellow-flowered hybrid, is a cross between* C. aclandiae *and* C. luteola.

If you can afford to purchase mature flowering-sized orchids, you should do so. These plants will be more tolerant of culture variations than younger plants or recently collected species. However, if you prefer not to spend the price of fully mature plants, buy seedlings or mericlone plantlets. These smaller plants may need two to five years of good care before flowering but they are less costly than mature orchids of comparable quality.

Buds of Potinara *Mariachi, an orange-colored hybrid, push from a sheath (common in cattleya hybrids), which opens to make room for flowers.*

Avoid buying small seedlings in community pots (which are usually shallow and hold ten to thirty seedlings), or pots smaller than 3 inches, if you are just starting to grow orchids. Learn about orchid plants with well-grown established specimens before trying more delicate seedlings. Once you have mastered the watering techniques for orchids, and are sure that your environment is suitable, then you might even enjoy growing orchids from the flask stage.

COMMERCIAL SIZES

Orchids in catalogs are offered by two different measuring systems. One method refers to the size of the pot in which the plant is growing. Since one nursery may have a 3-inch-tall cattleya in a 4-inch pot while another grower has a 7-inch-tall cattleya in a 4-inch container, the pot size measuring system is not precise, only general. Some growers clearly state in their catalogs what you may expect in various pot sizes.

The second measuring system refers to the actual plant size. This system is often used for monopodial genera which grow tall or wide faster than they fill a pot. For example, phalaenopsis hybrids are frequently sold by the inch, measuring across the seedling leaves. One then selects the seedling in the desired size and pays accordingly. Paphiopedilums and vandas may be sold according to their height. Cymbidium seedlings are frequently offered as one or two pseudobulbs (swollen, water-storing stems) plus active growth. Flowering-sized cattleyas are usually listed by the pot size and a minimum number of pseudobulbs.

WHAT ORCHIDS COST

Mature plants of popular large-flowered species currently sell for about $10 to $20. Imported jungle-collected species sell for several dollars less but one must wait until they have new roots and have grown for a season before you can expect flowers. Smaller flowered species, often called *botanicals,* are offered ready-to-bloom (called "established" in orchid circles) by some growers for $5 to $10 each.

The cost of hybrids offered in orchid catalogs ranges from several dollars for small seedlings to $50 or more for fully mature plants of good quality. Mericlone plantlets (excellent clones reproduced by tissue culture), which often receive awards from orchid societies, now sell for the price of seedlings. Before tissue culture was used, divisions of superior orchids, selected for good color, size, shape, and similar attributes, sold for hundreds of dollars. Now the modern technique of meristem propagation can produce thousands of identical plants and the price therefore drops to a level we all can afford.

Some outstanding orchid clones are not meristemed by their commercial owners but are propagated by dividing mature plants. Orchid connoisseurs often add expensive clones to their collections. In some cases, such a purchase may be considered an investment, but it is more practical to enjoy the orchids for their beauty, or the prestige of owning something exquisite and rare. Currently, costly orchids include a few rare species such as *Paphiopedilum elliottianum,* listed by one orchid supplier at $1,250, and the rare *Paph. volonteanum,* priced at $10,000.

Some cultivated hybrids, selected for outstanding quality, sell for hundreds of dollars. Consult a number of recent catalogs to determine which plants are in the price range you prefer.

Dwarf Ascocenda *Sauvanee 'Talisman Cove' came from Thailand as a seedling. Quality parents almost guaranteed that this plant would produce these perfectly shaped pink flowers with brown markings.*

Subjective Beauty Orchids, unlike gold and diamonds, have no set international value. There are general price ranges for orchids of various sizes and qualities, on up to about $500 for a sturdy, blooming specimen. Beyond that price, the value is strictly subjective. What a neighbor might pay a high price for might not appeal to you at all; yet your favorite orchid might be priceless to you, although listed as one of the least expensive orchids in a catalog.

Bargains Orchid bargains occur frequently in the special sales offered by commercial growers. Several species specialists give at least 20 per cent off list prices during summer sales. Other dealers offer good discounts on seasonal specials, usually advertised in the orchid publications and by mailings to previous customers. Some local orchid groups have plant sales tables where members offer extra orchids at reasonable prices.

The best bargain of all is to trade your extra plants with another orchidist who has plants that you want. Buying hybrid seedlings of good parentage is another way to get good-quality orchids at low prices. (Remember that seedlings may turn out to have rather ordinary flowers, but will need two to six years before they flower in any event.) Mericlone plantlets are often a good buy since you are sure of what the mature plant will produce.

ORCHID NAMES

Species are named according to a standard international system. Each type has a genus and species name. Printed matter lists the genus first, with an initial capital letter, followed by the species in lower case. The genus and species names are always used together—for example, *Laelia flava*.

Individual clones of species and hybrids are given a clone name which is put in single quotes, with each word having an initial capital. Thus, *Oncidium* Star Wars 'Palolo' is distinguished from all other clones of this cross by the fancy name 'Palolo'. Botanists also identify varieties of species that differ from the standard type by using a variety name. For example, a white variety of the normally purple *Cattleya skinneri* will be called variety *alba*. Variations occurring only in cultivation are called *cultivars,* distinguished by having clone names in single quotes, as in *Rhynchostylis gigantea* 'Pride of Thailand'.

Botanical names are printed in italics for species and genera. Cultivar names and those for man-made hybrids are printed in standard type with initial capital letters. The better orchid catalogs follow this code, or mention how their publication differs from the international standard. Orchid genera names have accepted abbreviations which are often used in catalogs. *Ascocentrum* is abbreviated *Asctm.* and *Cattleya* becomes *C.*

INTERGENERIC HYBRIDS

Hybrids between different genera are common in the orchid family. In contrast to most other ornamental flowering plants, different orchid genera are sexually compatible, easily producing mixed offspring. Sometimes different species cross in the wild, and rarely an intergeneric hybrid may be found in a tropical habitat, but most crosses between genera are man-made hybrids.

Crosses of *Cattleya* with compatible genera such as *Brassavola, Laelia,* and *Sophronitis* are very popular. Each of these created genera has a different name. *Cattleya* plus *Brassavola* creates *Brassocattleya.* Add *Laelia* and one gets *Brassolaeliocattleya,* abbreviated *Blc.* in writing. Add *Sophronitis* to *Blc.* and *Potinara* is created—a charming, usually compact man-made genus abbreviated *Pot.*

Hybrids between various genera are so popular that several times each year an entirely new combination occurs, resulting in still another new genus name. Sometimes the new genus is named for the genera involved, as in *Ascocenda,* a rewarding combination of *Ascocentrum* with *Vanda.* Other times the new genus is named to honor a person, as in *Goodaleara* (*Gdlra.*), a combination of five genera named in honor of W. W. Goodale Moir, a famous orchid breeder who has made some of our most unusual intergeneric hybrids. *Goodaleara* combines *Brassia, Cochlioda, Miltonia, Odontoglossum,* and *Oncidium.*

Colmanara *Moon Gold* (Mtdm. *Aztec Gold* X Odm. *Yukon Harbor*) *is a modern multi-generic hybrid with flowers on an arching spray.*

DUPLICATION OF ORCHIDS

When you admire an orchid flower and wish to obtain a plant that will produce the same bloom, be sure to make a note of the plant's full name. Giving a hybrid name, such as *Cymbidium* Showgirl, is not enough because you will not have specified a selected color form of this cross. Since each of the thousands of seedlings resulting from a seedpod will differ in flower form and color slightly, one must have a more specific form of identification.

The *clone name* identifies a single seed-grown individual and all vegetative propagations from that single clone. Therefore, orchid growers give their special clones fancy names in single quotes to identify them. *Cymbidium* Showgirl 'Malibu' has white flowers with clear red lips; clone 'Glamor Jane' has a more spotted lip.

One can be sure to obtain an almost identical flower just by obtaining the same species of an orchid, but even pure species can vary in color or form. To duplicate a specific clone one must make propagations by vegetative means, such as division or tissue culture. Seed-grown orchids, especially hybrids, differ from their parents.

Something to look for in catalogs are extra-fine forms of pure species. Growers cross these with other good plants of the same species, or self-pollinate the superior clone. The resulting seedlings usually produce flowers equal to or better than the select parents, almost always superior to randomly selected jungle plants.

Crossing hybrids produces seedlings with a wide variation of flower form and color. One of the pleasures of orchid growing is the anticipation of waiting for seedlings to produce their first flowers. After a few years of enjoying orchids, you will be able to make reasonable predictions regarding the hybrids produced from various parents.

Search through catalogs or commercial greenhouses to find crosses that incorporate clones you like. Often you can obtain a seedling for $5 to $10 from parents that sell for hundreds of dollars. If you do not like to gamble with seedlings, choose mericlones that will produce flowers identical to the donor clones, barring the very rare mutation.

CATALOG TRANSLATION

The best orchid catalogs show the full parentage of plants, plus precise descriptions or predictions. To understand a typical listing, keep in mind the orchid nomenclature mentioned earlier.

For example, *Blc.* Norman's Bay 'Hercules', FCC/RHS, JC/AOS (*Lc.* Ishtar X *Bc.* Hartland) 6″, $64.50, tells you the following: The offered orchid is a select awarded clone of *Brassolaeliocattleya* named Norman's

Bay. The specific clone 'Hercules' has been given a First Class Certificate (FCC) by the Royal Horticultural Society (RHS) and a Judges Certificate (JC) by the American Orchid Society (AOS). The parents, shown in parentheses, are *Laeliocattleya* Ishtar (the female or pod parent is always listed first) crossed with *Brassocattleya* Hartland. Plants offered in 6-inch pots are $64.50. The catalog will also mention flower color and usual flowering season.

Select seed-grown species may be listed with only a species name but the description or information in parentheses will tell you about the parentage. *Catasetum pileatum* (var. *aureum* 'Orchidglade', AM/AOS X 'Icy Green') tells us that seedlings were bred by crossing two select clones. The female parent, an awarded clone 'Orchidglade' of the botan-

Compact Paphiopedilum godefroyae *is a good species to grow under fluorescent lights.*

ical variety *aureum* (yellow flowers), was crossed with the clone 'Icy Green'.

Buying species grown from seed is preferable to purchasing jungle-collected orchids. Although one may occasionally encounter a superior clone from a random selection of jungle species, such an occurrence is rare unless thousands of individual clones are studied. Moreover, many species are now almost extinct in their tropical habitats. For conservation reasons, these rare orchids are usually protected by law. Commercial growers who offer seed-grown species are helping preserve rare orchids while offering us plants that are usually superior in quality and health.

COMPACT AND MINIATURE SPECIES

Within most genera one finds some especially compact species. Certain genera such as *Sophronitis* and *Stelis* are comprised mainly of miniature species. These compact to miniature orchids are good choices for light gardens and windowsill growing where space is limited but conditions are suitable. Some commercial catalogs include special sections for small-growing orchids, so check for these when searching for compact plants. Some of my favorites are:

Aerangis
Angraecum philippinense
  (botanically *Amesiella philippinense*)
Angcm. compactum, Angcm. magdalenae
Ascocentrum miniatum
Cirrhopetalum guttulatum
  (syn. *Bulbophyllum umbellatum*)
Dendrobium linguiforme
Gastrochilus species
Laelia pumila
Leptodes bicolor
Neofinetia falcata
  (botanically *Holcoglossum falcatum*)
Oncidium hybrids in equitant group
Onc. henekeni, Onc. onustum
Ornithocephalus species
Paphiopedilum bellatulum, Paph. concolor,
  Paph. godefroyae, Paph. niveum, and many primary hybrids with these
  species
Phalaenopsis cornu-cervi
Pleurothallis, most species

Rodriguezia
Saccolabium quisumbingii
Stelis species
Trichocentrum

FRAGRANT SPECIES

These selections are especially fragrant, in addition to having showy flowers and moderate mature height:

Aerangis species
Aerides odorata, Aer. Pramote
Angraecum species and hybrids
Brassavola species and hybrids
Catasetum species and hybrids
Cycnoches
Epidendrum (*Encyclia*) *atropurpureum,*
   Epi. fragrans, Epi. tampense
Neofinetia falcata
Oncidium lanceanum, Onc. ornithorhynchum
Rhynchostylis gigantea
Stanhopea species
Zygopetalum

In Chapter 4, "Sunlight and Artificial Light," I have included lists of orchids that thrive with very bright light, and others that tolerate low light situations.

3. Temperature and Humidity

WITH A SUITABLE environment of correct heat and adequate humidity your orchids are well on the way to healthy growth. Orchids are horticulturally divided into three groups, according to their temperature preferences. Traditionally temperatures given refer to the minimum temperature range at night. Light-hour temperatures should be 8° to 15° F. higher, which occurs naturally with the sun's warming rays or ballast heat from fluorescents in light gardens.

There are three general temperature classifications for orchids: Warm Preference, 65° to 70° F. (approximately 18.5° to 21.5° C.); Intermediate Preference, 55° to 65° F. (approximately 12.5° to 18.5° C.); and Cool Preference, 45° to 55° F. (approximately 7.5° to 12.5° C.).

An apartment becomes a suitable environment for an orchid collection when a humidifier and bright fluorescent lights are provided.

Most of the popular showy species will thrive in the intermediate range of temperatures and hybrids are usually even more adaptable. (See Chapters 11 and 12 which give temperature requirements for specific genera.)

Choose orchids that will thrive in the temperatures you are willing to provide. If you can heat a sunporch or greenhouse to 65–70°, then warm-preference orchids will do well. However, if you wish to economize on heating costs or prefer to keep orchids in a cool place, select those that thrive with 45–55° nights. By matching particular plants with proper environmental conditions, you will have success with your collection.

MICROCLIMATES

In your home or greenhouse there may already be one or more areas that are warmer or cooler than most of the other space. These microclimates are useful to know about because by using these temperature variations your collection can include orchids from different temperature preference groups.

For example, you may prefer to have mainly warm-growing types, such as phalaenopsis or vandas, but also wish to grow a few cool-preference species, such as cymbidiums or miltonias. If you locate a microclimate—perhaps a cool sunny window or a corner of the greenhouse away from the heater—you can put the cool-preference orchids there, while warm-growing types thrive elsewhere.

Keep in mind that in a light garden the top tiers are warmest because hot air rises. In a sunporch or greenhouse the outside sections may be several degrees cooler at night than the inside portions.

By hanging plastic curtains or partitions near home windows or outside greenhouse walls you can form microclimates that are cooler at night than other sections. To check high and low temperatures in any given environment, use a maximum-minimum thermometer. This instrument registers both the highest and lowest temperatures where it is placed. You can reset the gauges by using the small magnet supplied with the thermometer or with a hard shake of the wrist.

TEMPERATURE RANGE

In their tropical habitats orchid species experience a difference in temperatures during the day and at night. Usually the sun warms the plants during daylight hours; then temperatures cool naturally at night. In rain forests or shady sea-level areas, the temperature differences may be slight, while in dry regions of Central America or in the mountains of Asia the difference may be 15 or more degrees F. Orchids grown indoors will do best if given similar variations between day and night temperatures.

*The maximum-minimum thermometer at the
right shows a temperature range from 62°
to 82° F. The thermometer at the left shows a
range from 62° to 74° F.*

Fortunately, the species joined together in many hybrids have varied
temperature preferences. Offspring with such mixed parentage usually can
adapt to a considerable range of minimum night temperatures. A cross
between a cool-growing *Odontoglossum* and a warm-growing *Aspasia*
produces *Aspoglossum,* a man-made genus that will grow with a 55° to
68° F. night range and produce good-quality flowers.

By crossing cool-preference, large-flowered cymbidiums with small-
flowered, warm-growing species, a new hybrid type called "miniatures"
was created that grow and flower under cool to intermediate temperatures. The large-growing cymbidiums have big long-lasting flowers but
need six to ten weeks of 50° to 55° F. nights or they will not bloom. The
miniature cymbidiums flower easily with 60° to 68° F. nights but will do
well with night temperatures in the 50s.

Some pure species and hybrids directly derived from similar species
may need a period of cool nights in order to bloom satisfactorily. The
large cymbidiums are one example. *Dendrobium nobile* hybrids must

High humidity, fresh air, and bright light provide an excellent envi-
ronment for these Ascocendas, Dendrobiums, and Rhynchostylis on
an outdoor porch over a Bangkok canal.

have a similar cool period. Although these orchids may thrive with warm nights while making their new growth, they need nights in the 50s to initiate flower buds. When *Dendrobium nobile* has warm nights after its pseudobulbs have completed their growth, the plants develop offsets rather than flowers. If a species needs such a cool rest period to bloom, I have noted this in Chapters 11 and 12.

Night temperatures on the warm side, in any of the three temperature preference groups, will encourage growth. Seedlings in any genus will do better with the warm end of the genus preference range. For example, although mature *Phalaenopsis* will accept night temperatures as cool as 55° F., they will grow and bloom with greater abandon with 68° to 70° F. nights, provided that night temperatures drop into the low 60s in the fall in order to encourage the initiation of flower spikes.

Vanda hybrids will also accept 55° to 60° F. nights, but do better in the 65° to 70° range. When nights are kept on the warm side, daytime light must be bright enough for sturdy growth. High night temperatures with low intensity light during the day encourage weak growth and poor-quality flowers. Keeping temperature, light, and humidity in correct balance is the way to grow healthy orchids.

HUMIDITY CONTROL

Warm air holds more moisture than cool air, so relative humidity usually decreases as temperatures rise. It is important to provide a minimum of 50 per cent relative humidity for orchids. A few deciduous types, such as catasetums, can survive lower humidity when they are leafless, as can some species from dry regions. However, for maximum flexibility in growing healthy plants, maintain a humidity between 50 and 60 per cent around the orchids. Hygrometers to accurately measure relative humidity are offered in orchid catalogs. (See the "Source List" in Chapter 16.)

Water on a plant's roots is not a substitute for adequate humidity. Even with sufficient water in the potting mix, a growing orchid will not thrive in an environment with 20 per cent relative humidity. You can furnish humidity by growing orchids above trays of water, moist gravel, or in an area where moist air will remain, such as an enclosed sunporch with a damp brick floor or in a damp basement light garden.

If these techniques are not enough to maintain a 50 per cent relative humidity, you may need to obtain a humidifier.

Inside a basement greenhouse, wire benches, with water trays below, offer orchids good air circulation and humidity. A thermostat (top) controls the minimum night temperature, and a hygrometer (center) shows 71 per cent relative humidity.

Humidifiers Small humidifiers designed for home use must be filled manually. Although inexpensive and portable, these are only practical for use in a small area or where only a slight increase in humidity is needed. Larger units are more efficient but may require filling by hand. The most efficient types, and those needing the least care, are attached to the waterline.

I have two types in my greenhouses. One humidifier blows a fog out in all directions through holes in a plastic dome. After a few minutes, the mist evaporates into the air. The regular dome has 8 holes but some can be taped to restrict fog flow. A second sort of dome has one large opening which permits you to direct the fog flow.

Another humidifier I use is a floor model with a three-speed fan inside that I have set on low at all times. However, when the humidistat calls for moisture, the fan automatically goes to its top speed and a jet of fine mist spurts from the nozzle tip.

Both humidifiers need a free space in front of the mist exit, otherwise the moisture turns into liquid water, dripping off whatever it hits. Each machine is attached to the waterline with a thin copper pipe and was installed quickly with no extra plumbing. The electricity required comes from a standard wall outlet where the cord is plugged in. A humidistat mounted on the wall controls the wet cycle, calling for mist or fog when humidity drops below the desired level.

Fogging and Misting Besides using trays of water, wet gravel on the floor, and a humidifier to raise humidity, you can also provide a fine mist or fog manually by lightly wetting the leaves on bright mornings. This is a useful way to supplement humidity but should not be the only method you use. The fog or mist quickly evaporates when the air is dry.

It is best to restrict misting your orchids to sunny mornings because having foliage wet at night encourages fungus rots. In any case, relative humidity will rise at night as temperatures drop. In some areas like the South, orchid growers have problems with excessive humidity, but for most collectors the task is to maintain enough humidity for healthy growth of plants.

Recently potted orchids need high humidity to prevent damaging dehydration, until new roots can absorb enough water to keep the plants from shrinking. When all other methods fail, one can hold humidity directly around a plant by using clear plastic, but this is not recommended as a regular routine.

Species which require ultra-high humidity are best kept in large glass cases or terrariums. For example, "Jewel Orchids" such as ludisias and anoectochilus look best in a terrarium setting, especially when grown under lights. The consistently high humidity lets the glittering foliage expand to maximum size.

Ecuadorian boy shows Oncidium (*right*) *and* Anguloa *species he found growing on the eastern Andean slopes, about 1,200 meters in elevation.*

AIR CIRCULATION

Orchids require an exchange of air for sturdy growth. Epiphytic species usually do best when there is constant air circulation. I find that keeping a fan blowing in an orchid collection encourages healthy growth and lowers the frequency of fungus rot. The fan should be kept far enough away from the orchids and at a low speed so that a breeze gently ruffles the leaves.

Constantly moving air keeps temperatures more even, thus preventing pockets of damp cool air which fosters rot on plants. Some greenhouse heaters have built-in fans which work when heat is being produced. This forced air helps distribute the heat. If a heating system doesn't have a fan, it is wise to use an auxiliary fan to blow warm air around.

In a living-room growing area, a constantly rotating fan may not be necessary, but in places with relatively still air, such as basements, the orchids will do better with a fan nearby, constantly moving air around. Avoid strong gales of air directed at plants from close distances since this causes plant tissues to lose water faster than roots can replace it. Strive for a refreshing atmosphere rather than windy weather or tropical torpor.

PROLONGING ORCHIDS IN BLOOM

When orchids have flowers, you can help the blooms to last by keeping the plants in a slightly cool atmosphere. For example, you should give them night temperatures of 58° to 60° F. rather than 65° to 70° F. In a sunporch or greenhouse, place the orchids in bloom in a separate area, so that you can water them individually and make sure that their flowers are kept dry. Dry buds and blooms are much less likely to get fungus spots. This is especially important for genera with short-lived or thin flowers such as *Gongora*.

Flowers such as paphiopedilums that are likely to hold water should be shaken out if they are wet. If fungus does spot the flowers, spray the buds and unmarred blooms with a fine mist of Physan solution, ¾ teaspoon per gallon of water at room temperature. You should also increase the air circulation.

Orchids with many buds which open over a period of weeks, such as *Cymbidium, Paphiopedilum* multiflowered hybrids, and *Phalaenopsis,* must receive enough light for the buds to mature normally. This light can be dimmer than the amount of light required for growth, but still strong enough to preserve normal color in the flowers. In fact, green cymbidiums may not be true green in color unless the plants are shaded as they develop. Flowers developing in bright light often become blushed with red or yellow tones.

Plants with fully developed open flowers can be kept in dim light for one to two weeks with no harm. For example, a blooming cattleya or paphiopedilum may be kept on a prominent table or sideboard while it is in full flower. When the flowers fade, return the plant to diffuse light, and in a few days to its normal light intensity. If your collection is crowded, put active orchids in the brightest light; place those that are resting or have fully completed their growth cycle in dimmer places.

4. Sunlight and Artificial Light

BRIGHT LIGHT is a requirement for sturdy orchids. Sun is the most popular light source for growing orchids but orchid plants also thrive under combinations of sun and fluorescent lamps, or even entirely under fluorescent lamps. When selecting orchids to grow, match the kind of plants you choose with the light intensity you can provide them, so that they will grow and bloom normally.

Among the numerous popular orchid genera there are some plants, such as vandas, that need very intense light to grow well. Others, from the shadier habitats, thrive under diffuse light. Paphiopedilums and stanhopeas, for example, will bloom with the intensity needed for African violets. Still, when compared with other ornamental flowering houseplants, orchids bloom best with relatively strong light.

In their tropical habitats, epiphytic species often grow high in the trees where sun is intense. Some orchids from Central America and parts of

In a hot dry region of El Salvador, Epidendrum atropurpureum (*in boy's hand*), Brassavola nodosa, *and* Laelia rubescens *thrive on a tall tree's trunk.*

Asia live in deciduous trees. When tree leaves fall, these species are exposed to direct sun, often during a cooler dry season. Water-storing pseudobulbs and tropical dews help such orchids survive under these conditions.

Other orchids, adapted to live on the forest floor or under tangles of jungle vegetation, prosper with less intense light. However, the hot sun does break through overhead foliage to briefly light the orchids directly, but for only a few minutes in any given pattern.

In a home or greenhouse, direct sun through glass during warm months of spring into fall is usually too strong for orchids. Even plants that thrive outdoors in direct sun are subject to sunburn when glass concentrates the sun's rays and indoor temperatures rise. Greenhouses are shaded to soften the sun and open-weave curtains will protect plants inside home windows.

LIGHT INTENSITY

Some commercial growers measure light intensity with footcandle meters to obtain a precise measurement of light intensity. Although home orchid growers need not make such precise measurements to grow healthy

Light coming mainly from one direction caused this Potinara Neopolitan *to develop a leaning growth, but the light was strong enough for healthy flowers to develop.*

plants, there are similar methods that can be used to measure light intensity, such as with a standard photographic meter. For example, I have a meter with a footcandle table on the back that enables me to convert what the meter scale says into approximate footcandles.

The footcandle measurement is precise, but a species can thrive over a range of light intensity. Even commercial growers vary the light intensity they use for different genera. One grower may give cattleyas 2,000 footcandles while another grower provides 1,200 footcandles. The total environment, especially humidity and temperature, determines how much light an orchid will accept.

As the sun's intensity increases, the temperature also rises. By using cooling devices, greenhouse operators can keep orchids under very intense light without harmful effects. Naturally the relative humidity must be maintained at a high level (usually above 50 per cent) when maximum light is provided. In bright sun without humidity, orchids lose more moisture through their leaf pores than their roots can absorb. The result is stunted growth, shriveled plants, and yellow or burnt leaves. One interprets footcandle recommendations with this in mind.

Footcandle ranges for the most popular genera are:

Cattleya	1,200 to 2,000 fc
Cymbidium	2,000 to 4,000 fc
Dendrobium	1,500 to 3,000 fc
Paphiopedilum	800 to 1,000 fc
Phalaenopsis	1,000 to 2,000 fc
Vanda	3,000 to 4,000 fc

Outdoors in the tropics many vandas and dendrobiums will accept full sun, yet growers often provide some degree of shade.

PRACTICAL APPLICATION FOR DIFFERENT SPECIES

Observing your orchid plants is the best system for perfecting culture in each specific environment. A useful way to judge if the sun is bright enough for your plants is to observe shadows. Hold your hand about 6 inches away from a leaf. If the sun casts a sharp-edged shadow for more than a few minutes, the sun is too intense for medium to low light-preference orchids. A soft-edged shadow indicates ideal sun intensity. No shadow at all means that the sun is too weak for sturdy flowering growths. Orchids will grow with very little sun but they will hardly, if ever, bloom.

Here are some attractive orchids that need only diffuse light. Remember that although these thrive with diffuse sun, they will often accept rather strong fluorescent light. The fluorescent lamps are an even, cool source compared with the sun, which can easily scorch these orchids from the shade.

Anoectochilus	*Pleurothallis*
Gongora	*Polyrrhiza*
Masdevallia	*Stanhopea*
Paphiopedilum	*Stelis*

If you have a greenhouse or sunporch with strong direct sunlight, you can succeed with species that need intense light to bloom. Some good choices include:

Ascocentrum
Brassavola
Broughtonia
Dendrobium
Epidendrum radicans and *Encyclia* types,
     such as *E. atropurpureum*
Laelia dwarf types, such as *L. anceps, L. milleri*
Oncidium species with thick succulent foliage
Renanthera and its hybrids
Vandas, especially terete or round-leaf sorts

DIFFUSING THE SUN

Early morning and late afternoon sun (sunrise to about 10 A.M. and 5 P.M. to sunset) seldom causes even orchids with a low light tolerance to turn yellow or burn. However, the stronger midday sun must often be diffused.

In the home, sun coming through windows can be pleasantly diffused with frosted plastic sheeting. Diffusing material sold for photographic uses is efficient since it spreads light evenly while still permitting maximum brightness to shine through. Choose diffusing material with a white or neutral color, not green or blue. Plain frosted plastic sheeting and fine thin curtains will also do.

Another approach is to break up the sunrays so that only a limited quantity can come through the glass over a given period of time. By using bamboo slats, blinds, or lath, direct light can shine in on plants, but since the sun keeps moving, the rays only stay on a given area for a short while. (Lath is a standard shading used outdoors, sometimes combined with plastic screening called shade cloth.)

Special shade cloth designed to hold back specific percentages of sun can also be used to control the sun's rays. This plastic screen-like material is sold by greenhouse supply firms. In Hawaii, Thailand, Malaysia, and other tropical places where the sun is intense, great expanses of outdoor bench space are protected by such shade cloth so orchids receive maximum light for good-quality flowers but they never burn.

One brand of shade cloth is a polypropylene fabric which can be purchased in 74-inch-wide by 30-foot-long sections from some orchid growers. Cattleyas and other genera that thrive in bright light will prosper under the 53 per cent shade mesh. If the sun in your area is especially hot, a 60 or even 73 per cent shade weave is available. Some firms will sew a heavy hem and eyelets into the shade material for a slightly extra charge. This is especially useful for summer shade on greenhouses. When the sun gets less intense in the fall, one can easily take down the shade cloth.

In a greenhouse I diffuse sun by using frosted fiberglass over the glass roof. White greenhouse shading paint shades the sides where the sun enters directly. Many growers leave the glass clear in the winter, since the sun is less intense. Then they spray on shading paint as the light intensity increases in the spring. Finally, during warm summer months, several coats of white shading paint may be required.

A special diffusing solution for glass can be made with water-soluble latex paint (white) or even powdered household cleaning powder mixed to a thin paste and applied with a cloth or sponge pad. The proper greenhouse shade paint or other means of diffusing sun is best for long-term use.

Adjustable Venetian blinds protect orchids from the midday sun but permit less intense rays in the morning and late afternoon to reach the plants directly.

FLUORESCENT LAMPS

You can grow most orchids successfully in your home under strong fluorescent light. By choosing broad-spectrum lamps you will be providing the most useful type (color) of light for flowering plants. Even plain cool-white fluorescent lamps will provide enough light to grow orchids, but I find broad-spectrum fluorescents produce better flowering growths. Commercially available broad-spectrum tubes include Wide-Spectrum Gro-Lux, Vita-Lite, Verilux, and Agro-Lite.

The easy way to install fluorescent lights is with standard fixtures that hold two-pin-type lamps, available at hardware stores and mail-order firms. I use mainly 40-watt tubes. Larger industrial fixtures, and some models designed for commercial greenhouses, are efficient but not practical in the average home or moderately sized greenhouse.

Industrial-type Very High Discharge lamps produce an abundance of useful light but are noisy, give off more heat than home fixtures, and

Fixtures with eight broad-spectrum fluorescent tubes furnish adequate light for a collection of orchids and companion plants. Inverted pots enable shorter plants to get nearer to the light. Mirrors reflect the growing plants.

require professional installation. If you are planning an extensive indoor light garden room or a large greenhouse, consult a local electrical contractor to obtain the latest costs regarding installation fees and equipment for your particular needs.

My favorite fluorescent fixtures are made of aluminum, with a one-piece top. The single metal top keeps splashed water from getting inside. Fixtures with two 40-watt tubes are adequate for supplementing sunlight.

If your orchids rely totally on fluorescents for light, use fixtures with four or more lamps. For example, when orchids are grown in a light garden in a cellar or spare room in the home, you should provide them with high intensity light from four or more 40-watt tubes in order to ensure the best flowering. Less light means fewer flowers for many orchids.

My basement light gardens have two types of fixtures. One area holds a compact Flora-Cart with two tiers of growing space, each lit with four 40-watt tubes. A sturdy fiberglass tray holds moist gravel for added humidity. The area covered by each fixture is 48 by 20 inches. Since the lamps provide the brightest light at the center of the fixture, I put mature plants in the middle section. Seedlings and companion tropicals thrive toward both ends of the tubes. By keeping the lamps 3 to 6 inches above the orchids' foliage, I can provide sufficient light for many genera to grow and bloom.

Reflectors By using reflective surfaces around a light garden, one can get maximum use from each fixture. Some light fixtures come with built-in reflectors. To increase the efficiency of reflectors near the plants in my home, I paint nearby walls matte-white and sometimes use mirrors to reflect light back into the plants. Over some trays I place white wooden slats on which the pots rest. Trays are kept filled with water, thus increasing humidity, while the white surface bounces light into the leaves.

If you install plain fluorescent strip lights, with no built-in reflectors, provide a flat white surface or aluminum foil above the tubes for efficient light use. Dark surfaces absorb light and waste energy; light surfaces reflect light into the plants and use more of the light output from each fixture.

Combine Sun with Fluorescents In a greenhouse you can increase growing space by installing fluorescents under the benches and against a house wall in lean-to models. Even where a greenhouse has glass-to-ground construction, supplemental fluorescent light helps grow sturdier plants.

My own collection of orchids, at my home in southern New York, is in a temperate zone climate with warm summers and cold winters. Many days are cloudy but fluorescent lamps help the orchids continue sturdy growth. Even at bright picture windows I have fluorescents behind overhead valances. These lamps illuminate flowers at night and supplement the sun.

Laeliocattleya *Gold Digger, a deep-gold-flowered
compact hybrid with red lips, was grown under
a combination of broad-spectrum fluorescents
and morning sunshine.*

LIGHT GARDENS

Several commercially manufactured light gardens offer two, three, or four tiers of growing space. Tiered gardens may come in a plain aluminum color but this can be adjusted to fit your taste. You can apply a paint to metal surfaces, but leave the inside sections of all reflectors white.

Some aluminum fixtures have external surfaces that look like wood. Decorative fixtures are nice for light gardens located in living rooms or dens. Other modern light gardens look like sideboards or cabinets, but these designs seldom have more than two lamps inside, enough for displaying orchids but insufficient for total growth.

Tiered light gardens offer the convenience of a professionally designed unit ready to be plugged in. Many orchids can be grown in limited space on three to four tiers. The main disadvantage of commercially available tiered gardens is their limited range of height adjustment. When plants get too tall in a tiered garden, they must be grown elsewhere.

Unlike tiered gardens, single fixtures which hang from rafters or other overhead support can be made lower or higher easily by adjusting a link chain. Leave the chain long to hold lamps 3 to 4 inches above short seedlings, then take up slack chain to raise the lamps as the plants grow. Once orchids mature and begin to bloom, be sure to check carefully that the plants' flowers have not grown into the lamps. Phalaenopsis have fast-growing inflorescences (flower spikes) that can reach the lamps in a few days.

It is good to keep lamps close to the foliage for compact growth and for best blooming, but buds pushed against light bulbs will burn. Some orchids with long inflorescences may have to be moved out of smaller light gardens when spikes get too tall. An easy solution is to place plants on the floor right next to the light garden fixture where they can still receive light. Let the inflorescences continue to grow in the same direction, toward the lamps.

Once buds start to open, put the plant where it can be enjoyed, perhaps at a bright window or on a dining table where it will get diffuse light. Orchids with long arching inflorescences look best if kept where the light comes from the same direction in which the buds develop and the blooms open. If you change light direction by moving your plant or light fixture, the growing inflorescence will reorient the direction in which it grows. This phototropic response makes the spike crooked and interferes with symmetrical flower display.

Electrical Considerations Since light gardens will be subject to splashed water and high humidity, all plugs should be of the three-pin grounded type. The three-pin plug provides an electrical grounding to prevent dangerous shocks. Before installing an extensive light garden, check with an electrician to be sure your current wiring is adequate.

Older buildings may need new wiring for light gardens that require a lot of power. If you plan to have an electrician build a custom light garden, consider locating the fluorescent ballasts away from your plant shelves since the ballasts produce noise and heat.

On tiered light gardens, which come with wired fixtures, it is best to leave the ballasts alone. Ballasts produce a small amount of heat that is advantageous in cold weather. Therefore, the uppermost tiers will be warmer than the bottom shelf because heat from the lower ballasts will rise. Use this microclimate to grow seedlings in the top tiers and cool-preference orchids below. I find warmer top tiers useful places to sprout backbulbs, too.

Timers You can use an electric timer to control when fluorescent lights come on and how long they will glow. In my orchid collection I use grounded (three-prong plug) air conditioner timers. Each timer has a plaque listing how many watts it will control. Always use a timer that can accept slightly more wattage draw than you plan to use. The least expensive models accept up to 800 watts, more than enough for two or three fixtures of four 40-watt tubes each.

Fixtures designed for light gardens often have an electrical outlet where another lamp can be connected. By plugging another fixture into this outlet you can use a single timer to control more than one fixture.

Timers should be set to provide fourteen to eighteen hours of light over seedlings in order to encourage growth and early bloom of the orchids. Mature orchids should receive a maximum of fourteen hours of light. This reduction in light hours saves electricity and encourages blooming on orchids that flower best with short days. Some cattleya species, such as *Cattleya trianaei,* may not bloom if they are given continuous long days of twelve or more hours. Commercial growers carefully monitor the flowering times of their plants so that peak blooming occurs at times of maximum cut-flower demand.

If you have some mature cattleyas or phalaenopsis that refuse to bloom under days of fourteen or more hours, reduce the light hours to eleven or twelve for six to eight weeks each season, as growths near maturity. In *Phalaenopsis schillerana* and *Cattleya warscewiczii,* cool temperatures also encourage maximum bloom. Strive to give these species and their primary hybrids 50° to 55° F. nights during the short-day weeks.

Avoid buying hybrids described in catalogs as "light controllable," because they need short days to bloom well. The most popular orchids being grown today bloom easily with fourteen- to eighteen-hour days.

Seedlings mature one to three years sooner under fluorescents because they get 365 "sunny" days in which to grow each year. By giving them long days, up to eighteen hours, seedling orchids make amazing progress under broad-spectrum fluorescents. If you have a greenhouse for orchids, consider using fluorescents over seedlings to help them bloom sooner. Even small seedlings can accept bright fluorescent light without burning. Giving them a similar intensity with sun would be risking sunburn and too much heat.

Lamp Maintenance Fluorescents gradually lose brightness as they age. For top efficiency of electricity and maximum light output, change the tubes every year. This may be too expensive if you have several four-lamp fixtures, so you might change tubes in every other lamp. This means, in my own light garden, that most of my four-lamp fixtures have two tubes of twelve or more months' age and two tubes up to twelve months old.

Be sure to install tubes with the metal ends correctly aligned. Fluorescent lamp metal caps have a reference indentation or raised nub. This point should be directly opposite the lamp holder opening. Incorrectly inserted tubes may light but they burn out sooner than those that have been correctly seated.

5. Containers and Supports

MOST OF THE orchids in your collection will succeed in containers. A few of the smaller epiphytic orchids thrive on slabs of cork, tree fern, or various hardwood logs. Here are some recommendations for containers to grow different kinds of plants: sturdy clay pots for top-heavy species; plastic pots for species that must be kept evenly moist or small seedlings; slabs of cork for small epiphytic orchids that require very free air circulation; poles of tree fern for rambling epiphytes that are difficult to keep in a pot. Plants in pots and baskets are easy to place on benches, shelves, or tables in your home. Specimens in baskets can be hung from rafters, hooks, greenhouse pipes, or placed on inverted pots.

CLAY POTS

Clay containers are valuable for orchids that must dry out slightly at the roots between waterings, or for an annual rest period. This includes catasetums, cattleya types, and bulbous epidendrums. Since clay pots are heavier than most plastic containers, they are also the best choice for tall top-heavy orchids that might topple in lightweight plastic pots.

Unglazed clay evaporates moisture quickly, a healthy characteristic for

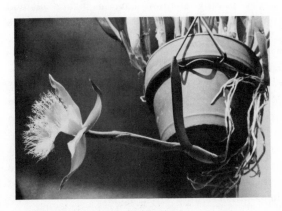

Brassavola digbyana, *in a clay pot supported by a metal pothanger, grew out of the bottom drainage hole and produced a flower.*

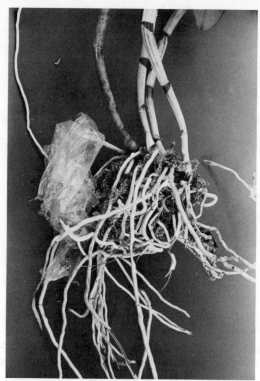

*When this cattleya hybrid grew over the edge
of its pot, a plastic bag with unmilled sphagnum
moss wired in front of the growth gave room
for new roots. Later repotting is easy since
the plant has a full root system intact.*

epiphytes which need free circulation of air around their roots. Clay pots
are also useful for terrestrial genera if you give them frequent attention
and prevent the complete drying of the potting mix. After a few months
of practice you can learn when the potting mix is dry by hitting the clay
pot with a ring or other hard object. Pots with wet mix make a thud
sound, while those with a dry potting medium have a higher pitched
sound. I use a long metal pot waterer as a tap to sound out the clay pots
as I'm watering my plants.

Potting Techniques Before using new clay pots, soak them in a solution of water overnight, then rinse them off again before use. Add 1
teaspoon of Physan per gallon of soak water to kill any harmful bacteria
and fungus spores. If the pots have been used, clean them first, then make
a stronger Physan solution of 2 teaspoons concentrate to each gallon of
water. A Clorox solution may also be used to kill harmful organisms on
used containers. Mix 1 part household bleach to 9 parts of water, soak the
containers for 10 minutes, then rinse and soak in plain water for at least
15 minutes. Before using the containers, rinse them again.

An alternative to using Physan or Clorox to kill disease organisms on used clay containers is to put the pots in the dishwasher or pour boiling water over the clay. Using uncleaned clay pots increases the chance that newly potted orchids will develop a disease or virus from the pots' previous occupants.

Orchids which grow ahead on rhizomes, such as cattleyas, should be given the most room in front of their active lead. At potting time, hold the oldest lead against the pot wall, thus giving maximum space in front of the new growth. Choose a container that gives room for two to three new pseudobulbs or mature growths. Plants with multiple leads growing in various directions are best positioned in the center of a pot. This gives room for the plant to expand in all directions, thus filling the container with multiple flowering growths.

Genera which grow taller each year, or lean forward only slightly, such as *Angraecum, Phalaenopsis,* and *Vanda,* should be centered in the container, with roots spreading in all directions. Rapidly growing monopodial genera with abundant thick roots along the stem can be better supported with a branch or tree fern pole set in the pot.

A slightly unwieldy growth of vine-like Epidendrum radicans *is controlled with a stake and plastic plant ties.*

Drainage Clay pots made for orchids have extra drainage and aeration slits. Clay containers made for terrestrial plants usually have a single hole in the bottom center of the pot. For all clay containers, place a curved section of clean broken pot over the center drainage hole. Add other large chunks of crock, or medium to large pieces of gravel, to form a ½- to 1-inch drainage layer. Then put in a few chunks of hardwood charcoal. On top of this drainage material, add an inch of potting mix, then the plant, followed by more potting mix around the plant's roots.

For terrestrials you may also add a thin layer of unmilled sphagnum moss over the drainage material before adding any potting mix. This moss keeps fine terrestrial potting mixtures from clogging the drainage area. In the case of epiphytes without pseudobulbs—phalaenopsis, for example—the unmilled sphagnum moss holds additional moisture. This is a good idea if your plants are in clay containers or baskets, but sphagnum moss is not usually required in plastic containers. (Chapter 6 discusses potting materials and mixtures in detail.)

PLASTIC POTS

Containers made from plastic vary greatly in quality. Some of the inexpensive plastic pots are so thin that they may even crack or break when one picks them up by the rim to move a potted plant. In contrast, some high-quality, more expensive plastic pots are tough and will accept a lot of handling without cracking or chipping.

Medium-weight plastic pots are suitable for growing orchids of many genera, especially seedlings, and they are used often by commercial

This display shows cattleya hybrids in various stages of growth, from flask (right) to fully mature plant (left). (Photo courtesy of Rod McLellan Co.)

growers. One must balance cost with projected use to choose a suitable container. For mature orchids that will be put on display when they are in bloom, I prefer the more expensive, high-quality plastic pots, which are also attractive and long lasting. Some containers look just like wood or ceramic clay although they are created from plastics.

If you plan to grow epiphytic orchids in plastic pots, it may be necessary to add extra holes in order for the plants' roots to get more air. Plastic pots with aeration slits up the sides will not require additional holes. However, plastic containers with only bottom drainage holes can be made more suitable by drilling extra holes, or by burning more holes in the pot with a soldering iron or a screwdriver that has been heated over a flame. In very dry regions these extra holes may not be required.

Do this work in a well-ventilated room or outside because the fumes from melted plastic should not be inhaled. With care this can be done even though an orchid is growing in the container.

Advantages Plastic pots are generally less expensive than clay pots, mainly because clay is heavy to ship and breaks easily. Plastic pots usually can be put in a dishwasher for cleaning, and the plastic does not absorb minerals from fertilizer or hard water. Old roots and dirt usually come off plastic easier than clay. Plastic containers are lighter in weight than clay, less expensive to ship, and less of a strain on hangers or supports. A row of plants in plastic pots is less of a strain on shelves or light garden carts than a similar row of orchids in clay containers.

Disadvantages Inexpensive plastic cracks and splits easily. Since smooth plastic does not evaporate moisture, the roots of a plant stay moist longer and get less air circulation. This is a disadvantage for most epiphytes but it can be modified by using a coarse potting mix and by burning extra holes in the pot for aeration. Some plastics melt when put in the dishwasher.

Drainage Material Use the same drainage material in plastic pots as recommended in the clay potting techniques. If you grow orchids on trays of moist gravel, add extra drainage material in the plastic pots, to ensure that the potting mix never sits in water. An inch of gravel plus a few chunks of hardwood charcoal in the bottom of plastic pots is sufficient.

FOAM PLASTIC CONTAINERS

Containers made of plastic foam are suitable for orchids. I grow both terrestrial and epiphytic genera in plastic foam pots and find that these lightweight containers are excellent. Foam, unlike smooth plastic, does permit air exchange, and it is unlikely to split or crack. However, foam containers are not sturdy enough for constant lifting at an angle or for heavy hangers attached to the pot which could crush or snap the foam. Plastic foam pots are available in white or terra-cotta color. Extra holes easily can be punched or burned into the container for aeration. In addition, foam pots can be safely cleaned in a dishwasher.

One slight disadvantage of foam containers for growing epiphytes is that the orchids' roots may grow very tightly onto the container and become difficult to remove at repotting time. However, orchids can stay in foam pots longer than smooth plastic pots before they need to be repotted. Since the foam permits air circulation through the pot's walls, the potting mix in a foam container (especially coarse tree fern or coconut fiber) lasts much longer than in a smooth plastic container. Epiphytic orchids should be repotted before the potting mix is totally decomposed. Rotted organic media hold too much moisture and encourage root rot.

BASKETS

Baskets are useful as containers for epiphytic orchids, especially those species that have arching or pendant inflorescences. A few of the miniature cymbidiums have strongly pendant spikes and are best grown in hanging pots or baskets. For example, the species *Cymbidium finlaysonianum* is an epiphyte with a strongly pendulous inflorescence and is best seen in a hanging position.

Although some people think that wooden baskets look best for orchids, the metal types are also useful when they are lined with sheet moss or coarse coconut fiber. Plastic baskets are useful when moisture should be maintained in the potting mix, such as for genera without pseudobulbs and for terrestrials.

Hanging containers are suitable for genera that normally grow in trees, such as epiphytes with long sturdy roots. I do not recommend placing paphiopedilums or terrestrial jewel orchids in such containers.

Aerial Roots Vandas and other genera such as *Ascocentrum* and *Rhynchostylis* form thick aerial roots. In tropical habitats these roots often hang free from tree branches, swaying in the air for 3 or 4 feet, receiving all the moisture and air needed by a growing epiphyte. In your home or in a greenhouse, these thick roots should not be forced into a container. However, since hanging roots all over an orchid collection can be a nuisance, you might want to reach a compromise between unrestrained freedom for roots and rot-producing total confinement.

Growing such plants in slat baskets is a useful method which produces healthy roots and floriferous plants. After roots get to be a few feet long, they can be gently turned around and around the basket or held out of

Aerides *Pramote is growing in a teakwood basket with tree fern and coconut fiber around its roots. Thick aerial roots grow into space.*

the way with plastic-covered wire. Where space is available, vandas grow beautifully in baskets with space below for roots to hang free.

Another horticulturally sound method of controlling aerial roots is to provide an exposed support to which the orchids' roots can cling. Mounting vandas and monopodial epiphytes on slabs of cork bark is a useful way to make the plants happy and keep your collection under control.

If pots are preferred, use large chunks of hardwood charcoal and broken pot pieces or gravel combined with a minimum of coarse tree fern. If conditions are rather hot and dry, you can add some redwood bark to hold moisture. This will provide the plants with both support and moisture-holding materials which are much coarser than for epiphytes with finer roots.

HANGERS

Sturdy galvanized pot hangers in several lengths are sold by mail-order orchid dealers and some local garden stores. These clip onto pots easily but they may cause thin plastic containers or foam pots to crack or break. Clay pots are safe to use with sturdy pothangers. You can also attach pothangers on baskets by tying the clip sections to the basket with plastic-coated wire. The wire can be easily cut if you wish to remove the hanger at repotting time.

Cord hangers and small platforms supported by thin monofilament lines (almost invisible) are suitable for orchid pots that might otherwise

After six years in a plastic pot, the Rhynchocentrum *is ready to be transplanted into a metal basket. The sprawling growth, with three active leads, is easier to control in this new container.*

be placed on a shelf or bench. These holders are offered in most local garden centers for other houseplants but are perfectly acceptable for orchids. Personally I avoid the ornate macrame creations because they distract from the orchid flowers. Plain coconut-husk cord hangers and clear-plastic hangers are aesthetically compatible with orchid flowers.

WOODEN CONTAINERS

Orchids look lovely in wooden containers. Terrestrials such as cymbidiums thrive in redwood tubs, while epiphytic genera do well in baskets of teak or other hardwood. Rafts of wood are appropriate for epiphytes and baskets with slat construction are the best containers for larger orchids that have sharply pendant inflorescences, such as stanhopeas. In a basket or raft made from wood slats (spaced ½ to 1 inch apart), the inflorescence will push into the air so flowers can open normally below the hanging plant. In a pot the spike usually rots in the potting mix.

Choose wooden containers made from long-lasting woods such as cypress, redwood, or teak. These woods do not require any chemical preservative to last many seasons. Other woods will last longer if given a treatment of a wood preservative such as Cuprinol. Do not use common creosote paints (oil-based paints used to preserve wood) since these are toxic to plants. In contrast, Cuprinol-treated wood containers can be used for orchids after a few weeks of weathering outside or a brief rinse after fully drying indoors. Cuprinol does not have to be used with long-lasting woods but it is useful for pine, oak, sassafras, and similar woods that rot quickly when subject to constant moisture and high temperatures.

WOODEN SLABS AND BRANCHES

Miniature orchids, such as the succulent oncidiums and small *Aerangis* species, thrive on slabs of wood or branch sections. Buttonwood, oak, and sassafras have all been used with success. Slabs of teak and cypress are also suitable.

Small orchids do well on slabs when relative humidity is above 50 per cent. Growing small orchids on slabs is not easy if your growing area has low humidity and you are unable to mist the slabs on bright mornings. Slabs and branches are especially appropriate for epiphytes that come from relatively dry regions such as the Caribbean islands and for epiphytic orchids that grow outdoors in areas of high rainfall.

Since wooden slabs drain and dry out quickly, they may be inappropriate where humidity is low, light is intense, and winds are strong. Inside a light garden, sunporch or greenhouse, wooden slabs and branch sections are useful. Cork bark is a thick lightweight material with an attractive rough surface and is suitable for mounting many orchids.

Cork lasts for years so orchids usually outgrow a slab before replacement is required. A cork slab that is still sound can be mounted on top of another larger slab so that the orchid plant will not have to be disturbed when it is moved elsewhere for remounting.

By pushing heavy hooks of galvanized metal into the cork, slabs can be hung. Inconspicuous twine made from hemp or coconut husk is also useful for hanging slabs.

Trichocidium *Elvena is shown here mounted on a slab of cork bark. U-nails and heavy twine will hold the clump until new roots take over.*

TREE FERN SLABS AND POLES

Most of the same considerations for using cork or wooden slabs as supports for epiphytic orchids also apply to tree fern slabs and poles. The single most important exception is durability. Tree fern often has a shorter life than cork or hardwood slabs. Some tree fern is quite hard while other types are soft and hold much more moisture. The hard types are best for hanging slabs or poles.

If the orchid species you want to mount needs very sharp drainage and will not accept moisture around the roots, position the tree fern so that the grain points down. By doing this, you will enable water to run rapidly away from the plant's roots, preventing it from becoming watersoaked. If the species needs more moisture around its roots, such as an epiphytic genus without pseudobulbs, have your plant mounted with the tree fern grain running horizontally, causing the slab to remain moist longer after each soaking.

Poles of tree fern are good as backing material for rambling species, such as some oncidiums and reed-stem epidendrums, such as *Epidendrum radicans* (syn. *E. ibaguense*). Some pseudobulbous bulbophyllums and maxillarias (see Chapter 12) have several inches between growths so growing them on poles is the most practical way of keeping them under control. A tree fern pole can be hung or set in a clay pot with heavy stones or gravel to anchor the base.

Mounting Techniques Fasten orchids on slabs with plastic-covered wire or thick twine. Avoid ultra-thin cords, lines, and bare metal wire, since these may cut into the above-ground stems and roots. Tie or twist the cord or plastic-covered wire until the orchid cannot turn or shift on the support. If the species has no pseudobulbs, a small wad of unmilled sphagnum moss or dense osmunda can be used to retain additional moisture, but if the orchid can be kept in a humid place this will not be necessary. The moisture-retaining material is best avoided where orchids are growing outside in high rainfall regions.

Most orchids will establish best when kept in diffuse rather than very bright light. In a light garden, put unestablished mounted orchids toward the ends of the fixture or else farther away from the lamps than for established specimens. Mist the slabs and roots every sunny morning or at the start of a light period for plants in fluorescent light gardens. As new roots begin to grip the slab, heavier misting should be necessary. Finally, when the orchid has several healthy new roots attached to the support, you can water the orchids thoroughly. Avoid keeping slabs constantly moist for unestablished plants, but *do* maintain high humidity.

6. Potting Materials and Methods

ORCHIDS GROWN in containers usually need a medium to support the roots. Rarely, except in wet tropical regions such as Southeast Asia, are epiphytic orchids grown without some sort of mix around their roots. Terrestrials must have compost to keep the roots alive. The potting medium you choose depends upon several factors:

1. Suitability to the orchids being grown
2. Availability and cost
3. Growing techniques
4. Conditions under which orchids are grown

The suitability of a potting medium for growing a particular kind of orchid is probably the most important, yet the least troublesome factor, because orchids adapt to so many potting materials.

The availability and cost of potting media are related. For example, on the East Coast of the United States, fir and redwood bark are not available and so they must be shipped over two thousand miles from the West Coast. While bark is relatively inexpensive on the West Coast, shipping costs make bark relatively expensive in the East. One has to keep in mind that bark mixes usually rot within three years, making repotting mandatory.

Hardwood charcoal is a good buy for orchid growers who live near timber supplies. In some regions volcanic stones or other rock aggregates are also inexpensive. Since epiphytic orchids thrive in these materials if fertilized regularly, some orchidists pot orchids in stones or bricks, whatever is available locally. Naturally such heavy potting media would not be practical if it had to be shipped very far.

Throughout the Asian tropics I have seen orchids grown in coconut husks. The coconut tree is fast-growing and much appreciated for its leaves, sap, nut meat, milk, oil, husks, and even its wood which is used for building. Orchids thrive in coconut-husk chunks or shredded fiber.

Some orchid growers pot their plants mainly with tree fern fiber, which is not overly expensive. In the United States most tree fern is imported from Guatemala and Mexico. Tree fern can be soft or hard, and the shredded hard fibers last at least three years. Hard tree fern slabs endure six or more years under most conditions.

Other interrelated factors which will influence the kind of potting medium you choose are your growing techniques and the conditions under which you grow orchids. If you have time to water your orchids every day and your growing area is not too hot or dry, then a potting medium consisting of gravel or rocks is practical. If you grow plants in plastic pots but have high humidity, or if you tend to overwater your plants, then a coarse mix is best. Orchids grown outside in regions of high rainfall will soon rot if given too dense a mix. In fact, in tropical Asia some genera are grown in baskets with no media, or under translucent waterproof roofing so that water can be strictly controlled.

The most commonly used materials for growing orchids are fir and redwood bark, tree fern, osmunda fern root, unmilled sphagnum moss, coconut fiber, hardwood charcoal, coarse perlite, and gravel. These can be bought from mail-order firms, local garden stores, and most commercial orchid nurseries. To obtain unusual material, check with orchid growers at orchid society meetings.

POTTING MEDIA

Fir Bark   Bark from fir trees can be used alone as a potting medium but more frequently it is mixed with coarse perlite or gravel. I mix fir bark with perlite and shredded tree fern to form a blend useful for many epiphytes. Fir bark is sold in fine, medium, and coarse grade sizes. Genera with fine roots, such as miltonias and oncidiums, should get fine to medium grade fir bark, while genera with thick roots, such as cymbidiums or vandas, should get medium to coarse grade. Seedlings in all genera accept a finer, more moisture-retentive blend than mature plants. Bark from other evergreen trees, such as pines, is usually not as good as fir bark because it has a high resin content.

Redwood Bark   Redwood bark chips are also available in fine, medium, and coarse grain sizes. The fine material is useful in terrestrial mixes while the medium and large chunks are suitable in mixes with tree fern and fir bark. Redwood bark chips are seldom used alone, and when mixed with other media they discourage bark fungus. Redwood wool, the shredded inner bark of redwood that is moisture-retentive, is frequently used in mixes with fir bark and perlite for orchids in clay pots. I find that redwood wool holds too much moisture for epiphytic orchids in plastic pots under greenhouse conditions, but in dry areas, such as the Southwest, it can be useful.

Tree Fern   Tree fern is available as trunks, slabs, poles, or in a shredded form, usually in several grinds. The coarse type is good for mature orchids; the medium type is useful in mixes with bark; the fine type is good for seedlings, especially in clay pots. Tree fern lasts a year or two longer than bark.

For a good basic mix, blend 2 parts of shredded tree fern with 1 part redwood bark or ⅓ tree fern, ⅓ redwood, and ⅓ fir bark. This combination will satisfy most epiphytic orchids. Unmilled sphagnum moss and coarse perlite can be added when additional moisture is required, as for seedlings, or when clay pots are used.

In Hawaii, tree fern trunks (logs) are used in gardens as supports for orchids and bromeliads. In most parts of the Hawaiian Islands they last many years.

Osmunda   The roots from osmunda ferns have been used since the nineteenth century for potting orchids. Like tree fern, osmunda comes in several grades, varying from "soft" (that holds lots of moisture), to hard, coarse osmunda (that resembles tree fern). Osmunda is generally expensive to buy.

Osmunda ferns live in swamps where the slow-growing clumps are difficult to harvest. Sometimes harmful fungus is present in the roots so the osmunda must be steam-sterilized. Even with these disadvantages, some orchidists prefer osmunda for most of their orchids.

To pot your orchids with osmunda, first wash the big chunks of osmunda in plain water, then soak them in a solution of 1 teaspoon Physan to 1 gallon of water to discourage fungus. With a durable pair of shears or a knife, cut the osmunda into 2-inch chunks. Suit the size to the orchid being potted.

Osmunda must be firmly pushed into a pot which has good drainage. Orchids are hard to establish if they move around in the medium too much. Therefore, use clay pots or slat baskets if you plan to use osmunda. Most plastic pots will split or crack before the osmunda is firm enough around the rhizome and roots.

Hold a chunk of osmunda under the orchid, spread the roots over the chunk, then place the plant in the pot, over drainage crocks, holding the rhizome firmly against the pot wall. Allow more room in front of the main lead than behind to allow for growth. Push additional chunks of osmunda in from the side and front, forcing the medium toward the orchid until the plant will stand firmly alone. Trim off excess osmunda with sharp scissors. A pot stake may be required for large orchids. It is possible to grow orchids in osmunda without additional fertilizing since the fern root supplies some nutrition, but using water-soluble fertilizer will help orchids grow faster. (See Chapter 7 for details about fertilizers.)

Osmunda fiber cut with clean tools is soaked before being used. An aluminum potting tool (center) is used to firm the fiber in the pot. Crocks and gravel help provide good drainage. When Trichocidium Elvena *is correctly potted, there is room for new growth in the clay pot.*

This odontoglossum is thriving in a clay pot filled with osmunda fiber.

Unmilled Sphagnum Moss Sphagnum moss, a long-fibered swamp-dwelling moss, is useful in mixes for terrestrial orchids and for seedlings. It also helps to keep moisture around the roots of monopodial epiphytes that might otherwise dry out too rapidly. Sphagnum moss has antibacterial qualities and at one time was used to dress people's wounds.

Disa, Habenaria, and some terrestrial jewel orchids thrive in plain unmilled sphagnum moss. In my own orchid collection I have some fine-rooted miltonias and odontoglossum hybrids in unmilled sphagnum moss over hardwood charcoal. Since sphagnum moss holds lots of water I pack it loosely and use relatively small pots.

Orchid backbulbs should be placed in a tray of unmilled sphagnum moss to encourage sprouts. A similar technique is useful for establishing newly imported orchids which often have few live roots. Unmilled sphagnum moss is available in small bags (relatively expensive) or a bale (less expensive).

Coconut Fiber Plain coconut fiber can be used to grow various epiphytic orchids, with good results. The fiber is golden brown, pleasant to work with, lightweight, porous, yet retains some moisture. When

Brassolaeliocattleya *Herbert William Tickner 'Talisman Cove'* (Blc. *Fleur de Lys 'Dark Splash'* X C. *Bella Simpson 'Flamboyant'*).

Potinara *Magic Lamp (right) is a hybrid of* Blc. *Fortune* X Lowara *Trinket. At left is* Blc. *Golden Slippers, a modern hybrid* (Blc. *Helen Morita* X Blc. *Golden Galleon*).

Cattleya aurantiaca *(bottom) and hybrids bred from this compact bifoliate species—* Lc. *El Cerrito 'Talisman Cove' (top) and* Lc. *Chit Chat 'Tangerine', HCC/AOS, an orange flowered mericlone.*

Cattleya *Porcia 'Cannizaro', a bifoliate hybrid* (C. *Armstrongiae* X C. bowringiana), *has received Awards of Merit from three orchid societies as well as a Certificate of Cultural Merit.*

Sophrolaeliocattleya *Madge Fordyce 'Red Orb', a modern mericlone with dwarf growth, is a cross between* Sc. *Doris and* Slc. *Jewel Box.*

Miniature cymbidiums bloom from winter into spring. At left, yellow mericlone Cym. Mary Pinchess 'Del Rey', HCC/AOS; in center, Cym. Leodogran 'Cradlemont', AM/AOS; at right, Cym. Showgirl 'Talisman Cove'.

Dendrobium phalaenopsis *hybrids decorate a shrine in Thailand.*

Dendrobium *Otohime 'Talisman Cove', a modern* Den. nobile *Yamamoto hybrid.*

switching from bark mixes to coconut fiber, most growers find that they must reduce the frequency with which they water their plants. However, I have found that loose coconut fiber needs water more often. With my plants usually in plastic pots, I use lots of gravel and hardwood charcoal in the containers. Plastic mesh baskets, which are used to hold berries in some supermarkets, can also serve as a potting container for coconut fiber.

Although coconut fiber does have nutrients that orchids need, the plants do much better if given regular applications of fertilizer (see Chapter 7). I sometimes use coconut fiber around the aerial roots of monopodial genera to encourage their growth, or to cover new roots, even though the plant may be potted in another medium. Since coconut fiber is lightweight, it is useful to put in wads around new roots which grow over the pot rim, prior to repotting the whole plant. The very fine coconut fiber is almost like peat moss and makes a good ingredient for terrestrial mixes.

In the tropics, whole chunks of coconut husk are used for orchid growing. My friend Michael Ooi, a commercial grower in Penang, Malaysia, establishes newly collected phalaenopsis directly on chunks of coconut husk. Elsewhere in the tropics, husks are used to support orchids grown in raised beds outdoors.

Coconut-husk potting fiber is being used to grow this cattleya seedling in a plastic mesh basket. A coconut shell is a suitable container once the drainage holes have been drilled.

Phalaenopsis *Talisman Cove* seedlings will be transplanted from a community pot into separate pots, using coconut fiber over gravel and hardwood charcoal.

Rootone powder is dusted on the base of the seedlings when the dead roots and old stem are removed.

These Phalaenopsis *seedlings have just been transplanted and will receive individual labels. The center seedling was large enough to be potted in a coconut shell; the other seedlings are in 3½-inch plastic pots.*

Hardwood Charcoal Hardwood charcoal (not powdered, re-formed cubes) is a good material for potting vandas, cattleyas, and other genera, and as an additive in the bottom of containers. The charcoal absorbs excess minerals and gases that sometimes harm roots. Epiphytes can be grown in charcoal alone but must be regularly fertilized. More often, orchid growers use a basic epiphyte mix, such as tree fern/perlite/bark combinations, and then add chunks of hardwood charcoal in varying amounts. For mature ascocendas I include about 50 per cent charcoal, while for cattleyas I may use only ¼ charcoal. (The different amounts of charcoal are used because of the plants' root structure.) Some slow-growing monopodial orchids can be kept in the same containers for years without being repotted, if grown with hardwood charcoal and gravel. Avoid any type of charcoal that has additives, such as some products sold as cooking fuel or to start fires.

Perlite Perlite is a volcanic rock that is usually white and is offered in several grades. The coarse type is most useful for orchid culture. Perlite is lightweight, yet it can hold moisture and air around a plant's roots. Since it lasts for many years it also enables organic mixes to maintain good aeration and drainage.

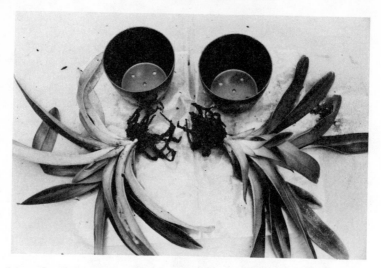

A mature clump of paphiopedilums has been divided into two clumps after its flowers have faded. Each division will be potted in a well-drained plastic container.

After pebbles and charcoal are in the pot for drainage, hold the ball of terrestrial potting mix under the plant's roots and gently settle the orchid in the center of the pot.

Fill in the potting mix around the roots. Lift the pot, then tap sharply on a firm surface several times to settle the mix around the roots.

Correctly potted and labeled, the paphiopedilum divisions will grow several years before needing a new potting mix.

Gravel Gravel, lava rock chunks, and other types of small stones that do not have an alkaline reaction can also be useful for orchid potting. I avoid using limestone pebbles for orchids except as drainage in the bottom of pots or for a few paphiopedilums that thrive with a slightly sweet mix. Yellow gravel and other kinds of gravel sold for building and concrete mixes are suitable. To make sure that the gravel you use for potting carries no harmful organisms, pour boiling water over it before use.

Hard terra-cotta gravel can also be used to pot orchids. This inorganic material lasts for years so that plants only need repotting when they grow out of their containers. Since this material, like lava rock, holds some moisture, orchids with pseudobulbs should be dry between soakings. Plants potted in rock materials should receive a diluted, balanced, water-soluble fertilizer every other watering.

BASIC MIXES

Orchid potting mixes should be chosen with the specific growing conditions and individual plants you have in mind. Avoid trying untested materials as potting mixes unless you are willing to lose a few orchids during your experimentation. As with other indoor plants, it is wise to avoid using common garden soil and leaf molds that have not been pasteurized in a potting mix. Material from the garden often harbors harmful fungus spores and pests.

For Terrestrials Terrestrial orchids such as most cymbidiums and paphiopedilums need a well-drained mix, yet one that also retains sufficient moisture to keep a plant's roots from drying out. Plain osmunda is suitable for growing terrestrials but a mixture of various materials is more practical in most regions. A basic terrestrial mix can be formulated with equal parts of a pasteurized houseplant potting soil, such as Jungle Growth or Jiffy Mix, medium- to fine-grade fir bark, coarse perlite, and fine redwood. Some growers use redwood wool or coconut fiber in combination with sharp sand, pea gravel, and fine fir bark. Commercial growers offer their own versions of terrestrial potting mixes.

For Epiphytes A general mix for seedlings is 8 parts fine fir bark or tree fern, 1 part coarse perlite, 1 part fine redwood or redwood with some redwood wool. Genera with fine roots, such as miltonias or oncidiums, need a finer textured but still well-drained mix. Genera with thick roots, such as cattleyas and vandas, thrive with an open, coarse mix. Seedlings of terrestrial species can be potted directly in the terrestrial mix used for mature plants, or you can add some chopped sphagnum moss to retain moisture if the mix seems too coarse.

The basic mix for epiphytes with fine roots is the same as for seedlings but it has more coarse perlite or pea gravel, especially if you use plastic pots. Epiphytes with medium to coarse roots thrive in a mix made from medium-sized fir bark with redwood bark and perlite added. Fir bark used alone sometimes rots too quickly from snow mold or similar fungus, so 1 part of redwood is added to each 6 to 8 parts of fir bark to help the mix last longer.

Coarse perlite keeps any potting mix airy and can be used with tree fern or bark. Packaged orchid-growing media offered by commercial growers are helpful and will produce excellent plants when used according to the directions on the bag. Check to see whether the packaged mix has added fertilizer. Some growers add timed release nutrients to their formulas so you will need less fertilizer with these mixes, at least for the first few months.

Until you have a large collection of orchids, the most practical alternative is to purchase a ready-to-use orchid potting mix. Get hardwood charcoal and gravel locally. If your orchid collection is large and you have room to store large bags of a mix, some money can be saved by buying your favorite ingredients in bulk, then mixing a medium as required. Tree fern, redwood bark, and coconut fiber are all available in large bags from some suppliers. Sometimes it is possible to pool your orders for certain potting mixes with members of a local orchid society, thereby saving considerably on shipping charges for bulky items that are shipped from many miles away.

Ingredient Ratios Vary the ratio of potting mix ingredients according to the genus of your orchids, growing conditions, and type of container you have. For example, if you grow phalaenopsis in baskets where air circulation is excellent, the mix can contain more unmilled sphagnum moss than if the same plants are grown in plastic pots on a bench. Epiphytes such as cattleyas will thrive in clay pots and a mixture that contains redwood wool. However, if you water your plants frequently and prefer to use plastic pots, the mix for your cattleyas should contain no redwood wool, which holds too much moisture.

Orchids are tolerant plants, especially hybrids. Crosses between various species and hybrids generally have more vigor than pure species. If you watch your orchids for signs of water needs, they will grow in a wide variety of materials, from plain air with the plants' roots just grabbing the pot, to many combinations involving the media mentioned in this chapter.

PREPARING THE POTTING MEDIUM

Organic potting materials absorb water and should be lightly moist before being used or directly after the orchid is potted. It is better to have the mix slightly moist rather than dusty dry because a very dry mix is unpleasant to work with and will draw water from the roots under some conditions. Clay pots also absorb moisture from the potting mix.

Before using a mix I put the required quantity in a big plastic tub, then pour a warm solution of Physan on the mix to encourage new roots while discouraging fungus. After the mix is stirred thoroughly, I use it for potting. An alternative method is to pot with a dry mix, then thoroughly soak the orchid until water pours out of the drainage holes.

During the potting procedure with bark or tree fern, tap the container on a hard surface several times to settle the mix around the plant's roots. With coconut fiber this is not required because the fiber needs to be tucked loosely around the roots. With osmunda the material is forced into the pot tightly. A stiff aluminum or sturdy wooden rod is often used when potting with osmunda since strong pressure is needed.

Potting with mixtures that are mainly bark, or with gravel type mixes, is easy. The material will fall in around the roots just the way soil does, especially with an occasional tap of the container on a table or bench. When orchids wobble too much, I use a stake to which the stem can be tied, or mulch around the rhizome with gravel chips to steady the orchid until new roots take over.

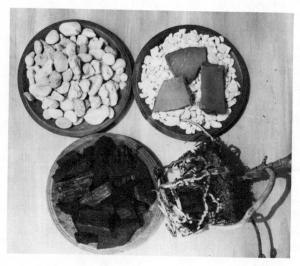

Drainage materials include gravel, broken pots, and hardwood charcoal. Roots of Ascocentrum (right) are well attached to the charcoal at potting time and can be left intact.

REPOTTING

Repot orchids when they have grown too big for their container or the mix has deteriorated. Organic mixes last two to four years. Tree fern, or tree fern with perlite or gravel, lasts longer than bark under most conditions. Inorganic materials last for the life of the orchid. Gravel or lava rock, for example, never rots.

Wooden slabs, tree fern slabs, and branches last for varying times, but usually at least four to six years, depending upon the conditions and original material. For example, teak lasts longer than sassafras. Orchid growth slows and some roots stop growing or rot when the potting mix

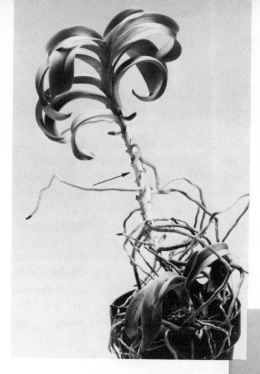

Renanthopsis *grown leggy, but with healthy roots on the stem, can be cut down (where arrow points) and repotted.*

The cut stem is dusted with a fungicide/rooting powder before being potted.

The top cutting is then potted much lower in a container filled with coconut fiber over gravel and charcoal.

or support is no longer sound. If this happens, repot the plant at once, removing all dead roots and dusting the cuts with a fungicide and hormone powder called Rootone.

Water orchids prior to removing them from their old pots. Wet roots come free more easily from containers than dry roots. This is easily accomplished by inverting the pot and striking it on a hard surface such as the side of a table or bench. Sometimes a *gentle* pull will dislodge stubborn roots. If the plant does not drop from the pot, use a clean, sharp knife to run around the inside of the container, thus freeing the roots. Epiphytes are most likely to grip the container with tenacity.

Terrestrials come out of their pots more easily than epiphytes because their mix is much looser and the plants' roots do not grip the pot walls with such vigor. Occasionally mature cymbidiums must be cut from a container or the container has to be broken to get the orchid out. Any wounds caused during potting procedures should be dusted with a fungicide or Rootone powder.

This overgrown Oncidium splendidum *is ready for repotting.*

The mature plant with a new active lead (left) has been separated from older pseudobulbs (right).

The oncidium is then potted in a clay container, filled with an epiphyte mix of tree fern, redwood bark, and perlite, over charcoal and gravel.

CARE AFTER POTTING

Orchids with pseudobulbs establish fastest when they are not too wet at the roots. Humidity must be kept high and unestablished plants should be protected from direct sun until new roots are established. Encourage roots by misting the mix surface every bright morning. As roots begin, increase the quantity of water. For newly potted epiphytes, never keep the mix constantly moist.

Terrestrial orchids need to be thoroughly watered after being potted, then kept slightly dry at the roots until new growth is well under way. As with epiphytes, terrestrial orchids establish best in diffuse light and high humidity. Once new roots have grown, usually in four to eight weeks, the orchids can be given light intensity suitable to their genus. If a recently potted orchid looks weak but tries to bloom, cut off the flower spike to conserve the plant's energy.

7. Watering and Fertilizing

GENERAL RULES FOR WATERING

PROPERLY POTTED, planted, or mounted orchids kept in a suitable environment with adequate light will thrive when watered correctly. How often to water your plants depends upon a number of factors:

1. Temperature
2. Relative humidity
3. Light intensity
4. Growth stage of the plant
5. Container size and type
6. Support media or potting mix ingredients

All of these factors work together, influencing how much water an orchid needs at the roots. As temperatures rise, orchids lose more moisture through their pores so they take up more water through their roots. When humidity is high, a potting mix dries out more slowly, orchids lose less water through their pores, and plants require water less often.

When light is strong, especially if temperatures are high, orchids grow faster and can be watered more often. Outdoors during the summer, established orchids in clay pots and those grown on slabs may need watering every day. In a humid greenhouse during the winter these same orchids can go a week before they need water.

Orchids that have just finished flowering often go through a brief rest period. Some species may lose all their leaves for a few months each season. Such relatively inactive plants need water infrequently. In contrast, seedlings continue to grow when other environmental factors are suitable. Seedling orchids in a light garden in your home or in a warm greenhouse usually need water every day, while mature plants in the same situation need water only every week.

Orchids with pseudobulbs can dry out at the roots. While still growing, orchids with pseudobulbs should become partially dry before being soaked. Very succulent orchids from dry regions can become dry between waterings too, but not to the point of shrinking. Keep the newest growth plump. Watch pseudobulbs just behind the active lead. When these shrink slightly, it is a signal that water is needed.

As long as humidity is adequate, you can delay watering orchids that do not clearly need more water. Overwatering orchids is more harmful than occasional drying. Mist the plant's roots if you are not convinced that the plant needs thorough watering.

Large containers dry out more slowly than small pots. Orchids in plain clay pots need water more often than those in plastic containers. Orchids grown on cork slabs dry out faster than those on fern slabs because the cork support absorbs much less moisture.

Terrestrials that retain their leaves should dry slightly between waterings, so that the compost never has a chance to get soggy. Terrestrials without pseudobulbs require more even moisture than those without these water-storing organs. Recently potted orchids require less water than well-established specimens. Dry roots are usually white; wet roots, gray-green.

FERTILIZERS

Orchids in nature live upon trees, mossy ground, or even on rocks, where countless tiny bits of organic matter that accumulate around orchid roots are gradually decomposed by bacteria. The ubiquitous bacteria of decay turn dead leaves, insect bodies, bird droppings, and similar organic debris into basic chemicals for the plants. Nitrogen, phosphorus, and potassium are the most important of these chemicals. Rain or heavy dew dissolves these elements sufficiently so that they can be absorbed by orchid roots. These nutrients, in combination with air and light, provide the building blocks for sturdy growth.

In contrast, the orchids that you grow in your home or greenhouse can be given chemical fertilizers, dissolved in water, that orchid roots can absorb at once. Most commercial growers rely on water-soluble chemical fertilizers for their orchids. They are easier and more pleasant to use than organic materials, such as emulsified seaweed, fish, or by-products, although both types have their value.

To be useful for orchids, a fertilizer need not be called an "Orchid Fertilizer." Popular brands such as Hyponex, Miracle-Gro, Tender Leaf House Plant Food, and similar products designed for indoor plants are suitable, especially when used at ½ strength or weaker. For example, if the package says to mix 1 tablespoon per gallon, you should use only ½ tablespoon per gallon or 1 heaping teaspoon, especially for epiphytes.

Some fertilizers are formulated specifically for orchids and the directions are very clear regarding how they are to be used. These are the safest to use on a regular basis since the chemicals in these orchid formulas are specially suited to the plants. Fertilizers made for terrestrial plants and outdoor farm crops are likely to be too harsh for indoor orchids and tender epiphytic roots.

Some epiphytes, such as this hybrid of Cattleya *Louise Georgiana and* C. aclandiae, *will thrive even after growing out of their pots if they receive regular applications of water-soluble fertilizer and bright light.*

Chemical Types Fertilizer packages list the percentages of nitrogen, phosphorus, and potassium that they contain. A popular balance for orchids in fir bark mixtures is 30-10-10. (This water-soluble fertilizer has
· 30 parts of nitrogen, 10 parts of phosphorus, and 10 parts of potassium or potash. The other 50 per cent contains minute quantities of trace elements and an inert carrier.) Usually only the three most important major nutrients are listed on fertilizer packages but some manufacturers go into greater detail regarding trace elements, acidity of the fertilizer, types of nitrogen, and similar information.

Orchids grown in tree fern thrive with less nitrogen so a balanced ratio is used, such as 18-18-18 or 20-20-20. Fertilizers with high numbers are more concentrated than those with low numbers, but the ratio of nitrogen to phosphorus to potassium can be the same. A 3-1-1 fertilizer has the same nutrient ratio as a 30-10-10 ratio.

Organic fertilizers are generally weaker than chemical types. For example, one fish emulsion brand has a 5-1-1 concentration, which is weaker than the popular chemical 30-10-10 of the same ratio but still useful for growing orchids.

Which ratio of fertilizer to use for your orchids depends on:

1. Potting media used
2. Age of the plants, that is, seedlings or mature orchids
3. Growth stage, that is, just starting or completing annual growth

You need not be fanatic about which ratio fertilizer to use, but following general guidelines will help your plants grow better because each of the three major chemicals has a slightly different influence on growth.

Orchids in bark need some extra nitrogen since bacteria that decompose the bark temporarily hold nitrogen. The 3-1-1 ratio is good for active orchids in bark. Mature orchids in tree fern, coconut fiber, and osmunda thrive with a balanced formula in a 1-1-1 ratio or thereabout. Similarly orchids grown with inorganic mixes such as cinders, gravel, bricks, and charcoal do well with balanced water-soluble fertilizers such as 18-18-18.

The age of orchids also helps determine the best fertilizer. For example, seedlings should receive nitrogen to encourage growth and flowering, and therefore a 30-10-10 formula is suitable. In contrast, mature orchids should make steady, sturdy growth, but not at the expense of long-lasting blooms, so growers should alternate a 30-10-10 formula with a formula that has less nitrogen.

Orchids need the most nitrogen from the time they begin growth until their growth is about ⅔ complete. A cattleya hybrid that begins growth in March can well utilize a 30-10-10 water-soluble chemical fertilizer, diluted according to directions, every other watering, until its new pseudobulb is ⅔ grown. At this stage, change the formula to one with less nitrogen to encourage slower mature growth and formation of flower buds. I use a fertilizer with a 3-1-1 ratio for active plants under bright conditions, then switch to a 1-1-1 ratio.

The three major elements—nitrogen, phosphorus, and potassium—work together and the lack of one will upset your plants' health. However, we can regulate growth patterns somewhat by controlling nutrient concentrations and ratios. You do not need to be a chemist to do this. Just follow some basic guidelines and watch your orchids for signs of too much or too little fertilizer.

Too much nitrogen produces very dark green leaves, weak growth, short-lived flowers.

Too little nitrogen encourages yellowish foliage, slow growth.

Too little phosphorus causes abnormally small growths, few flowers.

Too much fertilizer causes leaf tips and new growths to turn black and die, and roots die from chemical salts. (Overfertilized orchids will recover when washed with a heavy drench of water. If the potting mix is saturated with fertilizer, then repot the plant.)

Fertilizer works in conjunction with light, air, and water to produce healthy orchids. Giving fertilizer to plants that have too little light will only encourage weak growth. Fertilizer that is too concentrated will "burn" roots by causing cells to lose water. Organic fertilizers and timed release pellets need heat and water to be effective.

After establishing a suitable environment for your plants, it is necessary to decide what fertilizers to use, keeping in mind the kind of potting mix and the stage of growth of your plants. Here are some basic guidelines:

High nitrogen (3-1-1):   Seedlings in general; orchids in bark mixes; orchids making new growth in adequate light

Balanced (1-1-1):   Orchids in osmunda, tree fern, inorganic mixes, or on slabs; alternate feedings for mature plants also given a 3-1-1 ratio

High phosphorus and potassium (1-2-3):   Mature plants completing growths, to encourage flowering

Variations in fertilizing patterns are common among experienced growers, although each person may produce healthy orchids with high-quality flowers. This occurs because of differences in environment, water supply, water quality, potting medium, and similar variables. Fertilizer can also be supplied in several ways. The simple way, most often used by commercial nurseries, is to rely on precise chemical formulas applied in dilute concentrations at regular intervals, usually at every watering.

Application   Water dry plants first, then several hours later apply the fertilizer solution. Moist plants can have the fertilizer solution applied without prewatering. In home collections it is often easier to apply water-soluble fertilizer every few weeks, but orchids keep growing so a steady dilute supply of nutrients can be utilized. It is biologically more productive to supply weak nutrients frequently than a stronger solution infrequently.

With this in mind, many orchidists use a proportioner device which attaches to the water supply. A very concentrated solution of water-soluble fertilizer is poured into the proportioner tank. When water is run through the proportioner, a minute quantity of fertilizer concentrate is automatically mixed with the water. This is the easiest way to apply fertilizer to many plants but it is not necessary for the average home collection.

For a small collection one can apply fertilizer easily enough by preparing a mixture every week and applying the dilute solution with some sort of spray device. For my collection I use a sprayer which draws fertilizer from a 3-gallon bucket where I can easily mix the solution and see how much is left as I spray the plants.

Indoors where orchids grow at a window garden or on light garden carts, it is best to apply fertilizer around the plants' roots from a 1-gallon watering can or sucked up from the can with a cooking baster and then applied to individual plants. Mix fertilizers with water that is at room temperature. Stir the solution thoroughly to completely dissolve all solid matter in the fertilizer crystals.

Fertilizer can also be absorbed through orchid leaves. However, since roots need to absorb the most fertilizer, if the fertilizer is applied as a spray, be sure it is a drenching spray that runs down into the root zone.

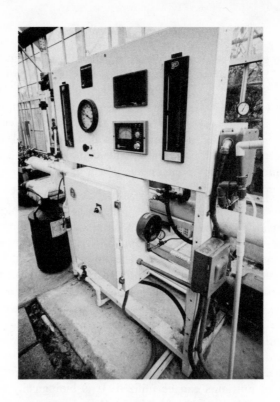

At the Marie Selby Botanical Gardens in Sarasota, Florida, this reverse osmosis system can make water with an unusually high mineral salt content safe for orchids. Less elaborate ways to avoid salt harm to roots include using rainwater or flushing pots well every few waterings.

TIMED RELEASE CHEMICALS

Timed release products for orchids are an alternative to water-soluble chemical fertilizers and can be used with equally good results. Plastic-coated chemical fertilizers are designed to release nutrients to a plant gradually, over a period of months. For example, Osmocote 14-14-14 formula releases nutrients for three to four months.

Some timed release products are safe for orchids in epiphytic mixes; most are safe for orchids in terrestrial mixes or outdoors in tropical areas. If no directions are given on the package for orchids, use only ½ the quantity listed for potted houseplants.

Late in the spring I feed all my orchids with timed release Osmocote. Then during the summer growing season I supplement the Osmocote with 2 or 3 applications of water-soluble fertilizer. Many of the mature orchids are outdoors on raised wire benches from June through September. If rainfall is sparse, the garden hose is used to soak pots every five to seven days, thus providing enough water to release nutrients from the timed release pellets.

Cymbidiums and other genera in terrestrial mixes can benefit from the slow release fertilizers stirred into the potting medium. Mag-Amp (7-40-6) is one formula suitable for promoting sturdy growths and flowers. Since the Mag-Amp formula is low in nitrogen, you should supplement it with a 30-10-10 fertilizer or an organic high nitrogen fertilizer, such as fish emulsion, during periods of active growth.

ORGANIC FERTILIZERS

Fish emulsion is the most popular organic fertilizer for orchids. This liquefied fish by-product is easy to mix with water and is compatible with other fertilizers. Organic fertilizers such as fish and seaweed emulsions contain useful trace elements.

An advantage of organic fertilizers is that they are usually inexpensive. A disadvantage is that organic materials must be broken down by bacteria before orchids can benefit from the nutrients. This may be an advantage because slow release of nutrients offers the orchid a steady supply of minerals for growth. However, the bacteria of decay encouraged by organic fertilizers also break down organic potting mixes. Actually orchids can be perfectly grown with only balanced chemical fertilizers. This is in contrast to farming practices where organic fertilizers make a very real contribution to the structure of soil.

Adding an occasional organic fertilizer to orchid-fertilizing solutions assures a supply of trace elements that are needed in minute quantity. I find, for example, that seaweed emulsion helps deepen the color in orchid flowers. In nature, epiphytic genera obtain mineral nutrients from dust which settles around the plants' roots and various organic matter such as rotted leaves and animal droppings.

A practical way to use liquefied organic emulsions is to add fish emulsion and seaweed fertilizer to watering solutions. The organic products can be safely mixed with chemical formulas.

In terrestrial mixes, or for orchids growing outdoors in tropical settings, applications of fish meal and bone meal will provide a steady supply of nutrients. Such meals can also be mixed in terrestrial composts before orchids are potted. Cymbidiums in terrestrial mixes can accept stronger fertilizers than most orchids, so some commercial growers offer dry fertilizer formulas to spread on top of the potting mix around cymbidiums. In my orchid collection I prefer to use pure chemical fertilizers in solution, or as timed release pellets, and apply an occasional organic fertilizer in solution during the summer months.

8. Orchids in a Window Garden

GROWING SHOWY orchids in a bright window or sunporch is easy and very enjoyable. By selecting species and hybrids that thrive in a sunny window or sunporch, you can have a wonderful orchid collection without ever needing a greenhouse. Large picture windows in homes or special sunrooms with windows that face south often provide more light than most orchids need.

However, even if you have windows with northern exposure where light is always reflected (never direct sun), it is still possible to grow orchids with low-light requirements. (See Chapters 11 and 12 for specific plants' light requirements.) An even wider selection of orchids can be grown when daylight is supplemented with fluorescent lamps.

HUMIDITY

Providing humidity is easiest in sunrooms and similar situations where plants can be isolated from drier living areas. However, a minimum humidity of 40 to 50 per cent is a healthy level for people in the house and also is sufficient for many orchids. With this in mind, you may want to increase overall humidity in your home by means of central humidifiers. In an apartment, or other places where large-scale humidifiers are not practical, consider smaller portable units.

Portable humidifiers range in size and price from inexpensive 1-gallon-capacity models to large console models that can be attached to the waterline. Sometimes a greenhouse humidifier is practical in a plant room. Before buying a humidifier, get a hygrometer to measure the relative humidity where you plan to grow orchids.

If your conditions are not very dry, you might raise the humidity level by placing 1 to 4 inches of gravel in waterproof trays under your orchids. Then add water to the trays until it almost reaches the surface. Pots of terrestrial orchids can be set directly on the wet gravel, but the water should not actually reach the pots.

Pots containing epiphytes should be held above the moist gravel on plastic, wire, or wooden grids. In my basement light garden, pots of epiphytic orchids rest on white wooden slats above trays filled with water. Humidity stays at an acceptable 50 to 60 per cent.

Window boxes or trays filled with moist perlite are also practical for orchids that are growing with companion houseplants. Terrestrial gesneriads, begonias, ferns, and other compatible tropicals make an attractive display when grouped with orchids in bloom.

WINDOW SHELVES

A wide windowsill will support moisture trays and single pots but this arrangement is less flexible than a 10- to 15-inch-wide shelf. A sturdy shelf with right-angle supports can be constructed to the length of each window. This makes a conveniently wide support for trays of gravel or water and an assortment of plants. Each orchid plant can be placed attractively on the shelf. In cold climates there should be space between the window glass and the plants to prevent frozen foliage. A wide shelf just below the window gives you maximum freedom to grow orchids in a safe and pleasant style.

HANGING CONTAINERS

To fully utilize window space, install plant hangers at the sides and above your window space. By grouping orchids all around your window you will create a lovely living frame. In cases where you do not like the view, string a sturdy wire across the window space and attach containers with miniature orchids to this. For an even nicer arrangement, use clear monofilament line or rustic rope to support hanging pots.

At the sides of the large picture windows in my home are sturdy birdcage hangers. These inexpensive metal hangers screw into the wall or a wooden window frame. The arm swings from one side to the other and the plants can be adjusted easily. Wire hangers which clip to clay or plastic pots are easy to use in combination with the birdcage hangers. A chain which hangs from an overhead valance or ceiling hook will also attach to the pothanger hook.

In some windows I use gold plastic chain hung as a loop from the window valance. Blooming orchids are hung on display by using the pothangers hooked into the ornamental chain. Since the chain can be adjusted in length, the position of each pot can be changed.

SHADE

Some orchids may require that full sun be diffused in order to prevent leaf burn. If the weather is bright and clear (and the windows clean!) some orchids develop burns where hot sun concentrates through the glass. Curtains of light open-weave materials are attractive and practical shade for living area gardens. Curtains also hold back the cold on chilly days.

Although heavy draperies can make a nice background for blooming orchids on display at night, close-weave material keeps away too much sun from the plants. Some windows have enough room for a double valance with rods for two different materials: a light, gauze-type curtain for daytime shade, and a heavy, ornamental fabric for nighttime insulation.

If you have adjustable curtains, take care that the moving fabric will not topple your plants. Leave enough space between the curtain and your plants to let drawstring curtains work smoothly.

Special precaution must be taken at sunny windows if you have moved your plants there from another location. For example, I often grow large orchids in a greenhouse and then bring them to a dining-room table by a southeast window when they are in bloom. If orchids are moved from diffuse light in a fiberglass-covered greenhouse into direct sun concentrated through window glass, they will burn. Using curtains as shade, or keeping orchids back from the glass and out of direct rays, solves the leaf burn problem.

Orchidist Margaret Lang designed this orchid garden in a living room where the plants can receive bright light all day. The orchids are grown with companion tropical plants in pots resting on moist gravel.

Thick-leaved sun-loving orchids, grown year-round in a sunny window, usually adapt to increasing light intensity. However, there is a difference between the quality of bright sun outdoors and the concentrated beams coming through glass. Air circulation and mist often cool orchids outdoors, but behind window glass these tempering factors are lost. Even thick-leaved orchids, such as *Oncidium splendidum* and *Brassavola nodosa,* may need the protection of a light, coarse-weave curtain.

Where no suitable window space is available, miniature orchids can be grown in an indoor growing compartment. This 4×2×2-foot unit; made of plastic, aluminum, and glass, is equipped with two 40-watt fluorescent lamps, sliding glass panels, a built-in heater, and light timer. (Photo courtesy of Coes' Orchid Acres)

SUPPLEMENTAL LIGHTING SOURCES

Sun is fine for growing orchids during the day, but to enjoy flowers blooming at night you will need supplemental light. Fixtures with a swivel base are the most useful because you can turn or tilt each lamp to illuminate the plants anywhere along the window. Reflector lamps have hot incandescent bulbs, so use them only in ceramic sockets and keep plants at least 3 feet away. Too much heat will make flowers fade fast.

Over my living-room picture windows, but hidden from view by a valance, are long fluorescent lamps which give diffuse light to all the plants below. Also hidden by the valance are some ceramic sockets for 40- to 75-watt reflector spot or flood lamps. These lamps direct light just where I want it, usually to illuminate a spectacular plant in bloom. A well-illuminated collection of orchids is a special pleasure in a home.

This unique sitting room, in the home of the Goodale Moirs in Honolulu, is filled with phalaenopsis, paphiopedilums, and companion tropical plants. In colder climates, one could add double-glazed windows or double-layer fiberglass glazing and supplemental fluorescent lights.

Track lights and fixtures are more expensive than lamps but are usually quite attractive. A dimmer switch can adjust the intensity of track lighting. Pure white orchids need less light in the evening to look nice than dark-colored flowers. For maximum visibility at night, and for full use of the sun during the daytime, paint surrounding walls and shelves a light color or install mirrors to reflect light on your plants.

Mirror panels are an inexpensive way to reflect light onto plants while also giving an impression of depth. The beauty of your plants is enhanced by placing mirrors behind your orchids so that their flowers are reflected from varying angles. Mirror panels come in self-stick squares which adhere to most surfaces. Custom-cut mirrors are more costly than stick-on panels but have an aesthetic advantage of being seamless. If you are creating a prominent orchid display, a custom-fit mirror is worth the extra cost. In situations where the mirror will be mainly hidden by a mass of plants, the self-stick panels are satisfactory.

An inexpensive light reflector can be constructed from foil which is then cut and pasted on cabinets or walls. Commercially made self-stick Mylar material, such as Con-Tact, is easy to apply and inexpensive, but gives a much more diffuse image than true mirrors.

Reflective materials and light-colored paints, especially matte-white, are useful under, above, and at the sides of windows. For displays against walls or in cabinets, use these materials behind orchids. Reflection material made for photographic use is also practical for lining window frames, light gardens, or wherever maximum light reflection is required.

9. Greenhouse Orchid Growing

A GREENHOUSE OFFERS you full control over the environment for your orchid collection. Even a small greenhouse can be arranged to provide two different areas of minimum night temperatures. If you have room for a greenhouse on your property, and funds to build one, check with major greenhouse firms who will discuss different models that might fit your requirements. From personal experience I know that a greenhouse can greatly increase your pleasure with growing orchids.

BASIC STYLES OF GREENHOUSES

A freestanding greenhouse is usually more expensive than a lean-to (built onto the side of your home) because construction costs are higher. Freestanding styles offer maximum growing space for your plants.

There are many prefabricated models of greenhouses to choose from and greenhouse firms will create custom designs and modifications to fit a greenhouse to your specific needs. Some examples include having a greenhouse enclose an existing terrace or building a two-story greenhouse.

Sketch a plan of where you want the greenhouse located and prepare a list of the features you desire. For example, how many doors do you want? What automatic controls do you want (such as automatic ventilation, heating, humidification)? Thermostatically controlled heaters, for example, are especially useful to see that correct day and night temperatures are maintained for your plants. What bench design will fit your needs? Photographs (prints) are useful if you must communicate with greenhouse companies by mail. If possible, speak with the firm's design consultant.

Many seemingly complicated problems are quickly solved by experienced greenhouse engineers, or even builders who specialize in greenhouse construction. A few of the inexpensive freestanding greenhouses are relatively easy to set up. However, more complicated or sophisticated models should be supervised by an experienced professional, especially for the electrical and water connections.

This example of a lean-to greenhouse is built onto the side of a house at the second-story level, situated to provide good light for plants. (Photo courtesy of Lord & Burnham Co.)

Orientation Situate your greenhouse for maximum light. If your plants can receive sun from early morning until late afternoon, they will be sure to flower well and heating costs will be lower. In very hot climates, a greenhouse may need extra cooling devices, such as wet pad coolers, air conditioning, and exhaust fans. Nearby deciduous trees can be an advantage in providing some shade where summers are hot; however, sunlight is easier to control with rolling shade curtains, blinds, and shade paint.

Foundation Most large greenhouses need a foundation. Often this is a simple 8- to 12-inch base of cement blocks or bricks. Some inexpensive models need only flat ground but larger models must be firmly attached to a ground foundation.

Floors Orchid greenhouses should have floors that are easy to keep clean. Plain concrete is a good choice. For a more interesting effect, brick paving, laid fieldstone, or slate are possibilities, although somewhat more trouble to keep clean. Wood floors are practical if made of rot-resistant redwood, cypress, teak, or other long-lasting woods. Wooden deck boards are good over concrete floors since you can use them to avoid stepping in puddles. Gravel is another flooring possibility but it doesn't offer the same easy maintenance as concrete. If a stone floor appeals to you, look into the various colors and textures available.

Incorporate a drain in a concrete or cement floor to avoid accumulations of water. Brick and gravel floors usually absorb enough water to prevent puddles forming. Cover drains with sturdy metal plates to prevent rodents from entering through drainpipes.

SHADING

Some form of shading is obligatory for summer months, except in northern regions, where the sun's heat is not intense. A usual method of shading that is relatively inexpensive is to use paint-on shade compounds. These white paints provide diffusion shade until they are washed off by rain.

Spray on the first coat as the sun begins to get hot and another coat as the weather gets progressively warmer. Under usual conditions a single application in the spring will be sufficient. However, since some shading compounds wash off easily, a midsummer reapplication may be required if orchids look too yellow or temperatures rise above 100° F. By fall, let the shade paint wash off so that the orchids receive all the light possible during the winter.

Fiberglass covers are another good way to diffuse sun, prevent leaf burn, and lower the temperature inside a greenhouse. Over my lean-to greenhouses I have a fiberglass cover held on a redwood frame 12 inches above the glass roof which helps to protect the structure from falling branches and hail in the winter.

Greenhouse supply firms and some orchid growers sell shading fabric in various mesh sizes to give different percentages of shade. Plastic fabric screen can be placed above a greenhouse's outside glass on a simple frame, or rolled down like a window shade.

A more sophisticated form of shading can be provided by electrically operated roller blinds that come down over the greenhouse's roof as temperatures rise. This permits orchids to receive maximum sunlight on cool or cloudy days and yet be automatically shaded when the sun is intense.

HUMIDITY

It is preferable to install a unit with an automatic humidistat which maintains adequate moisture in the air, depending on the temperatures desired within. Set the control for your orchids at 60 per cent. A hygrometer can check for the actual relative humidity maintained.

In a greenhouse a humidifier should be connected directly to a waterline so that no filling is required. Place the humidifier so that the mist or fog has several feet of free air space and is not too close to the plants. It is also helpful to mist your orchids in the morning and wet the floor on dry sunny days. (Refer to Chapter 3 for additional information about humidifiers.)

In the winter, when heaters dry out the air but cloudy days make direct misting inadvisable, soaking the greenhouse floor with a hose is a useful technique to increase the relative humidity. If you have a heater that blows out hot air, place a large pan of water directly in front of the heater, so that humidity is raised by the evaporating water.

VENTILATION

Fresh air is important, especially in a greenhouse that is crowded. Even in chilly weather one can open the vents just a crack, enough to let some air circulate but not allow cold breezes to come in. A healthy greenhouse for orchids is not a giant sealed terrarium.

This powerful humidifier sends out a fog to cover a large area inside a fiberglass greenhouse. At right are epiphytic orchid plants.

This double-height, lean-to greenhouse creates a spacious sunny room for growing orchids. When construction is completed, a raised bed will provide an attractive area around the foundation. (Photo courtesy of Lord & Burnham Co.)

Lean-to greenhouses with one or more entrances to a home can be partially ventilated in cold weather by leaving the door to the inside of the house open, a pleasant idea when fragrant orchids are in bloom. In one of my greenhouses I have a small fan blowing heated air from the basement (where there is a gas furnace and hot water boiler) into the greenhouse, and this fresh air helps to save heating costs.

Specific thermostat controls are available in which vents in the greenhouse roof open at a preset temperature. Side windows can also be kept open during the summer for full air circulation.

Frosted double-layer plastic sheeting with air bubbles diffuses light and conserves heat when placed against glass.

HEAT CONSERVATION

In cold climates, much heat is lost through cracks and plain glass construction. Using double glazing or double panels of acrylic rather than glass will save heat.

Plain glass can be insulated for the winter with air bubble plastic sheeting, offered in various widths and lengths by greenhouse firms. This plastic sheeting can be stuck on with glue, tacked to wooden frames inside, or just pushed against wet glass. Loose ends can be held with tape, but the plastic usually holds well on moist glass alone. In my greenhouses I use air bubble plastic between large plants and the glass to be sure that the foliage does not get frosted in bitter cold weather.

AIR CONDITIONING

Air conditioners are practical for limited areas, such as a sunporch or small greenhouse, during hot summers. Several drawbacks are that standard air conditioners are relatively expensive to run and they decrease the humidity in a room.

In areas where summers are hot but not too humid, you can use wet pad evaporative coolers to lower your greenhouse temperature. With this method, air is cooled by being drawn over a fiber mat in which water continually circulates. As outside air is drawn over the wet pad, it loses heat to the circulating water. The wet pad system works best with rather dry air, hence its popularity in the Southwest and California.

Before deciding which method of cooling is necessary for your greenhouse, it is helpful to discuss your needs with experienced orchid growers in your area. Find out what neighboring greenhouse owners have in terms of air conditioners, and get suggestions from American Orchid Society meetings and publications, so that you can plan for your new greenhouse using detailed regional facts.

In this greenhouse, orchids which require more light hang from the rafters. A sink and potting bench (back, left) make work with plants a pleasure. The floor is concrete and gravel. (Photo by Christopher Quinn)

10. Outdoor Orchid Culture

CHOOSING ORCHIDS for an outdoor garden is similar to selecting types to grow indoors because one must pick those plants that will adapt to the prevailing conditions. Orchidists soon learn that species from high mountains seldom thrive in warm lowland gardens. Similarly, warm-growing species often languish when brought into cool, moist-habitat gardens. Hybrids are generally more adaptable to outside temperature fluctuations, but it is still best to pick genera that prefer the climate in your area. A visit to a local orchid grower or regional orchid society meeting will give you some ideas about the best outdoor orchids for your garden.

A wood frame, raised wire-covered benches, and a cement-block wall with holes open for air circulation provide a suitable home for orchids at Goodale Moir's garden in Hawaii. A similar arrangement is practical for orchids outdoors during the summer in colder regions.

A vanda hedge is a popular way to grow terete hybrids in tropical climates.

CLIMATE

The weather conditions where you live will determine whether orchids can be grown outdoors in your yard all year round, or taken outside only during the summer months.

In dry hot regions, such as New Mexico or Arizona, orchids should be kept indoors because the outdoor climate is much too dry. Or, if you have a special collection of plants in a greenhouse where there is no over-crowding, you probably won't want to move your plants outdoors.

In temperate climates, one must grow tropical orchids indoors most of the year. Often indoor conditions are not ideal, perhaps quite over-crowded. With this in mind, I put many orchids outdoors during warmer months, and I see a marked improvement in their growth. In southern New York, orchids must wait until June before going outside.

In areas where frosts sometimes do occur, it is wise to select cold-tolerant plants, such as cymbidiums, and grow all other orchids where they can be given emergency protection if frost threatens. However, during the summer in most parts of the United States, where the climate is not extreme, orchids can benefit from the increased air, sun, and cleansing rain they receive outdoors.

If you live in a tropical area, you can grow showy orchids outdoors all year long. Many orchidists in warm areas have whole gardens overflowing with orchids. In the United States, Hawaii is thought of as our orchid state and indeed orchids thrive there. Commercial orchid nurseries in Hawaii grow millions of orchids for sale around the world. Some firms specialize in cut-flower orchids, whose blooms are used to decorate homes, restaurants, and hotels.

Southern Florida and California are other areas whose year-round climate is favorable for growing orchids outdoors, although their weather conditions tend to vary more than Hawaii's. Occasionally hard frosts occur in Florida and California, endangering all but the most cold-tolerant orchids. Still it is practical to grow many orchids outdoors if one selects them with cold tolerance in mind. Some good choices include: *Cattleya citrina,* a small Mexican pendant species; cymbidiums, especially standard-size hybrids; *Dendrobium nobile* hybrids; epidendrums from Mexico (some Encyclia types); *Laelia anceps* and its primary hybrids; masdevallias; odontoglossums; and pleiones.

Weather Watch The local agricultural extension agent can provide people in northern climates with weather data showing the last date of frost and anticipated first fall frost. Cool-preference orchids, such as cymbidiums and Mexican species of epidendrum and laelia, can be put outside when nights are at least 50° F. Other orchids should stay indoors until nights are in the upper 50° range. Warm-preference orchids should be kept indoors until summer has come, with nights in the 60s.

In the fall, reverse the procedure, bringing warm growers indoors first and cool growers indoors a week or two before the first frost. A cool fall will encourage blooming on cymbidiums and nobile-type dendrobiums.

WATERING

How much you will need to water your plants outdoors depends on the weather conditions in your area. If summer months are rainy, you may hardly need to water your orchids at all. For an average summer, neither too wet nor dry, outdoor orchids hung from trees or growing on slabs should get a heavy spray from your garden hose every sunny morning. Potted orchids on wire or wood slat benches under tall trees can go five to seven days between soakings, but should get sprayed if days are dry and sunny.

Because the sun is brighter and the air circulation is better outdoors, orchids can accept more watering than when grown inside. During some rainy summers my plants have been wet for two weeks at a time. In the greenhouse, their roots would have rotted, but being outside the orchids tolerated the excess water. Keep in mind that all of the epiphytes were in pots with excellent drainage and aeration.

BENCHES AND RACKS

Pots containing orchids can be placed on wire or wood slat benches where plants will receive plenty of air and where slugs and other insects

*Clean wire benches, sides open to the air, and a
plastic-covered roof to control the rain are a part
of the orchid nursery of Patrick Kawamoto
in Oahu, Hawaii.*

cannot reach them. Keep the pots close enough together so that they cannot blow over. If the plants' size prevents you from doing this, use empty clay pots or other weighted supports against each plant to keep them steady in gusty winds. Pots can also be hung from metal racks, horizontal poles, even clothes drying racks, by means of hangers. If you like, the rack can be painted white and used as a focal point in your yard to display blooming orchids. On the other hand, a coat of black or brown paint will make these racks unobtrusive in your summer garden.

If your summers tend to be windy, secure the pothangers to the rack with a twist of wire or strong twine. During the summer in New York, there are usually several storms which knock down the pots in my garden and blow off their hangers, unless I firmly secure them.

Locate outdoor benches and racks under the shade of a tall tree. In my garden I have large oak trees which protect my orchids from direct midday sun but still let some sun come through in a shifting pattern. Orchids grown under relatively low light during the winter must be moved to bright situations gradually. Fortunately the shade from tall trees and good air circulation protects all but the tenderest plants from burn.

LATH HOUSES

Orchids thrive under lath outdoors. These wooden slats act like trees in providing a shifting pattern of sun throughout the day. An attractive lath house can be made of redwood, a feature seen in many California and Florida gardens. Lath can be used just for the top of the structure or for the sides as well.

Since it is important to have good air circulation, solid sides should be avoided, except in regions with consistently strong winds or low humidity. Under such conditions, consider having cement-block, brick, or fiberglass sides for the structure. An interesting compromise are open-hole tile or cinder block walls which allow air to circulate through the openings. Porous blocks also hold rain and release moisture when the sun warms them, thus raising humidity.

TERRESTRIALS

Containers that hold terrestrial genera, such as cymbidiums, phaius species, and paphiopedilums, need not be placed on raised benches or racks, but they should be kept off the soil. Pots placed directly on the earth invite earthworms, sow bugs, and other creatures that will disturb the plants' roots. I keep shallow saucers under the containers holding terrestrial orchids and then put the containers on a bedrock area under a tall tree. Another alternative is to grow them in raised beds or to build a low platform of redwood in your garden on which to place orchids.

Cymbidiums will accept almost full sun outdoors if subjected to it gradually. Paphiopedilums, at the other extreme, do best in open shade, with direct sun only in the early morning or very late afternoon. Vanda hybrids which are often difficult to bloom in northern climates will grow satisfactorily when given strong sun outdoors from June until mid-September.

Raised Beds   One of the best places to grow terrestrial orchids outside is in raised beds, which are easy to construct and provide an area with ideal drainage and compost. One can construct a raised bed with cement blocks, 12 to 24 inches high; fill the area with volcanic cinders, gravel, or coconut husks over hardwood charcoal; and plant many orchids directly in the ground.

Drainage is good so heavy rains do not drown the roots. If soil tends to absorb water slowly, such as in heavy clay, dig a drainage area below the ground level and fill this with gravel or broken tiles so that the actual raised bed compost never gets soggy.

In regions where winters are occasionally cold, orchids are often cultivated in raised beds against house walls. Heat held by the building pro-

W. W. Goodale Moir, innovative orchid breeder, inspects orchids in his Honolulu garden. A plastic roof helps to shelter plants that need less water than the climate provides.

tects the plants at night from all but severe frosts. Cymbidiums, which are sturdy cold-tolerant orchids, actually bloom better when temperatures drop into the 40s at night.

EPIPHYTES

Epiphytic orchids thrive on big tree fern logs, tree branches, and in outdoor containers with a mix for epiphytes. In much of southern Florida, epidendrums, laelias, brassavolas, and certain cattleya hybrids thrive outside on trees. Although cold weather sometimes causes problems, orchids thrive and bloom there most years.

In tropical regions around the world, gardeners enjoy orchids outdoors. *Phalaenopsis, Vanda,* and *Dendrobium* are favorite genera to grow on trees in Asia. In Mexico and Central America, *Oncidium, Epidendrum,* and *Brassavola* are often seen. Cattleyas, laelias, and odontoglossums thrive in many South American gardens. In Tanzania and Kenya, *Ansellia africana,* a native plant, grows on garden trees.

Establishing Epiphytes on Trees To establish epiphytic orchids on trees requires extra care for at least one growing season. Seedlings two to three years old or young plants in general are easier to establish than large older specimens that often have damaged roots. Transferring older plants from containers is most successful if done just as new roots begin.

Orient the orchids according to their light preference and their growth habit. For example, put sun-loving epidendrums where they can receive direct sun, but keep phalaenopsis where branches give them shade, especially from the midday sun.

Let plants grow in a fashion appropriate to their nature. Epidendrums perch on tree sides; many small oncidiums like to cling to twigs; cattleyas often thrive in hollows of trees. Some vandas like to sprawl and anchor their extensive roots to branches, with other aerial roots hanging free.

Fasten orchids onto trees firmly. I prefer to use inconspicuous twine or dark-green plastic-covered wire which can be removed once the roots have established. Some growers staple or nail orchids to trees but this can damage the bark and encourage rotting. In dry regions a small wad of un-milled sphagnum moss between the orchid and the tree will retain moisture for seedlings that may dry too quickly until their roots grow longer. However, do not do this, if possible, because sometimes roots will form only in the moss and later the plants might fall from their perch.

Frequent misting of the newly fastened orchids is better than using wads of moss or tree fern between the tree and the plant. However, once roots have firmly grown onto the tree, one can add some moss around them to retain moisture, if required when climates are dry. As orchids are establishing themselves, give them several mistings each day in sunny weather. Add several drops of a rooting hormone such as Super-Thrive or Tender Leaf Plant Starter to a misting solution to help stimulate roots.

For newly collected species, add a tablespoon of sugar to each gallon of misting solution. Once the orchids' roots start to grow, add water-soluble fertilizer to the solution. This special treatment will help the orchids establish more quickly. Once the plants' roots have grown several feet along the tree, the orchids will usually be able to survive on their own. Watering may be required during droughts, unless the orchids happen to be dormant, as with some deciduous species.

OTHER OUTDOOR CONCERNS

In addition to natural hazards such as falling branches, hail, excess rain, or low humidity, there are other factors that can affect your plants outdoors—for example, insect pests and fungus attacks. My friend Goodale Moir, the famous orchid hybridizer, has a beautifully balanced garden in Honolulu where toads and lizards eat most of the annoying insects while good culture and excellent air circulation keep fungus problems under control. Since most of us are not as fortunate, one must occasionally resort to a pesticide or fungicide application.

To avoid transferring pests indoors, spray all orchids with a pesticide just before bringing the plants in. If you prefer not to use pure chemical pesticides, select an organic type which will at least kill some pests. (See Chapter 14 for details.)

Wash off containers with soapy water if pots have gotten splashed with soil outside. This discourages sow bugs which tend to hide under pots and removes any eggs that insects may have laid on the pots.

In Jakarta, Indonesia, Vanda hybrids planted in heavy clay pots are shaded by palm fronds until the orchids are well established.

11. The Six Most Popular Orchid Genera

OF THE MORE than seventy-five genera of orchids that are commonly grown, some are popular all over the world and six genera in particular find homes in almost every collection. The first orchids to gain favor in the early years of orchid growing were cattleyas.

CATTLEYA

The genus *Cattleya* (CAT-lee-ya) was named in 1824 by botanist John Lindley to honor Englishman William Cattley, owner of a comprehensive amateur orchid collection. Dr. Lindley named *Cattleya labiata* for its large lip and *Cattleya loddigesii* to honor the nineteenth-century firm of Loddiges and Sons, the nursery famous for bringing many showy orchid species to early European orchid collectors.

The sixty or so recognized *Cattleya* species are separated into two groups, according to how many leaves grow on each pseudobulb. *Unifoliate* cattleyas have one leathery leaf, usually about 10 inches long, 2 to 3 inches wide, as in *Cattleya labiata* or *C. mossiae*. Unifoliate species and their hybrids have three to five large flowers per stem, often with colored patterns in the lips.

A larger group of species classified as *bifoliate* has two or three leaves on each growth. Bifoliates usually have more flowers (more than ten to twenty per growth) than the unifoliates, but the blooms are smaller. Many bifoliates, such as *C. guttata,* have fragrant, waxy, thick-substanced flowers dotted with black, brown, or maroon. Bifoliates are crossed with unifoliates to produce hybrids with medium-sized colorful flowers that last a long time.

Bifoliate species popular in contemporary collections include compact *C. aurantiaca,* with brilliant orange to red flowers, and *C. bowringiana,* a tall species with clusters of sparkling rose-pink flowers atop 2½- to 3-foot-tall pseudobulbs. Most species of cattleyas are native to Central America and South America, especially Brazil, Colombia, Venezuela, and Mexico.

Cattleya dowiana aurea, *a unifoliate species, is often used in breeding yellow hybrids.*

Culture As epiphytes, cattleyas live in trees or on rocks in their habitats. Pot them in well-drained mixtures of tree bark, tree fern, and perlite or similar epiphytic medium. With regular fertilizer applications, cattleyas will thrive in gravel or stone aggregate and hardwood charcoal.

Clay pots are useful for their stabilizing weight and porosity, which encourages healthy aeration. Plastic pots are suitable for cattleyas if you add extra drainage holes and an inch or two of pebbles or crock in the bottom to ensure air circulation. Seedlings do especially well in plastic pots because they remain evenly moist. Foam plastic pots are excellent for cattleyas of any age.

Apply water-soluble fertilizers, as outlined in Chapter 7. Cattleyas often go through a brief rest after their flowers fade, at which time they require less water and no fertilizer. I alternate chemical formulas with organic fish emulsion for plants during summer months.

Light The best flower production and compact growth results from high light levels (up to 2,400 footcandles). Give cattleyas only enough shade to prevent leaf burn and yellow leaves. Foliage should be medium green. Many of my cattleya seedlings grow to maturity and flower under fixtures with four 40-watt broad-spectrum fluorescent lamps, fourteen to sixteen hours of light per 24-hour period.

Temperature Cattleyas thrive with intermediate 60° to 65° F. night temperatures. Most will also grow well with nights as warm as 68° F. if given high enough light intensity and good air circulation. Seedlings make the best growth with 68° to 72° F. nights. Daytime highs should be 10° to 15° F. more than evening temperatures.

Mature cattleyas will accept night temperatures in the 50s. Low night temperatures can be used to slow down flowering in *C. mossiae*. In fact, most cattleyas bloom more slowly if night temperatures are in the 50s.

Watering Since cattleyas have water-storing pseudobulbs, they can go many days before needing water. For growing plants, keep the new lead and just completed pseudobulb fully plump but permit the older growths to shrink slightly before soaking the plants.

Most mature cattleyas in a bark or tree fern mix need water every five to seven days, less often if the weather is cool or cloudy, or if the plants are not in active growth. Avoid keeping mature cattleyas constantly wet. Seedlings usually stay in active growth so they can be kept lightly moist. Soak the seedlings' pots, then soak them again when the potting mix starts to dry out.

Propagation To increase cattleyas, divide mature clumps into sections with at least one active lead and three to four leafed pseudobulbs. Cattleyas grown from seed take three to eight years before producing their first flowers. Most mature cattleya hybrids bloom two times per year but most species flower only once every twelve months.

Selections Cattleyas are a favorite subject with creative hybridizers. Hybrids between various species during the past hundred years have brought the pure *Cattleya* great fame. Many of the best pure white hybrids are pure cattleyas. More recently, multigeneric hybrids, involving *Cattleya* with related genera such as *Brassavola* (*Brassocattleya*), *Laelia* (*Laeliocattleya*), and *Sophronitis* (*Sophrocattleya*), are seen more often.

Exciting crosses of cattleyas with *Epidendrum, Diacrium,* and *Schomburgkia* are less common but well worth growing for variations in flower form, color, and fragrance. Some of the hybrids with *Schomburgkia* (*Schombocattleya*) have flower spikes 3 feet tall. Many hybrids with pseudobulbous epidendrums, some in the Encyclia section, have 4- to 8-inch-tall plants, 8- to 12-inch thin spikes of fragrant flowers. Current catalogs include cattleya hybrids with compact growth well suited to light gardens or windowsill shelves.

If large flowers are your favorites, you will be delighted with *Cattleya* hybrids, usually involving *Brassavola* and sometimes *Laelia* as well (*Brassolaeliocattleya*). Every year brings more offerings so that now we have thousands of attractive hybrids bred from cattleyas and related

Tall Cattleya *Porcia 'Canizarro' (see color plate) crossed with dwarf* Laelia pumila *produced this light-lavender-flowered dwarf hybrid which I raised under Wide-Spectrum Gro-Lux lamps.*

showy genera. Choice clones of pure species are sometimes offered, but more often the best species are crossed with themselves or other good clones, then raised from seed. Hybrids are often more floriferous than species, blooming two or three times a year.

The best clones are propagated by tissue culture and the resulting plantlets are reasonably priced, considering the quality of the flowers produced. A few visits to a commercial grower and an orchid show will expose you to a broad range of cattleya types, so you can choose those that you enjoy.

Fragrance is a pleasant bonus found in many cattleyas. The better orchid catalogs will list flower color, seasons of bloom, flower size, and may mention perfume when the cross is especially fragrant.

CYMBIDIUM

Cymbidium (sim-BID-ee-um) hybrids are most popular in temperate or semi-tropical regions where nights are cool enough to encourage abundant flower production. Recently smaller-flowered "Miniature" cymbidiums bred from warmer-growing small-flowered species have spread cymbidium fame. Now the miniature hybrids are grown everywhere because they will flower easily with intermediate-range night temperatures.

Cymbidium species include cool growers from mountains in India, and intermediate- to warm-growing types from the lowlands of tropical Asia. Hybrids between various species and highly developed modern clones are currently more popular than straight species because hybrid flowers tend

Cymbidium *Promenade is a modern white hybrid with pink blush and a darker pink in the lip.*

Cymbidium *Burgundian 'Sydney' is a standard-sized hybrid with buff-rose flowers and dark red-edged lip. This clone has received an Award of Merit from the American Orchid Society and the Royal Horticultural Society.*

to have better flower form (more rounded), clearer color, and greater substance. The name *Cymbidium* derives from the Greek *kymbes* (meaning "boat-shaped cup"), referring to the wide lip seen on many species.

Most of our cultivated cymbidiums are bred from terrestrial or semi-terrestrial species, although a few species do live as epiphytes on moss-covered tree branches, rocks, rough-barked palms, or in pockets of leaf mold on rocky ground. Well-drained terrestrial composts are suitable for cymbidium hybrids. A few strictly epiphytic species such as *Cym. finlaysonianum* do best in bark or coconut fiber.

Cymbidiums have long strap-shaped arching leaves and plump pseudo-bulbs varying in size from golf ball dimensions to baseball proportions. New growth sprouts from buds at the base of the previous year's pseudobulb. Abundant thick roots live for several years, and flowers are produced on an inflorescence from the completed pseudobulbs.

Most cymbidiums have erect spikes but some miniatures have arching or even pendulous inflorescences. The spike grows from the base of each pseudobulb, sometimes two may come from the same growth. For the first few inches, spikes are hidden by leaf-like sheaths, but soon they thrust free, growing 12 to 36 inches tall before starting to open buds. Modern hybrids have ten to thirty thick-substanced flowers per spike. Each flower will last four to eight weeks in perfect condition.

Blooms ripen from the bottom upward so the lower buds may develop into ripe flowers several weeks before the top buds open, extending the blooming period over several weeks. Some cymbidiums, like the miniature *Cym.* Peter Pan, are fragrant.

Temperature Large-flowered cymbidiums that are quite popular as cut flowers need cool (45° to 50° F., fall to early winter) nights to initiate abundant spikes. The miniature cymbidiums, bred from intermediate- to warm-growing species, thrive and bloom well with 55° to 65° F. nights, with 60° F. an ideal low temperature.

Culture Cymbidiums thrive in terrestrial mixes. Pot cymbidiums with their roots completely covered but their pseudobulbs exposed. Pure epiphytic species thrive in epiphytic mixes and look nice in slat baskets.

Active cymbidiums need to be well fertilized to develop their full potential. Use a balanced formula, such as 18-18-18, alternated with fish emulsion as new growths are forming. Some commercial fertilizers especially formulated for cymbidiums include Stewart's Top Dressing, which should be applied dry four times each year, and Q.U.E. "Fast Start" Slow Release (27-6-10).

When pseudobulbs are nearly completed, begin applications of low nitrogen formulas, such as Peters 10-30-20, to encourage spike formation. Keep established clumps constantly moist when they are growing. Well-drained composts in suitable containers will permit generous watering without having roots stay too wet.

Mature plants in clay pots may need watering every day during the summer. My cymbidiums grow well in tough rubber or flexible plastic tubes, used at garden centers for many outdoor plants. Even nicer are ceramic or wood-like heavy plastic pots, but remove the snap-on saucers for complete drainage.

Miniature cymbidiums are easier to care for and take less space than standard-size hybrids. Some miniatures bloom two or three times each year. Cymbidiums listed as miniature are smaller in size than standard hybrids, but they are *not* miniature compared to other genera. Most miniature hybrids which are bred from a combination of large- and small-growing species will reach 18 to 24 inches tall. Mature clumps need an 8- to 12-inch container size. Much more delicate, but with fewer flowers, are oriental miniature hybrids and several species, much appreciated for fragrance but not nearly as showy as more popular cymbidiums bred for larger flowers.

Light Cymbidiums need strong (2,000 to 4,000 footcandles) light. During warm months I put these plants outdoors where they receive full sun, except for midday hours when the sun is dappled by overhead tall trees or lath. Indoors I keep cymbidiums in bright light or in a combination of morning sunlight with broad-spectrum fluorescent lamps to provide fourteen hours of light even during winter months.

When cymbidiums are ready to bloom, you may wish to alter the light intensity according to the flower color. Greens and yellows are more pure and delicate when the blooms open under diffuse light. Dark tones such as maroons and reds are brighter when they develop in bright light. Some plants with white flowers, such as miniature *Cym.* Showgirl, develop a pink blush if they open in bright light.

Propagation Superior clones of standard and miniature cymbidiums are available as meristems (see pages 196–197). When selecting cymbidiums for your collection, read growers' notes in catalogs carefully and pick clones that bloom when you want flowers. Propagation of mature plants is best done at repotting time, after flowering, usually in late spring. Carefully pull the plant apart in the case of oriental miniatures, or cut with a sharp knife for tough, larger types. Each division should have at least one active growth plus three to five leafy pseudobulbs.

To sprout leafless backbulbs, put them in a tray of sphagnum moss, keep them in diffuse light with moss that is slightly moist, and pot when roots develop. Prize clones not available as meristems may be offered as backbulbs at a low price. Backbulbs take two to four years before developing into flowering-sized plants.

Cymbidium *Red Imp 'Red Tower' is a fragrant mericlone with velvety-red flowers, and yellow and maroon lips.*

Selections Any of the modern hybrids will provide beautiful blooms with a minimum of care. You can choose many colors, from pure white to pink, yellow, red, maroon, green, or combinations with red lips or contrasting colored dots.

Among the pure species sometimes offered in catalogs are:

Cym. eburneum var. *parishii* from Burma, a cool- to intermediate-growing type with an arching spray of 3-inch fragrant white blooms decorated with velvety purple lips.

Cym. ensifolium, a warm-growing miniature with 2-inch fragrant greenish-yellow flowers.

Cym. canaliculatum, an intermediate- to warm-growing plant from Australia, with maroon-red flowers.

An excellent miniature hybrid is *Cym.* Tiger Tail, a cross between warm-grower *Cym. tigrinum* from Burma and large-flowered *Cym.* Alexanderi 'Westonbirt'. *Cym.* Tiger Tail clones have yellow flowers with white lips with maroon spots. Christmas-blooming *Cym.* Red Imp 'Fire Balls' has pendant spikes and looks best in hanging containers. *Cym.* Mary Pinchess 'Del Rey', offered as a meristem, is a dwarf plant with erect spikes of waxy thick-substanced yellow flowers in midwinter.

Specialists' catalogs show many meristem selections in full color, so choosing your favorites will be easy. The main blooming season for cymbidiums is midwinter but hybridizers have been extending the season, especially with crosses involving miniatures. Catalog descriptions will provide dates of flowering for each clone.

DENDROBIUM

The genus *Dendrobium* (den-DRO-bee-um) has about fifteen hundred species which live over a wide area in the Asian tropics, India, Australia, New Guinea, and Fiji. The name *Dendrobium* stems from classic Greek, and means "living on a tree."

Although most Dendrobium species are epiphytes, their growth style varies greatly between types. Some miniatures are only 2 to 4 inches tall, while other dendrobiums grow 4 feet high before sending up 2- to 3-foot flower spikes. Certain species from high altitudes require cool nights to bloom, while others need a dry rest after growth is made. Others are evergreen and evergrowing, the type most famous in tropical regions of Southeast Asia and Hawaii.

Plant Groups Dendrobiums can be classified into three horticultural groups:

1. Evergreen species needing intermediate to warm temperatures, 50 to 60 per cent humidity, and constant moisture except for a slight drying at the roots as new pseudobulbs mature. *Dendrobium phalaenopsis* and *Den. discolor* (syn. *undulatum*) are examples.

2. Deciduous or evergreen species which grow with intermediate to warm temperatures but need a dry rest to bloom well. *Den. aggregatum* is an example.

3. Deciduous species which thrive with intermediate to warm temperatures but require six to eight weeks of cool 50° to 55° F. nights for best flowering. *Den. nobile* is in this group.

Growth styles range from *Den. cucumerinum,* which looks like a clump of 1-inch gherkin pickles, to pendant canes up to 4 feet long, as in *Den. superbum* (syn. *Den. anosmum*). Most popular for indoor collections are 18- to 24-inch-tall plants bred from *Den. nobile, Den. phalaenopsis* and, more recently, *Den. canaliculatum.*

Light and Humidity All dendrobiums thrive under bright light (1,500 to 3,000+ footcandles), at least the intensity needed to grow sturdy cattleya-type orchids. Gardeners in sunny tropical areas grow upright dendrobiums in garden beds with strong sun and sharp drainage. The evergreen species grow on trees in almost full sun in Malaysia, the Solomon Islands, and New Guinea. *Den. phalaenopsis* hybrids are grown throughout Thailand, usually in teak baskets hung from outside roof rafters.

Deciduous dendrobiums will tolerate less light when they are without leaves because they are not making new canes. Thick, succulent Australian species, such as *Den. cucumerinum,* accept full sun. A relative humidity of 50 to 60 per cent is ideal, although succulent sorts will adapt to slightly lower relative humidity.

Water and Fertilizer Active dendrobiums can use almost constant moisture as long as drainage is good and air circulation is constant. Drench roots until the water runs out of the pot. Then just before the mix dries out, soak the roots again. Compact creeping species, such as *Den. aggregatum* and *Den. linguiforme,* grow best on slabs of bark or tree fern and accept daily watering.

Provide active dendrobiums with fertilizer at every other watering or with a proportioner that provides fertilizer in special dilute concentrations each time that the plants are watered. Give no fertilizer to resting, leafless, or otherwise inactive plants.

Containers Evergreen dendrobiums grow well in fir bark or tree fern mixes in well-drained clay containers. If you use plastic containers, be sure to burn in extra drainage-aeration holes. All containers should have a 1- to 2-inch layer of drainage material at the bottom. I also add hardwood charcoal. Charcoal and gravel make a good mix for evergreen types grown outdoors in the tropics. Dendrobiums thrive in slightly small containers so that the roots will never be surrounded with soggy compost. Cork bark and tree fern slabs are best for dwarf creeping types and pendant sorts such as *Den. superbum.*

Selections *Den. aggregatum* is a compact 3-inch-tall creeping evergreen species from India and Southeast Asia which blooms well when given a dry, cool (50° to 55° F. nights) rest after its growth is complete. Orange-yellow flowers open on pendant spikes.

Den. cucumerinum is an Australian species, 1 to 2 inches tall, which forms a cluster of creeping stems with bumpy succulent leaves. The ¼-inch white flowers appear on short sprays and are attractive when seen as a mass.

Den. nobile is more popular in hybrid form since new types, such as outstanding Yamamoto crosses, have an abundance of 1- to 3-inch round flowers which last a month or more. Grow this type with intermediate nights until the last leaf begins to form on top of the pseudobulb, then provide nights about 50° F. to initiate flower buds. With warm nights *Den. nobile* types form plantlets, not flower buds, on the stems. Plantlets of select *Den. nobile* hybrids need one to two years of growing before flowers appear.

Den. phalaenopsis is often considered a robust variety of *Den. bigibbum,* but catalogs list the species and hybrids as *Den. phalaenopsis,* a reference to the flower form which is round and flat, resembling the blooms of *Phalaenopsis.* This evergreen species from Australia and adjacent tropical islands comes in several strains. The dwarf types grow 6 to 8 inches tall but most cultivars mature at 20 to 26 inches. The usual color is pink to magenta but white and white-with-lavender marked forms are sometimes offered.

Dendrobium *Golden Blossom is an advanced* Den. nobile *hybrid created by hybridizer Jiro Yamamoto. Similar hybrids are available with flowers that are white, pink, or dark lavender.*

Hybrids between *Den. phalaenopsis* types and compact *Den. canaliculatum* are good choices for bright light gardens and sunny windowsills. Most hybrids in this group are very sensitive to air pollution, and if smog is common in your area, bud blast may occur (see Chapter 14).

Dendrobiums with twisted petals are called "Antelope" types. These are usually tall growers which flower with great abandon if given bright light and warm conditions. *Den. D'Albertisii* (syn. *Den. antennatum*) and *Den. ionoglossum* are some "Antelope" type species.

Den. superbum (syn. *Den. anosmum*) from the Philippines and Southeast Asia has fragrant 3- to 4-inch pink flowers along 2- to 4-foot pendant stems. This is a deciduous type. A cross between *Den. superbum* and smaller *Den. pierardii* (syn. *Den. aphyllum*) is *Den.* Adrasta, which is charming and compact.

PAPHIOPEDILUM

For years *Paphiopedilum* (paf-ee-oh-PED-i-lum) species were grown as *Cypripedium,* but now all of the popular tropical types are known as *Paphiopedilum* or "Lady Slipper" orchids. About fifty species and thousands of hybrids are currently grown, all appreciated for their long-lasting waxy-textured flowers, many in unusual muted color combinations. Most species are terrestrial.

Hybridizers continue to make crosses between pure species. I find these graceful small- to medium-flowered hybrids and the pure species more charming than large modern hybrids. Nevertheless, the giant, round, waxy *Paphiopedilum* hybrids are dramatic, come in many different colors, and last for weeks in perfect condition. Some medium-sized hybrids have a multiple-flowered inflorescence but most large-flowered sorts have one single bloom per mature growth.

Some paphiopedilums have silver or maroon mottling on their foliage, an attractive feature found most often on warm-growing species and their hybrids. Other species have plain green foliage, 6 to 10 inches long. Most

Dendrobium *Adrasta* (Den. pierardii X Den. superbum) *has fuzzy-lipped pink flowers.*

plants are 8 to 12 inches tall, but some species, such as *Paph. bellatulum* and *Paph. godefroyae* from Thailand, are 3- to 6-inch dwarfs.

Temperature In captivity, paphiopedilums are divided into cool growers, which thrive with nights in the 50s, and intermediate to warm growers, which do well with 60° to 70° F. nights. Deciding which hybrids are cool growers and which might do better with warmer nights is not easy because modern hybrids frequently involve species from cool, intermediate, *and* warm habitats. A general rule is to treat plants with plain green foliage as cool growers and those with mottled foliage as intermediate to warm growers.

For best vegetative growth, in seedlings for example, all paphiopedilums will thrive with nights around 65° F. Mature plants should be given a month with nights in the mid-50s if they are reluctant to bloom.

Some green-leaved types bred only from cool-growing species will bloom well only if given four to eight weeks of cool nights around 55° F. When buds show from the center of the mature plants, nights can be in the low 60s. If you just want to grow a few paphiopedilums in a mixed orchid collection, select the types that thrive and bloom without any special night temperature drop. For example, *Paph.* Clair de Lune, *Paph.* Maudiae, and primary hybrids of warm-growing dwarfs such as *Paph. niveum* and *Paph. godefroyae*.

Light Paphiopedilums bloom most freely if given as much light as they can accept without their foliage yellowing. Furnish a relative humidity above 50 per cent so plants can grow well with bright diffuse light (800 to 1,500 footcandles), using shade only at midday or during summer months. These are perfect orchids for light gardens. Paphiopedilums thrive under broad-spectrum fluorescent lamps, 6 to 8 inches under tubes, with twelve- to fourteen-hour days.

Containers and Composts I use plastic pots for paphiopedilums so the roots have little danger of becoming completely dry. With good drainage from gravel and hardwood charcoal, plastic pots are the most suitable for terrestrial composts (described in Chapter 6). If the orchid nursery recommends a less acid compost for specific species, mulch the plants with oyster shell (sold in feed stores or pet supply departments) or stir in a teaspoon of ground dolomite limestone per 6-inch pot of compost.

Large-flowered hybrids thrive with even moisture at the roots, but never let them sit in water. Some of the species do better if permitted to dry out slightly before being soaked again. For example, *Paph. bellatulum, Paph. godefroyae, Paph. niveum,* and their hybrids can dry out slightly between waterings with no harm.

Paphiopedilum *Transvaal* (Paph. chamberlainianum X Paph. rothschildianum) *produces tall spikes with flowers in greenish-yellow tones with dark red-brown stripes and dots.*

Paphiopedilum bellatulum *from Thailand has low compact growth of mottled leaves and long-lasting white flowers with purple spots.*

Selections Although species come from Asia, the most highly developed hybrids are offered by European and American growers. Catalogs show hybrids involving multiflowered species such as *Paph. glaucophyllum* and dwarf *Paph. primulinum* in unusual types, but large-flowered hybrids are more common than multiflora types. Colors available in large types range from mahogany to brownish-red, light brown, green, cream, yellow, and bronze, most with contrasting black dots. One of the most famous parents in producing modern hybrids is round *Paph.* Winston Churchill.

Here are some of the charming pure species:

Paph. argus of the Philippines, an intermediate grower with tan flowers marked green and yellow, with black dots ("warts"), and decorated with hairs.

Paph. fairieanum from India, an intermediate grower with an adaptable nature, has flowers with a broad top petal, wavy side petals, an unusual red and white pattern, and a delicate brown pouch.

Paph. venustum from India, an adaptable intermediate grower with nicely mottled leaves, multicolored green, brown, and cream flowers marked red to orange, and black hairs.

Warm-growing dwarfs from Thailand and the Malay Peninsula include *Paph. bellatulum, Paph. concolor, Paph. niveum.* These species are used to breed compact hybrids with round, mainly white flowers dotted purple. All are excellent in light gardens.

Paphiopedilum *Diane is a primary hybrid of* Paph. chamberlainianum *and* Paph. fairieanum. *This is clone 'Pia de Luca', which received a Highly Commended Certificate from the American Orchid Society.*

Propagation Hybrids and select species are commercially grown from seed. Propagate mature clumps by dividing them at repotting time, usually just after their flowers fade (see Chapter 13, "Propagation Techniques"). Mericloning techniques are not yet widely used for *Paphiopedilum* because tissue culture techniques are not as successful as in other genera. When meristem propagation becomes practical for paphiopedilums, select clones will be available at lower prices than at present.

PHALAENOPSIS

The Asian genus *Phalaenopsis* (fal-ae-NOP-siss) was named in 1825. The name means "moth-like" in classic Greek, referring to the flat, white flowers typical of *Phal. amabilis,* the species from which modern white hybrids are bred. Smaller-flowered species with different-colored waxy flowers, such as *Phal. lueddemanniana,* are not as white but are still called "Moth Orchids."

Phalaenopsis are epiphytes without pseudobulbs. In their tropical Asian jungle habitats, they have sufficient rain and humidity to survive without water-storing stems. In your home or greenhouse, pot them in mixtures that permit good air circulation but still retain enough moisture to prevent their roots from completely drying. I use coconut fiber or mixes of bark and tree fern.

Keep plants evenly moist but never soggy. Their fleshy foliage stores some moisture, but phalaenopsis should never be subjected to weeks without water, in contrast to many orchids with pseudobulbs.

Special Features Phalaenopsis are champions for giving an abundance of flowers on relatively compact plants. The larger white-flowered hybrids do need 2 to 3 feet of space for arching spikes but the number of flowers produced per plant is outstanding. Each flower will last a minimum of three to six weeks on the spike.

An established mature plant can be encouraged to produce a secondary inflorescence, after flowers on the first have finished. To accomplish this, wait until the first group of flowers have faded or been picked off one by one. The whole front section of the spike can also be cut if you wish a spray of flowers. Then, with a sharp flame-sterilized knife or razor, cut off the inflorescence just above the second or third node. (My photo on page 108 shows where to make this cut.) In a few months a new inflorescence should form from the node just below the cut. This procedure sometimes encourages an established phalaenopsis to have two or three spikes of flowers at once.

Colors Traditional phalaenopsis have magnificent flat white, heavy-substanced flowers of smooth texture. Their lips are intricate structures

Old phalaenopsis flower spikes cut just above a live node (arrow) often produce a secondary inflorescence.

with delicate twisted tendrils on the tips of varicolored lobes. Most white-flowered hybrids have some yellow inside the lip and a few have a pink blush on the reverse of their petals. Modern hybrids are so uniform that it is easy to obtain excellent clones by buying seedlings bred from the best white parents.

Phalaenopsis with colored flowers are less uniform in breeding. To obtain a full, round, well-colored pink, apricot, or yellow flower is more of a challenge. Breeders are working with several rather small species which have yellow and pink flowers, or flowers with bars and stripes. By crossing these colorful small species with larger rounded phalaenopsis, new hybrids are being created to produce medium to large flowers of good shape and unusual colors. Since the background of these creations is so mixed, the seedlings vary greatly in color, even from a single cross. One hybrid I made has a deep-pink male parent and a buff-yellow female (pod) parent. Seedlings from this cross bloom in a range from pure white through light yellow, yellow-pink blends, to pink, many with fine dots inherited from the pod parent.

Pale-pink selections of normally white-flowered species have been interbred until we now have rich pink phalaenopsis with good shape and texture. By carefully selecting phalaenopsis hybrids bred from different species, you can have some plant in bloom every month. Since each flower lasts for several weeks, phalaenopsis are excellent orchids in all but the coolest growing conditions.

Phalaenopsis *Keith Shaffer, a modern white hybrid, contrasted with* Doritaenopsis *Purple Gem.*

Phalaenopsis *Pin Up Girl 'Carmen Vazquez' is a fine example of a modern white-with-pink-stripes phalaenopsis.*

Culture Provide phalaenopsis with 65° to 70° F. night temperatures. Seedlings prosper with the warmer 70° F. minimum, while mature plants do perfectly well with 65° F. nights. Bright diffuse sun (1,000 to 2,000 footcandles) is best, or broad-spectrum fluorescent light.

The species *Phal. schillerana,* and some of its primary hybrids, may refuse to bloom if given long days in the fall. Most large-flowered phalaenopsis are also temperature-sensitive. Mature plants bloom best when fall nights are long and 60° to 65° F. To encourage maximum flower production in a collection of mixed phalaenopsis hybrids, let night temperatures fall to the 60–65° F. range for four to six weeks at the end of each growing season, August into October in the northern hemisphere. This is when days are getting shorter.

The combination of long nights, at least thirteen hours of darkness, with 60° to 65° F. temperatures will encourage mature phalaenopsis to initiate flower spikes. Under warmer conditions, especially with less than thirteen hours of darkness, flower spikes may continue to lengthen without developing blooms, or may produce plantlets rather than flowers.

Luckily, in a typical collection of mixed genera, long nights at 60° F. minimum are acceptable. Other popular orchids such as cattleyas, dendrobiums, and paphiopedilums all respond well to long nights at 60° F. in the fall.

Hybrids with Other Genera   Phalaenopsis are now bred with related genera to produce flowers in different colors, shapes, and seasons. These complicated offspring are less sensitive to day length and night temperature than pure phalaenopsis. This is especially true when phalaenopsis are crossed with warm-growing genera such as *Ascocentrum, Vanda,* and *Renanthera.*

Similarly the dwarf phalaenopsis species from lowland tropical regions, such as *Phal. violacea* and *Phal. fuscata,* will thrive under warm conditions (65° to 70° F. nights) such as one might have around an indoor light garden. Some of the most charming hybrids are dwarf combinations between larger *Phal. amabilis* types and small but brightly colored species which are sometimes fragrant as well.

Orchid catalogs list an exciting array of colorful hybrids in all sizes and colors. Be sure to include some multigeneric combinations in your collection. By crossing phalaenopsis with *Ascocentrum,* breeders have created dwarf-growing *Asconopsis,* a group with yellow to apricot flowers on branched sprays. Combining phalaenopsis with *Renanthera* gives us *Renanthopsis,* compact creations with a multitude of pastel pink, yellow, or apricot blooms on branched spikes.

Growing Tips   The forming inflorescence of *Phalaenopsis* is very sensitive to light direction. Once the spike begins to elongate, it grows toward the strongest source of light. If you should turn the plant before the flowers open, the spike will readjust itself and continue to grow toward the brightest light. This results in a twisted disoriented display of flowers. For the most attractive arrangement of flowers on an arching spray (or upright on some Doritis hybrids), let the inflorescence develop and most of the buds open before changing the orchid's position.

Some of the smaller hybrids between species, or with one species parent, may continue to produce flowers on a continually growing spike over a period of months. This is also natural in *Phal. cornu-cervi,* which produces flowers from the same stiff stem year after year. Such long-flowering dwarfs are excellent in a light garden or where space is limited.

Some hybrids in my collection with this long-blooming habit are bred from *Phal. luddemanniana,* such as *Phal.* Tyler Carlson. Tiny *Phal.* Little Sister stays in bloom for months with small, red-spotted, white flowers. Its parents are *Phal. maculata* and *Phal. equestris alba.* Fragrant pink-flowered *Phal.* Violet Star (a cross between *Phal. violacea* and *Phal. intermedia* 'Portei') grows 6 to 8 inches and usually has a few flowers.

Phalaenopsis lueddemanniana *with plantlets on mature inflorescences has red and white waxy flowers.*

Terete Phalaenopsis Several species have round, succulent foliage, dwarf growth, and are classified in several ways. Taxonomist Dr. Herman R. Sweet puts these Bornean species into another genus, *Paraphalaenopsis*. However, horticulturally, terete species *denevei, laycockii,* and *serpentilingua* are considered *Phalaenopsis*. Each of these accepts brighter light than broad-leafed phalaenopsis. Even more adaptable to home collections are hybrids of terete species with other phalaenopsis and related genera.

VANDA

Vanda (VAN-dah) is a genus from tropical Asia. Its name derives from a Sanskrit word referring to one of the Indian species. The species grow in bright light on trees where some of the thick white roots can hang freely in the air. About seventy species are recognized but only twenty or so are common in collections. Most famous in the genus are the flowers

Vanda *Jennie Hashimoto* (V. sanderana X V. Onomea) *thrives in a teak basket under lath at T. Orchids in Bangkok, Thailand.*

on white- to pink-flowered terete (pencil-stemmed) hybrids that are used to make Hawaiian leis.

Vandas are monopodial, growing continually from a central stem. Offshoots may be produced around the main plant base. This often happens if the main growing point is damaged, or if the top is cut off to lower the stem. Because of their monopodial habit, vandas are slower to propagate in a home collection than sympodial genera. Commercial growers use tissue culture to increase good clones. (See Chapter 13, "Propagation Techniques.") Some terete types can be propagated by tip cuttings, too.

Most popular in greenhouses are strap-leaved species and their hybrids. These require less intense light than terete-leaved types. Strap-leaved types and terete vandas are crossed to produce semi-terete types. These plants require less light than pure terete vandas but still grow easily and propagate quickly from stem tip cuttings.

Flowers Blooms appear on upright spikes which sprout from between strap-shaped leaves, or directly from the round stem in terete types. Each spike has three to twelve flat flowers. The flowers are long-lasting, remaining in perfect form for twenty to thirty days. Well-grown modern hybrids often bloom two or three times each year. Vandas make excellent cut flowers.

Growing Techniques Vandas should be potted in coarse chunks of fir or redwood bark mixed with large perlite and hardwood charcoal over drainage of crocks or gravel. A tropical technique used outside in warm areas is to pot vandas in lava rock or coarse cinders, then water and fertilize almost every sunny day. Some of the smaller species, such as *Vanda cristata* and *Ascocenda* hybrids, are easy to grow in slat baskets filled with coconut fiber or coarse tree fern.

Mature 2- to 4-foot-tall vandas are top-heavy, so potted plants need enough weight in the container to prevent being tipped over. I use coarse gravel topped with hardwood charcoal for potted vandas and their hybrids. Large chunks of tree fern or coconut husk are also suitable potting media when used with gravel and charcoal.

Heat and Humidity Vandas thrive with 60 to 70 per cent relative humidity and warm temperatures. Nights of 65° to 70° F. are best for young vandas, while mature plants grow well with 60° F. nights. A few species from higher elevations, such as *Vanda coerulea*, accept nights in the 50s.

Daytime temperatures can go into the 90s with the sun's heat if the humidity is kept high as light intensity and temperature increase. I mist my vandas on bright mornings from spring until fall. When they are outside for the summer I also mist them in midafternoon when the weather is hot.

Vanda sanderana *from the Philippines has an excellent record as a parent for outstanding hybrids. It has 3- to 4-inch buff-brown flowers with rose blush and dark red-brown lips.*

Light and Fertilizer Vandas need strong light (3,000 to 4,000+ footcandles) to bloom well. Seedlings grow nicely with diffuse sun or under broad-spectrum fluorescent tubes. Mature vandas do best in a greenhouse, hanging close to the glass, and then outdoors in nearly full sun during the summer months in temperate climates. In subtropical southern Florida and tropical Hawaii, vandas flourish outside in raised garden beds, as they do throughout tropical Asia.

Fertilize vandas when they are making new leaves. I use timed release Osmocote 14-14-14 and occasional applications of water-soluble fertilizers diluted to half strength. During the summer I alternate chemical formulas with fish emulsion.

Special Growing Techniques Some of the vanda's thick roots grow naturally into the air. Let these aerial roots stay outside of the potting mix, an easy task for plants in baskets. For potted vandas, you can provide a support of tree fern or cork log for the roots to grab.

To shorten tall vandas, cut off the top with several live roots between spring and fall when plants are most active. Dust the cuts with Rootone powder or similar fungicide. Pot the top, place it in diffuse light, and mist every sunny morning to encourage new roots. Once roots grow into the compost, resume regular watering. Keep the old base since it may sprout a new lead.

Propagation Hybrids are grown from seed sown on nutrient agar. With good culture, seedlings begin to bloom after three or four years of growth. You can increase your vandas from an occasional *keiki* (small off-shoot or plantlet) or, in the case of terete types, from rooted tops. Superior clones are often propagated by meristem techniques.

Selections Vanda hybrids are generally superior in flower shape and vigor to pure species because they have been bred through several generations with these goals in mind. Pure species are still fun to grow and those plants raised from seed are often of excellent quality since breeders usually select top-quality clones to produce the seed.

In Thailand some commercial growers have whole lath houses filled with select forms of the famous indigenous *V. coerulea*. Another famous species, *V. sanderana* (botanically, *Euanthe sanderana*), has well-shaped cream and green flowers on upright sturdy spikes.

The most famous vanda hybrid around the world is *V.* Rothschildiana, a cross of *V. coerulea* with *V. sanderana,* registered in 1931 but still grown and often remade with select parents. *V.* Rothschildiana combines the floriferous habit and delicate tessellation lines plus some blue color of *V. coerulea,* with the better shape, substance, and lip of *V. sanderana.*

Since *V. coerulea* is a high-altitude species from Southeast Asia and India, it grows best with cool nights (50° to 55° F.). *V. sanderana* is from warmer habitats in the southeastern Philippines. Combining these two species produces a hybrid adaptable over a wide range of temperatures but intermediate to warm nights are preferable.

V. luzonica, like the species mentioned above, is a strap-leafed species, adaptable to indoor culture where light is bright. The flowers are thick-substanced, fragrant, and white with contrasting magenta to crimson blotches.

V. cristata is a dwarf species which is mature at 8 inches tall. Its fragrant 2-inch yellow-green to cream flowers are highlighted by a purple lip. This vanda species will fit well in a light garden or on a windowsill. It grows well with cool to intermediate range temperature conditions.

Round-leafed or terete vanda hybrids must have intense sun to do well so they are grown outdoors in the tropics or in greenhouses where sun is abundant. When the terete types are crossed with strap-leaf vandas, the result is semi-terete types which bloom with less light than the pure teretes. An example is the excellent *Vanda* T.M.A. (*V. sanderana* crossed with *V.* Josephine van Brero), a one-quarter terete hybrid adaptable to

Renantanda *Seminole* (Renanthera monachina *X* Vanda denison-iana) *has fragrant yellow flowers spotted red.*

full sun or bright diffuse light. Long-lasting flowers are apricot to buff-yel-low in color, with an orange to maroon lip.

Better than pure vanda hybrids for most home collections in temper-ate zones are hybrids of vanda with small-growing genera, such as *Ascocentrum* (*Ascocenda*) and *Rhynchostylis* (*Rhynchovanda*). These intergeneric hybrids need less intense light than pure vandas. They grow well in 4- to 8-inch pots, and many thrive in light gardens. Modern Ascocenda hybrids are so advanced that you can now find all the vanda colors available *plus* unusual blue and red tones not seen in any pure vandas. Currently the best Ascocendas and related hybrids are bred in Thailand or Hawaii, but orchid firms in Florida and California offer imported seedlings. Meristem plantlets are also offered.

Growers in semitropical to tropical regions give Ascocendas up to 7,000 footcandles of light. However, indoors these hybrids produce perfectly formed long-lasting flowers with the same light intensity that cattleyas are given—a minimum of four 40-watt broad-spectrum fluorescent lamps.

These large-flowered Paphiopedilum *hybrids were raised in a basement
light garden, then put on display in this sunroom.*

Paphiopedilum venustum.

Vanda *Chavananand* (V. *Jennie Hashimoto* X V. *Joan Rothsand*) *is an excellent hybrid bred from* V. sanderana.

This assortment of Phalaenopsis *flowers from my collection shows the wide variety of colors now appearing in hybrids.*

Ascocenda *Sauvanee 'Talisman Cove'* (V. *Jennie Hashimoto X* Ascocentrum curvifolium) *was bred in Thailand.*

Catasetum *Francis Nelson* (Ctsm. trulla *X* Ctsm. fimbriatum).

12. Orchid Genera:
Acineta to *Zygopetalum*

IN ADDITION to the most popular genera featured in the previous chapter, many more orchids are suitable for contemporary collections. In the tropics where plants are grown outside, genera are restricted to those that will adapt to prevailing temperatures. However, where orchids are given complete shelter, one can grow any desired species.

This chapter features more than sixty genera and hundreds of species. When one includes the man-made genera and their hybrids, the orchids you can grow run into the thousands.

Making a selection from among all these orchids is an exciting challenge. With good cultural practices and a balanced assortment of genera, your collection will always have orchids in bloom.

Acineta (ah-see-NEH-ta) is a Latin American genus of epiphytes with plump pseudobulbs and pendulous inflorescences. The broad leaves may reach 24 inches long. Grow acinetas in slat baskets or on tree fern slabs in diffuse light with intermediate to warm temperatures. Avoid having water accumulate in the funnel-shaped new growth and provide constant air circulation to discourage fungus. *A. chrysantha* has fragrant 2-inch yellow flowers spotted red-brown. *A. superba* has a fragrance of tropical spices from slightly larger flowers with waxy substance and creamy yellow tones. Acinetas bloom mainly in the spring. They look best in a hanging pot since the flowers open on a sharply pendulous spike.

Ada (AY-da) is a genus of two cool-growing epiphytes related to *Odontoglossum*. *Ada aurantiaca,* an orange-flowered species, is sometimes grown where cool conditions can be provided. *A. lehmanni* has less intense orange flowers and foliage dappled with gray. Adas thrive in small well-drained pots of unmilled sphagnum moss or any epiphytic mix suitable for odontoglossums. Grow them in diffuse sun or under broad-spectrum fluorescents.

Aerangis (ay-er-ANG-giss) species are related to *Angraecum* and come from similar habitats in tropical Africa, including Madagascar (Malagasy

Republic). About ten of the estimated sixty species are seen in cultivation. *Aerangis* thrives under intermediate to warm conditions with 60 to 70 per cent relative humidity and diffuse light.

The compact species are suitable in light gardens. I grow these on coffee trees or in small well-drained pots with an epiphyte mix, often adding some coarse unmilled sphagnum around the stem base to prevent roots from drying out completely. *Aerangis* species are monopodial and have no pseudobulbs. *Aergs. biloba, Aergs. citrata, Aergs. kotschyana,* and *Aergs. mystacidii* are all dwarf species, resembling 4- to 8-inch leathery phalaenopsis plants.

Aerangis flowers are white to cream-colored, and are produced on thin pendulous racemes. *Aergs. rhodosticta* is similar but the white flowers have a red center. Like their *Angraecum* relatives, *Aerangis* flowers are fragrant at night. Some species, such as *Aergs. calligerum,* have an upright stem with an arching inflorescence. A few rare hybrids are occasionally offered by specialists such as Fred Hillerman of Angraecum House.

Aeranthes (ay-er-AN-theez) is similar to *Aerangis* and both genera come from the same area of Madagascar and Mascarene Islands in the Indian Ocean. The white to green flowers vary in size from 1½ to 8 inches.

Aerangis calligerum *is a species with 10- to 15-inch-tall upright stems and fragrant white long-tailed flowers.*

The flowers are on wiry upright to gently arching spikes, often with buds opening over a period of days. Sometimes the same spike produces more flowers the following year. The stemless monopodial plants have leathery leaves and resemble dwarf angraecums.

Grow *Aeranthes* on tree fern slabs or in well-drained pots with an epiphyte mix. Give them intermediate to warm nights and provide bright light (as for cattleyas).

About thirty species are recognized but only a few are offered in specialists' catalogs. Here are some good choices: *Aeranthes grandiflora* with a 1- to 2-foot inflorescence and yellow-green 6-inch flowers opening over a period of months; and *A. arachnitis* with 2- to 3-inch green and white fragrant flowers. Leave the old flower spikes after the blooms fade because the spikes often live for several years.

Aerides (air-EE-deez) is a genus of monopodial orchids from tropical Asia. The species thrive on trees in bright light, high humidity, and intermediate to warm temperatures. Some of the species and hybrids are dwarf, 6 to 12 inches, and suitable for light gardens. I grow these in baskets with chunks of tree fern and unmilled sphagnum moss to hold extra moisture. Well-drained pots with a medium to coarse epiphyte mix are also suitable. Flowers are fragrant when warmed by the sun. *Aerides* crossed with *Vanda* produces *Aeridovanda,* a genus with larger flowers.

Aerides bred with *Ascocentrum* creates *Aeridocentrum* hybrids with compact growth and tightly flowered spikes of small flowers. Most hybrids with *Aerides* are made by hybridizers in tropical Asia where the

Rhynchorides *Blue Princess* (Aerides odoratum *X* Rhynchostylis coelestis) *has light-lavender-blue flowers on 2-foot-high plants.*

genus is widely grown. An excellent species is *Aer. crassifolia* from Thailand with a 1- to 2-foot gracefully curved inflorescence of perfumed white flowers marked lavender and green.

A delightful dwarf hybrid is *Aerides* Pramote (*Aerides houlletiana* X *Aerides flabellata*) with 6- to 8-inch spikes of fragrant yellow flowers and a white lip, spotted lavender. The hybrid has excellent shape and is small enough to be grown at a window or under lights. *Aer. multiflora* is an adaptable species from Southeast Asia and India. The thick-substanced 1-inch pink to purple flowers appear in the spring on pendulous 8- to 15-inch spikes.

Angraecum (an-GRAY-kum) species are monopodial epiphytes from tropical Africa, mainly Madagascar, and nearby islands in the Indian Ocean. This is one of my favorite genera because the pristine white-greenish or cream-colored flowers have such unusual form and night perfume. Plants range in size from dwarf species, which can grow to maturity in 3-inch pots, to handsome strap-leaved types that are 2 feet across by 4 feet tall with 12-inch-long flowers.

Angraecums are named after the Malay word *angurek,* which refers to orchids resembling *Aerides* and *Vanda*. Actually, angraecums do have the same monopodial habit, with leathery leaves and thick roots.

The most famous species is *Angcm. sequipedale.* In 1862 naturalist Charles Darwin predicted that its long-spurred flower would be pollinated by a nocturnal moth with a proboscis (tongue) long enough to reach nectar at the bottom of the plant's 10- to 12-inch spur. Years later, in 1909, a night-flying hawkmoth (*Xanthopan morganii praedicta*) with a 12-inch proboscis was discovered living near *Angraecum sesquipedale.* Darwin was right again, as the moth's name "praedicta" (as predicted) confirms.

The waxy white flowers of *Angraecum* lure the moth with an intoxicating night scent. To reach the sweet nectar, the insect inserts its long tongue into a flower. As its tongue is withdrawn it usually consummates pollination on the bloom.

Some commercial firms are creating hybrids from original *Angraecum* species. The oldest hybrid, *Angcm.* Vetchii, registered in 1899, combines the best features of *Angcm. eburneum* and *Angcm. sesquipedale.* My *Angcm.* Vetchii has waxy white fragrant flowers with 8- to 10-inch spurs every winter.

A more recent hybrid, *Angcm.* Ol Tukai (*Angcm. comorense* X *Angcm. sesquipedale*) faithfully blooms for me every Christmas, a perfect "Star of Bethlehem." These are 24- to 36-inch-tall plants; dwarf hybrids are also available. *Angcm. compactum* is 4 to 6 inches tall when mature and has 2- to 3-inch white flowers. *Angcm. magdalenae* has 4-inch white flowers but compact growth.

Angraecum philippinensis (syn. *Amesiella philippinense*), with 2-inch white flowers, is 2 to 4 inches tall and grows well in a light garden.

Angraecum compactum, *a dwarf species.*

Culture: Pot the large growing types in coarse bark mixes or tree fern chunks with hardwood charcoal. Rather than constantly repotting mature clumps, shake or pull out rotted bark or tree fern, then add new chunks every few years. Keeping established roots intact helps plants produce a bountiful display of big flowers. My mature large hybrids are in 10- to 15-inch pots.

The smaller species and their hybrids thrive in mixes of tree fern with perlite or coarse sphagnum moss and medium-sized bark, each of which is over hardwood charcoal. *Angcm. philippinensis* can thrive in a 2½-inch drained Bonsai pot, I have found. Provide all types of Angraecums with 50 to 70 per cent relative humidity and full sun during winter months. Give plants shade from direct midday sun as the weather gets warmer.

Fertilize active plants with balanced water-soluble fertilizers every other watering. Well-grown angraecums often produce plantlets at their base. These can be twisted or cut off once they have several roots, if you wish to propagate the clone. If you leave the offsets with the main plant, the large specimen clump will make quite a nice show at blooming time.

Anguloa (an-gyou-LOW-ah) is a genus of sympodial Andean species with plump pseudobulbs, wide-arching palm-like leaves, and waxy fragrant flowers on short upright spikes. Its popular name, "Tulip Orchid," derives from the flowers' resemblance to tulip blooms. Taxonomists recognize ten species and several of these are available in catalogs.

In my orchid collection, anguloas grow in relatively small clay pots with pure sphagnum moss. Although species may occasionally grow as epiphytes, I find them more often in humus accumulations or as terrestrials in sandy soil at medium to high elevations. The plants do best with nights at cool to intermediate temperatures (see Chapter 3) and a potting mix that retains moisture but never gets soggy.

Angulocaste *Memoria Abbott Robinson is a modern hybrid of* Angulocaste *Georgius Rex with* Lycaste macrophylla. *Its waxy yellow flowers are 4 inches across.*

A terrestrial mix such as used for cymbidiums is suitable in clay pots but under most conditions the mix would hold too much moisture in plastic containers. Since these sturdy orchids have broad leaves and big pseudobulbs, they are better suited to clay pots or very sturdy heavy plastic pots with extra drainage.

Fertilize growing anguloas at every other watering. They should receive bright diffuse light but no direct midday sun. Flowers appear when the new lead is ⅓ to ½ mature. When pseudobulbs mature, leaves fall and the plant is often left bare until a new lead sprouts. Keep leafless anguloas slightly dry at the roots but resume normal watering as the new growth expands.

Hybrids with *Lycaste* make *Angulocaste,* a genus of waxy-flowered fragrant orchids adaptable to intermediate conditions. Angulocastes grow up to 30 inches tall and 30 inches wide. *Anguloa clowesii* from Colombia and Venezuela has yellow flowers. *Ang. uniflora* from the Andean mountain ranges has creamy white flowers, dotted pink.

Anoectochilus (ann-EK-toe-chi-lus) is a genus of about twenty tropical Asian species called "Jewel Orchids," named for their shimmering olive-green leaves that are heavily veined in gold, silver, or red. These terrestrial plants are difficult to import so only three or four species are usually offered in catalogs.

Anoectochilus species are creeping, ½ to 3 inches tall, with an informal foliage rosette up to 3 inches across. Each rosette has a short stem sprouting from an above-ground rhizome. Although olive-green is the basic leaf color, it is usually hidden by a dense pattern of metallic-colored veins, further enriched by an overall velvety sheen.

These are some of the few orchids grown for their foliage alone, but the small ½-inch greenish-white flowers on 6- to 10-inch upright spikes are attractive, too. Cutting off the spike before it opens will turn energy back into the foliage, but an established clump can bloom without losing any of its leaves. Plant these "jewels" in a loose airy mix of pasteurized top soil with ⅓ chopped sphagnum moss or fine redwood bark. Packaged terrarium soils are also suitable when mixed ⅓ to ½ with fine bark or coarse moss.

For the richest leaf color, provide a relative humidity of 70 per cent in a terrarium or a large glass case. In a drier atmosphere, mist leaves on bright mornings. One of my *Anct. sikkimensis* plants thrives in an open dish garden with ferns in a living-room setting when misted on bright mornings. In a damp basement light garden, its leaves grow larger.

Diffuse light and 60° to 70° F. nights are ideal. Fertilize with dilute ½-strength water-soluble formulas alternated with fish emulsion as plants are making new leaves. You can propagate mature clumps by dividing them, leaving at least one sturdy rooted rosette per clump. Sections of the rhizome will also sprout.

Dust each 1- to 2-inch piece with Rootone powder, then place the rhizome cuttings flat on moist sphagnum moss in a warm place with diffuse light. Cover the cuttings with clear plastic, such as a plastic food dish turned upside down. A slight bottom heat from a soil cable or placement on the top tiers of a light garden will encourage root formation.

Anoectochilus sikkimensis *is a terrestrial orchid with gold-veined leaves.*

Anoectochilus roxburghii has a network of golden veins on copper-green leaves. *Anct. sikkimensis* has olive-green foliage with a filigree of yellow to white veins. The entire leaf has a velvety-red blush. No hybrids are currently offered in catalogs, but a cross between *Haemaria (Ludisia) discolor* and *Anct. roxburghii* was registered many years ago as *Anoectomaria* Dominyi, a genus now listed as *Ludochilus.*

Ansellia (an-SELL-e-ah) *africana* from Liberia to East Africa and *A. gigantea* found across a broad area of central, east, and south Africa are highly variable in flower characteristics. The flower color ranges from pure yellow to almost black when the brown to black bars dominate. Ansellias thrive in intermediate to warm greenhouses or a bright window, but they are too tall (up to 3 feet!) for most light gardens.

The name *Ansellia* honors British gardener John Ansell, who collected the first *Ansellia* in Africa around 1841. The popular name is "Leopard Orchid." Ansellias form a clump of slender golden-green pseudobulbs, 15 to 24 inches tall, topped with four to seven leathery arching leaves. The branched inflorescence grows from the top of the ripe pseudobulb, reaching 18 to 36 inches.

Ansellias' flowers are long-lasting, yellow with varied intensities of brown to black-brown bars. Each flower is only 1 to 1½ inches across, but a spray with twenty or more blooms makes a striking show for weeks.

Pot ansellias firmly in relatively small, squat clay pots with sharp drainage. I use a mix of tree fern, but bark mixes are also suitable. When new roots are established and pseudobulbs are enlarged, keep the mix evenly moist, with only slight drying between soakings. Fertilize every other watering. When the final leaf is made, stop adding fertilizer and reduce watering. Let the mature plant rest with its roots on the dry side but without excessive shrinking of the pseudobulbs. When flower spikes are seen, increase watering.

Do not be alarmed if your ansellia stays inactive for several months. Wait until new growth starts before disturbing an established plant for repotting or dividing. Ansellias do well with 60° to 68° F. nights, on the warmer side when plants are most active. Provide bright diffuse light from spring until fall, and full sun during the winter.

Arachnis (a-RACK-nis) is a tropical Asian genus of about fifteen species, all monopodial and with large waxy flowers, popularly called "Scorpion" and sometimes "Spider" orchids. In Southeast Asia, *Arachnis* species and hybrids are common garden plants, grown with the same techniques used for vandas. Indoors, *Arachnis* plants need strong light, warm temperatures, and considerable space for the tall viny stems.

A tree fern pole or similar upright support such as a wire mesh cylinder stuffed with unmilled sphagnum or coconut husk is needed for the vine types. The most famous plant is hybrid *Arachnis* Maggie Oei (*Arach. hookerana* X *Arach. flos-aeris*), a vigorous vine-like hybrid registered in

1940. It is popular throughout the Asian tropics for its long-lasting red and yellow spidery flowers.

Hybrids with *Vanda* (*Aranda*) are usually more compact, although they still reach 3 to 4 feet. Arandas have fuller flowers on long sprays.

Arachnis crossed with *Renanthera* produces *Aranthera,* mainly tall thin plants with sprays of bright red to orange flowers which are excellent for cut-flower bouquets. This can be grown in a sunny greenhouse or outdoors in a humid tropical region.

Arundina (a-run-DEE-na) is a tall Asian terrestrial with reed-like stems and cattleya-shaped flowers, considered as one variable species, *Arundina graminifolia* (syn. *A. bambusifolia*). Clumps I saw in Fiji and Java were 6 to 8 feet tall and reminded me of palm seedlings with their thin stems and grassy leaves. The slightly scented flowers open at the top of each stem and last only two to three days, but a healthy plant produces a succession of 1½- to 2-inch flowers throughout the year. Flower color ranges from white to brilliant rose-purple. Arundina is best grown in raised beds outdoors in full sun. Indoors it needs a spacious sunny greenhouse and a large pot of sharply drained terrestrial mix, even moisture, warm temperatures, and constant fertilizer.

Ascocentrum (as-co-SEN-trum) is a genus related to *Vanda,* with species native to tropical Asia, including southern China, the Philippines, and Malaysia. The species are popular for their vibrant yellow, orange, red, or rose-pink flowers in tight spikes on dwarf plants. The name comes from the Greek *ascos* (meaning "bag"), referring to a spur or tail-like extension seen on the flower lip.

Ascocentrum species often have brown or red spots on their foliage. These are seen on Ascocenda hybrids as well and are quite normal.

Ascocentrums thrive with warm temperatures, high humidity, and bright light. Species I studied in Thailand grow on rocky cliffs in almost full sun near the sea. Since these monopodial orchids have no pseudobulbs, they store some moisture in fleshy leaves which grow 3 to 8 inches horizontally from upright stems. After several seasons a plant may arch or trail slightly, often sprouting plantlets at the base.

Flowers appear on upright 3- to 6-inch spikes which sprout from between the leaf base and stem. The tightly packed spike contains many ½- to 1-inch blooms, nearly hiding the dainty plants in a vibrant flowery mist.

Culture: Provide bright light but protect ascocentrums from the midday sun which may scorch their foliage. A minimum relative humidity of 60 per cent and 65° to 70° F. nights are ideal. Ascocentrums also thrive under broad-spectrum fluorescents. These are perfect epiphytic orchids for growing in small teak baskets with chunks of tree fern or coconut husk. In pots, provide excellent aeration and good drainage of gravel or crocks with hardwood charcoal under a medium to coarse epiphyte mix. Let the potting mix dry slightly between soakings.

Apply balanced fertilizer alternated with fish emulsion during periods of most rapid growth, mainly spring into fall. Keep water out of the growing point unless it will dry by nightfall. It is perfectly safe to spray foliage and roots with dilute fertilizer solution if plants have good air circulation and are dry by nighttime.

Among the five or six species offered in catalogs, the most popular is spring-blooming *Ascocentrum curvifolium* from Thailand. This species is seldom over 5 inches tall. The 4- to 6-inch spikes have a multitude of long-lasting orange to vermilion flowers. This is a favorite species to use as a parent in crosses with *Vanda* to create compact *Ascocenda* with larger flowers. An outstanding example is *Ascocenda* Yip Sum Wah (*Vanda* Pukele X *Ascocentrum curvifolium*).

Ascocentrum ampullaceum, from tropical Himalayan regions and Burma, has pink to dark rose flowers nearly hiding the plants. This species has been crossed with the dwarf white-flowered *Neofinetia falcata* to produce *Ascofinetia* Cherry Blossom. A similar hybrid with clouds of

Ascocenda *Erika Reuter* (Vanda sanderana X Ascocentrum curvifolium) *is a compact dark-orange-flowered hybrid.*

Schafferara *Martha Schaffer,*
a complex hybrid of Beallara
Tahoma Glacier and Aspasia
epidendroides, *has long-lasting*
maroon and white flowers.

pink flowers is *Ascofinetia* Peaches (*Neof. falcata* X *Asctm. curvifolium*).

Dwarf *Ascocentrum hendersonianum* from Borneo is worth growing for its mildly fragrant, coral-pink flowers on upright 4- to 6-inch spikes. *Asctm. miniatum,* from warm altitudes on the Malay Peninsula, is the smallest species generally grown, hardly 4 inches tall, but showy for sprays of orange-yellow flowers each spring.

Ascoglossum (as-koh-GLOS-um) *calopterum* from New Guinea resembles a tall ascocentrum and is considered as such by some taxonomists. The 1-inch magenta flowers are produced on 15- to 18-inch arching branched spikes. *Ascoglossum* has been crossed with related genera such as *Arachnis* (*Arachnoglossum*) and *Renanthera* (*Renanthoglossum*) to make rather tall-growing genera, most suited to outdoor culture in bright humid tropical regions.

Aspasia (ass-PAY-zee-ah) is a genus from Central America, Colombia, and parts of Brazil, where species live under intermediate to warmly humid conditions. Several species are popular in collections, the best known being *Aspasia epidendroides* and slightly larger *Asp. principissa.* This genus of epiphytes is related to the oncidium subdivision which contains *Brassia, Oncidium,* and *Odontoglossum,* all genera recently bred with *Aspasia* to produce unusual hybrids.

Aspasia flowers are heavy-substanced, almost waxy, with a longer-than-wide look and subtle spicy fragrance during warm daylight hours. The flowers appear on short spikes which grow from between the pseudobulb and thin leaf, with a cluster of buds opening over a period of weeks. Each flower lasts fifteen to twenty days.

One of my *Aspasia principissa* plants, growing in a mix of ground tree fern and unmilled sphagnum moss, gave this typical performance: In early March, the first flowers on two spikes from a single new growth began to open. By the end of March, several flowers were fully ripe but still in perfect condition. By mid-April, the original flower spikes which had started to bloom in early March were still covered with perfect flowers. Finally, by early June, I had to repot the orchid as new growth began, yet the flowers were still so attractive that I cut them off to put them in water, where they lasted another week. By this time the new growth was 2 inches tall, with new roots creeping over the pot edge, a signal that repotting was required.

Culture: Aspasias thrive under intermediate to warm conditions with an epiphyte mix. Since the roots are thin and close together, add some unmilled sphagnum moss if your tree fern or bark mix is coarse. Use a container that is no more than 1 inch ahead of the active lead. Provide bright diffuse light but avoid direct sun in the summer. Keep active plants evenly moist.

Selections: *Aspasia epidendroides* and *Asp. principissa* have yellow-green petals with brown stripes, a white lip marked purple. The white lip often turns yellow after several weeks. *Aspasia* crossed with *Odontoglossum* produces *Aspoglossum,* a genus of compact hybrids which thrive under intermediate temperature conditions. Crosses with *Oncidium,* called *Aspasium,* have slightly smaller flowers. As a parent, *Aspasia* contributes compact growth, heavy flower substance, and long flower life. *Aspasia* and its hybrids are fine orchids under lights.

Bifrenaria (BY-fren-AR-ee-a) is a genus of Latin American epiphytes related to *Lycaste.* Several species are grown for their 2- to 3-inch fragrant flowers, which appear from the base of plump pseudobulbs. Grow bifrenarias with intermediate temperatures, bright diffuse light, and good air circulation. Pot them in clay containers with a mix of tree fern or medium-sized fir bark plus about ⅓ unmilled sphagnum moss over sharp drainage. Maintain an evenly moist compost while pseudobulbs are forming, then keep roots slightly on the dry side after flowers fade. Bifrenarias are often inactive for six to eight weeks after blooming.

Bif. harrisoniae from Brazil has 3-inch fragrant white flowers with contrasting purple lips; *Bif. tyrianthina* is similar but with a slightly larger plant and 3½-inch purple flowers. *Bifrenaria* is sometimes crossed with *Lycaste* to make *Lycasteria.*

Bifrenaria harrisoniae is an epiphytic orchid from Brazil.

Bletilla (blee-TILL-ah) is a genus from temperate China and Japan, so some species actually survive in protected garden beds as far north as Boston in the United States. *Bletilla striata* is offered in garden catalogs as "Hardy Chinese Orchid" or its synonym *Ble. hyacinthina*. I grow this species outdoors in well-drained acid soil under oak trees. Indoors it will succeed in pots of terrestrial mix or ½ loam with ½ acid leaf mold.

Bletilla sprouts from underground corms, producing an upright stem of grassy palm-like foliage, then a spike of six to twelve lavender flowers which resemble miniature cattleyas but have lacy lines on the lips. A white variety is rare. Indoors the plants need cool nights, bright light, even moisture while active, less moisture when corms are dormant. Grow outdoors where possible, saving indoor space for genera that require the warmth.

Brassavola (brah-sa-VOL-a) is a genus of pseudobulbous epiphytes from Latin America. The most famous is *Brassavola nodosa,* called "Lady of the Night" because of its delightful nighttime perfume. One clone I collected in Mexico smells just like cloves. Another famous member of the genus is *B. digbyana* (syn. *Rhyncholaelia digbyana*). This species has been crossed many times with *Cattleya* and *Laelia* to produce large flowers, plant vigor, and a big ruffled lip. Most cattleya-brassavola hybrids are fragrant.

The genus name honors Antonio Musa Brassavola, an eighteenth-century Venetian botanist. Since popular brassavolas are so adaptable and produce multitudes of night-fragrant white to greenish-white flowers, they should be grown in every collection.

In Central America and along the Mexican coast I found *B. nodosa* growing in full sun, but growing indoors it will thrive with the same light intensity as cattleyas. Several of my plants do well under broad-spectrum fluorescents. Because species *B. nodosa, B. glauca,* and *B. digbyana* are adapted to live through dry seasons, they will accept lower humidity than many orchids. Growing them at a sunny window with 40 per cent relative humidity is easy.

Species thrive in clay pots tightly filled with an epiphyte mix or mounted on slabs of cork bark. Hard tree fern slabs are also suitable for mounting brassavolas. *B. acaulis* and *B. martiana* grow strongly pendant, so they are best mounted on slabs. Other species are adaptable to pots.

Fertilize active plants every other watering for best growth. *B. nodosa* typically continues growth all year, often producing flowers two or three times, but *B. digbyana* and *B. glauca* usually rest several months after flowering, at which time they need much less water and no fertilizer.

Minimum nights of 60° to 65° F. are suitable but the species from Mexico and semi-tropical parts of Central America can endure cool nights in the 50s. A relative humidity of 50 to 60 per cent is ideal but the sturdier types mentioned above will tolerate less humidity. Let the compost dry out between watering. My *B. digbyana* goes six weeks in a winter

This is a secondary cluster of Brassavola nodosa *flowers, from an inflorescence that was cut just below the first blooms.*

greenhouse before needing water, but a clump of *B. nodosa* under the same conditions required water every three or four sunny days. As usual with orchids, it is best to evaluate each plant under your own conditions.

Selections: B. nodosa belongs in every collection. Select clones are offered by several growers but even seed-grown plants are nice. Growth is close together, foliage succulent, narrow, 4 to 12 inches tall, depending upon the clone and light intensity. Flowers vary from pure white, with minute purple dots in the lip, to creamy white or greenish-white. Hybrids with *B. nodosa* as one parent inherit its compact growth habit and flower shape but not always its night fragrance.

B. digbyana has large lemon-scented greenish-white flowers, 8- to 10-inch growths covered with a silvery sheen. This glaucous coating makes *B. digbyana* and *B. glauca* attractive even without flowers.

B. glauca has smooth lips and heavy waxy creamy-white flowers with a purple dot inside the lip. As a parent it contributes fragrance, compact growth, and heavy substance to its offspring.

Brassavola Moonlight Perfume (*B. nodosa* X *B. glauca*) has flowers that combine features of both parents. *B. David Sander* (*B. digbyana* X *B. cucullata*) has narrow pencil-like growth and the flower shape of *B. cucullata* but a fringed lip from *B. digbyana*. I have yet to find hybrids between any of these species that do not deserve space in a collection. You will enjoy brassavolas, especially when the flowers emit their nightly perfume.

Brassia (BRASS-ee-uh) is a Latin American genus of about fifty recognized species often called "Spider Orchids" because of their long sepals. The genus name honors William Brass, an eighteenth-century botanical artist and plant collector. *Brassia caudata* is a rare species in Florida. Other brassias are from the warmer climates of Mexico, Central America, northern South America, and parts of Brazil. Orchid catalogs list five or six species, all with compact growth and graceful sprays of long-sepaled 4- to 8-inch cream or yellow flowers, spotted dark brown or maroon.

These epiphytes have flat pseudobulbs, two or three thin green leaves, and are 8 to 12 inches tall. Flower spikes come from between partially completed pseudobulbs and grow 15 to 18 inches long in an arching fashion. My brassias succeed in a greenhouse, basement light garden, and at a sunny window but with protection from the midday sun.

Culture: Pot brassias in epiphyte mixes which contain some material to retain moisture without getting soggy. I use unmilled sphagnum mixed with bark. Other brassias thrive in plain coconut fiber, either in clay pots or plastic pots with extra drainage and air holes. Another alternative is to use a mix of 7 parts fine fir bark, 1 part charcoal, and 1 part peat moss.

Brassias can be propagated like other pseudobulbous orchids, using simple division, but sometimes they grow plantlets on top of mature pseudobulbs. These plantlets can be twisted off once they have a few roots, then put into 1½- to 2-inch pots and grown like seedlings. Mature brassias do well with intermediate temperatures, but seedlings will bloom faster if given 65° to 70° F. nights.

Selections: Brassia maculata is an easy-to-grow fragrant yellow-flowered species. For maximum adaptability and some hybrid vigor, grow the crosses between various species. *Brassia* Rex (*Brs. gireoudiana* X *Brs. verrucosa*) and *Brassia* Edvah Loo (*Brs. longissima* X *B. gireoudiana*) are excellent crosses with big yellow flowers nicely marked with brown spots. Popular intergeneric crosses which usually inherit the brassia spidery flower shape include *Brapasia* (X *Aspasia*), *Brassidium* (X *Oncidium*) and *Miltassia* (X *Miltonia*).

The flowers of Brassia *Edvah Loo 'Talisman Cove'* (Brs. longissima *X* Brs. gireoudiana majus) *are yellow with brown markings.*

Broughtonia (brow-TOE-nee-ah) *sanguinea* is a dwarf creeping epiphyte from Jamaica, sometimes crossed with related genera such as *Cattleya* to produce compact, well-formed Cattleytonia hybrids. The species has brilliant red flowers but white and pink variations occur. Clone 'Carmen Gauntlett' is yellow. Some taxonomists include another species in this genus, *Bro. negrilensis,* a variety that is slightly larger and has 2-inch lavender to pink flowers in clusters on wiry 15-inch spikes. The flower lips have darker-colored veins, although *Bro. sanguinea* lips are marked deep inside with yellow lines.

Mount broughtonias on slabs of hard tree fern or cork bark, or you can pot them in small clay pots with tree fern or medium bark over charcoal. Provide bright light, intermediate to warm temperatures, good air circulation, and slight drying between soakings.

An outstanding hybrid available as a mericlone is red-flowered *Cattleytonia* Keith Roth (*Cattleya bicolor* X *Broughtonia sanguinea*).

Bulbophyllum (bulb-oh-FILL-um) is a genus of tropical Asian epiphytes with about two thousand recognized species, making it the largest grouping in the family, followed by the genus Dendrobium, which has

Bulbophyllum medusae has 5- to 6-inch, creamy-yellow flowers in a medusa-like bunch.

only slightly fewer species. Many bulbophyllums are rampant growers, needing too much room to justify their inclusion in a collection. However, the popular species have less rampant growth and produce showy flowers in odd shapes. A few, such as *Bulb. beccarii,* smell like putrified flesh but most have inoffensive scents. Some taxonomists put various species into the related genus *Cirrhopetalum.*

Grow the smaller bulbophyllums on slabs of tree fern or in small pots of coarse chopped sphagnum moss or osmunda. The larger growers succeed in tree fern mixes or trained on tree fern poles. Provide intermediate to warm temperatures, diffuse light, and slight drying between waterings. Permit plants to develop into clumps for best flowering.

Interesting species are Indonesian *Bulb. lobbii* with egg-shaped pseudobulbs 2 to 3 inches tall. A single tan and purple flower is 2½ to 3 inches across, with a quivering lip. Malaysian *Bulb. medusae,* a compact species that is 4 to 6 inches tall, has short spikes of 5-inch-long creamy-white flowers marked with purple spots.

Calanthe (kal-AN-thee) species come from Africa, Asia, and Australia, with only one species, *Cal. mexicana,* found elsewhere. Indoors calanthes are treated as terrestrials. A few species may live as semi-epiphytes in jungle regions.

Some species are evergreen and have clumps of broad foliage and tall spikes of flowers. These thrive in a terrestrial mix with even moisture. Other species form pseudobulbs and usually lose their foliage before blooming. These pseudobulbous types need a more open compost and much less water when leafless. After the plants bloom, separate the clumps into portions of 1 to 3 pseudobulbs. Dust the cut surface with Rootone and trim away all dead roots. Set the cleaned, separated pseudobulbs in a tray of damp sphagnum moss in diffuse light, and with intermediate to cool temperatures, until new roots appear. Then pot in relatively small containers with a coarse terrestrial mix.

The evergreen types grow best when permitted to establish clumps. The broad thin leaves of all species are subject to fungus attacks. Keep calanthes in situations with excellent air circulation. Avoid having foliage wet at night. *Cal. vestita* from Asia has attractive silvery pseudobulbs, 6 to 8 inches tall, and arching 24- to 36-inch spikes of 2- to 3-inch flowers. The flowers are white to rosy pink, with orange inside the lip, but white and dark-purple types are also found.

Calanthe masuca, an evergreen species, grows with cool to intermediate temperatures and has 2-foot spikes of 1½-inch magenta flowers. *Calanthe* is occasionally crossed with *Phaius* to make *Phaiocalanthe.* A few species from semi-tropical regions in China and Japan, such as *Cal. striata,* succeed in a very cool place, with temperatures just above freezing when plants are dormant, 50° to 55° F. as new leaves grow.

Calanthe vestita *is an easy-to-grow terrestrial orchid for intermediate to warm conditions. Its flowers are white with a vivid pink to red blotch.*

Catasetum (kat-a-SEE-tum) is a genus of more than seventy species, up to a hundred species according to certain taxonomists. However, only about twenty species are popular and available in specialists' catalogs. The species' habitats include Mexico, Central America, and tropical South America. Catasetums have plump pseudobulbs ranging from egg-shaped 2- to 3-inch dwarfs (*Catasetum warscewiczii*) to larger types, mature at 8 to 12 inches (*Catasetum macrocarpum*).

The plants' foliage is thin and graceful, usually arching out toward the top of each pseudobulb. Catasetums are deciduous. The swollen pseudobulbs conserve moisture during dry seasons by losing all their leaves. After several months of dryness, except for nightly dew and humidity, rains start the plants' growth.

Catasetum *Rebecca Northen is ready to be potted when new growth begins.*

Catasetum *Rebecca Northen* (Ctsm. *Grace Dunn* X Ctsm. roseum) *has pink flowers with a ginger fragrance.*

The deciduous habit gives us a culture key: Give catasetums a dry rest when leaves begin to yellow and drop, usually from fall into winter. Provide only enough water to stop the plants from excessively shrinking. Resume watering gradually as new leaves sprout from the base of last year's pseudobulbs. Once roots penetrate several inches into the compost, maintain even moisture.

Provide balanced half-strength water-soluble fertilizer alternated with fish emulsion every other watering. Catasetums respond well to adequate fertilizer when active. Keep water out of new foliage clusters.

Watch the undersides of leaves for signs of red spider mites, the worst pest for these thin-leaved orchids. Spray with Kelthane or malathion if mites are seen.

Some species produce unisexual (male *or* female) flowers on the same plant but usually at different times. The most popular species have bisexual flowers with complete reproductive parts, or unisexual flowers that look quite similar. Catasetums, like *Mormodes,* shoot pollen if you touch the pollen trigger of a ripe flower. *Catasetum pileatum* has a gluey substance with attached pollen sacs (pollinia), designed to stick on an insect's back, to carry pollen to the next flower for nectar.

Daily Care: Catasetums grow well in bright diffuse light. They accept full sun in cooler months but keep humidity between 40 to 60 per cent. Growing plants thrive with 65° to 68° F. nights, resting plants accept nights down to 60° F. Pot catasetums in epiphyte mixes of bark or tree fern in relatively small clay pots or very well-drained plastic pots.

Selections: Among the pure species, *Catasetum pileatum* is my favorite for 2- to 3-inch waxy, fragrant, creamy-white to yellow flowers and compact plant habit. This is an excellent parent, too, used to create the popular hybrid *Catasetum* Orchidglade (*Ctsm. pileatum* X *Ctsm. expansum*), usually creamy-yellow with brown or orange spots. *Ctsm. roseum* (light pink) and *Ctsm. warscewiczii* (creamy-white, green stripes) are both dwarf species with fragrant flowers on pendulous inflorescences, and do well in small clay pots or slat baskets. *Ctsm.* Francis Nelson (*Ctsm. trulla* X *Ctsm. fimbriatum*) is a hybrid created from two Brazilian species. It has fragrant green and maroon flowers with fringed lips nicely displayed on an arching to pendulous spike. *Ctsm.* Rebecca Northen (*Ctsm.* Grace Dunn X *Ctsm. roseum*) is a delightful 4- to 6-inch-tall hybrid with light-pink, ginger-scented, fringed-lip flowers on a sharply pendulous spike. *Catasetum* is crossed with *Mormodes* to make *Catamodes,* and with *Cycnoches* to make *Catanoches.*

Cattleyopsis (kat-lee-OP-sis) species are dwarf epiphytes related to *Broughtonia* and thrive with the same care. Three species are currently recognized, all from Cuba and the Antilles islands. Flowers are light pink to deep rose, and have been crossed with *Laeliopsis, Cattleya,* and *Broughtonia* to make floriferous dwarf hybrids.

Chysis (KYE-sis) is a genus of several epiphytic species from medium to low altitudes in Mexico, Central America, and northern South America. Pseudobulbs are pendulous, 10 to 18 inches long, spindle-shaped, and have thin foliage resembling catasetums. Flowers appear on an inflorescence which appears from the new growth several weeks after it sprouts.

Chysis thrive in relatively small clay pots with tree fern and unmilled sphagnum moss. Provide bright light but no direct sun during the summer. Intermediate to warm temperatures and high humidity are best. However, upon the completion of each new pseudobulb, the leaves drop, the plants need much less water, and they can be moved to a cooler location with 60° F. nights. Resume watering when new growth begins.

Chysis aurea has heavy-substanced, fragrant, 2- to 3-inch flowers, usually cream with yellow to caramel markings. An excellent hybrid is *Chysis* Chelsonii (*Chy. bractescens* X *Chy. laevis*) with orange and white flowers. Let *Chysis* form clumps since they produce better flowers when undisturbed by frequent repotting. Slat baskets filled with tree fern or osmunda are suitable for mature clumps.

Chysis *Chelsonii is an epiphytic orchid with orange- and cream-colored flowers.*

Cirrhopetalum (see-row-PET-a-lum) is a genus of miniature and dwarf epiphytes which is considered a section of Bulbophyllum by some taxonomists but horticulturally retained as *Cirrhopetalum*. Popular species are compact, with 1- to 2-inch-tall stems on creeping rhizomes. Plants have intricately formed white, yellow, or tan flowers marked in red or brown. Currently available species suitable for intermediate to warm conditions include *Cirr. bhutanense* (white, marked maroon), *Cirr. guttulatum* (syn. *Bulbophyllum umbellatum*) with 6-inch spikes of yellow flowers, and *Cirr. ornatissimum* with tan-yellow flowers marked reddish-purple and unusual mobile lips that quiver in a breeze. All these are from India. Any small species you can locate are worth growing in a light garden. These do well mounted on tree fern slabs or in small pots of tree fern with unmilled sphagnum moss.

Cochlioda (kok-lee-OH-dah) is a genus of about five epiphytic Andean species noted for their bright-red or deep-pink flowers. *Cochlioda* is most famous as a parent used in breeding bright colors, mainly in *Odontoglossum* hybrids. Species that I have studied in the Andes grow at medium to high elevations where humidity is high and nights frequently drop into the low 50s. Although species grow as epiphytes, their roots are frequently in moss, sometimes in gravelly soil.

Coelogyne speciosa *from Indonesia thrives with intermediate to warm temperatures. It has 3-inch yellow-green flowers with white and tan lips.*

Grow *Cochlioda* in small pots of unmilled sphagnum or fine bark mix with diffuse light and cool temperatures. Much more adaptable are larger-flowered hybrids which have inherited the red color, such as *Vuylstekeara* (*Cochlioda* + *Miltonia* + *Odontoglossum*) and *Odontioda* (*Cochlioda* X *Odontoglossum*).

Coelogyne (see-LAW-ji-nee) is a large genus of species from high elevations in China and India and warm tropical lowlands of Southeast Asia. I have found species growing on well-drained gravel or lava-flow areas. However, the most popular types are epiphytic and thrive in mixes of bark, tree fern, or plain osmunda.

Large-growing coelogynes are easier to control when grown in flat baskets or rafts hung from a sunporch rafter or greenhouse, but compact sorts are suitable in pots. Species from high elevations, such as *Coel. cristata* need cool conditions, while species from lower altitudes, such as *Coel. dayana,* thrive with intermediate to warm temperatures. Provide excellent drainage for all species and let them become well established for maximum flowering. By using wooden baskets, rafts, or clay pots with coarse osmunda or tree fern, pseudobulb clumps will grow several years before new compost is required.

Comparettia macroplectron *is a light-pink Colombian species with arching inflorescences of 2-inch flowers.*

Coel. cristata, which prefers cool nights, has compact clusters of pseudobulbs, 10- to 12-inch-long leaves, and arching spikes of white fragrant flowers usually from late winter into spring. *Coel. dayana,* which prefers warm temperatures, grows 10 inches tall and has a pendulous 2- to 3-foot-long inflorescence with 2-inch tan to creamy-yellow flowers. *Coel. pandurata* is a warm grower with arching spikes of 2½- to 3-inch fragrant black-lipped green flowers. Keep fungicide sprays on hand (refer to Chapter 14), since this genus frequently suffers from foliage fungus problems.

Comparettia (kom-pah-RET-ee-a) species are dwarf epiphytes from Andean South America. The small pseudobulbs are almost hidden by leathery 3- to 4-inch leaves. I have found comparettias growing in trees and bushes, often along streams where humidity is consistently high. Plants should receive bright light and excellent air circulation, indoors or outdoors, in order to thrive. Plants should grow in intermediate temperatures, potted in small containers of tree fern with sphagnum moss or mounted on tree fern or cork slabs.

Comp. coccinea has 1-inch red flowers on an arching inflorescence. *Comp. macroplectron* is an outstanding beauty with 1½- to 2-inch white to pink flowers, dotted dark violet. *Comparettia* is crossed with *Oncidium* to make *Oncidettia* and with *Rodriguezia* to create *Rodrettia,* all compact hybrids with sprays of small flowers.

Coryanthes (ko-ree-AN-theez) is a genus of Latin American epiphytes known as "Bucket Orchids" because their fragrant flowers have bucket-like lips. In the tropics, coryanthes' clumps are infested with fire ants which contribute some organic nutrients to the orchids. Coryanthes thrive with diffuse light, 65° to 70° F. nights, and high humidity. Grow them in hanging slat baskets like Stanhopeas, to which they are related. *Coryanthes maculata* has pendulous inflorescences of several fragrant 3- to 4-inch yellow to tan flowers marked with purple spots. None of Coryanthes' flowers last more than a few days, but they are spectacular while they are around.

Cycnoches (sik-NO-keez) species are epiphytes from tropical Mexico, Central America, and South America. I recommend that you include at least one species in your orchid collection because the flowers are so delightfully fragrant and unusual. The most well-known species is the "Swan Orchid," *Cyc. ventricosum* var. *warscewiczii,* more commonly called *Cyc. chlorochilon.* (See color photograph.)

Culture: Pot Cycnoches in relatively small clay pots of tree fern or bark mix over hardwood charcoal. Give them bright diffuse light, intermediate to warm temperatures, always above 60° F. nights, and slight drying at the roots between watering. Repot only as new growth is starting. Plants drop most of their leaves after blooming and remain inactive for four to

Cycnoches *Cygnet* (Cyc. chlorochilon X Cyc. haagii) *has fragrant buff-yellow flowers with white lips.*

eight weeks before sprouting new growth. Growing cycnoches respond well to constant dilute fertilizer. My plants of *Cyc. chlorochilon* often make a second spike of flowers a month or so after the first one fades.

Cycnoches species may produce only male flowers one year, female flowers the next year. High light intensity encourages female flowers, as it does in the related genus *Catasetum*. The form of these imperfect bisexual flowers is almost the same in large-flowered *Cyc. chlorochilon*. In *Cyc. egertonianum* and related species, male and female flowers differ. The male flowers, on pendulous inflorescences, are more common; female flowers are larger, with waxy lips resembling "Swan Orchid" form. *Cycnoches* is crossed with *Mormodes* to make *Cycnodes* and with *Catasetum* to make *Catanoches*.

Cyrtopodium (seer-toe-POE-dee-um) is a genus of robust epiphytic to terrestrial species from subtropical Florida to Latin America. I have found them thriving as terrestrials in lava rock and as epiphytes in tree forks with abundant humus around the roots. "Cowhorn Orchid" is the genus' popular name, referring to the plants' pseudobulb shape.

Flowers are produced on a branched upright inflorescence which bears numerous 2-inch yellow and brown blooms plus some odd bracts, usually on clumps which have lost all their leaves. The deciduous habit helps cyrtopodiums survive long dry seasons in their tropical habitats.

Most practical in containers are compact species such as *Cyrt. andersonii* with fragrant yellow-green flowers, and *Cyrt. punctatum* which has a branched spike 3 to 5 feet tall covered with yellow and brown flowers. Plants need intermediate to warm temperatures, bright light, and frequent fertilizer for growing clumps. Keep roots on the dry side after the pseudobulbs are mature and leaves begin to fall. Cyrtopodiums in my orchid collection grow in relatively small containers of cymbidium mix.

Dendrochilum (den-dro-KYE-lum) species are epiphytes from tropical Asia. They are distinguished by their long pendulous inflorescences of small yellow or cream flowers resembling fine chains. Popular species thrive in clay pots with tree fern and sphagnum moss, or mounted on a chunk of tree fern log. Provide intermediate to warm temperatures, bright diffuse light, and slight drying between soakings. Permit plants to form clumps for best flower display, but repot at once if the compost has rotted. The former name of *Dendrochilum* was *Platyclinis*.

Diacrium (dye-AK-ree-um) species have been renamed *Caularthron* (kawl-AR-thron) but horticulturally they retain the old name, as do the hybrids such as crosses with *Epidendrum* (*Epidiacrium*) and *Cattleya* (*Diacattleya*). These are epiphytes with hollow pseudobulbs which harbor ants in the wild. *Diacrium bicornutum,* a compact 9- to 12-inch-tall plant, has fragrant white flowers on an erect inflorescence. Diacriums can grow in tree fern or bark mixes. Permit them to form clumps before dividing. Plants should have intermediate to warm conditions, bright light, and frequent fertilizing when new growths are forming. Hybrids with cattleyas, epidendrums, and laelias are all showy and adaptable, and often have white flowers with colored lips.

Disa (DEE-zah) is a genus of terrestrial African species. Very few of these plants are in modern collections, although many years ago ten or twelve species were popular in European greenhouses. Disas should grow in a well-drained terrestrial mix, diffuse light, and cool to intermediate night temperatures. One of the most adaptable and beautiful species is *Disa uniflora,* with pink to nearly red 3- to 4-inch flowers on an upright spike. One of my friends grows lovely disas in unmilled sphagnum moss.

The main caution with disas is to avoid having water collect in the leaves since this genus is very susceptible to rot. If local water has a high mineral content or is alkaline, use rainwater or bottled spring water of neutral to slightly acid pH.

Doritis (doe-RYE-tis) *pulcherrima* is the single variable species in this genus from Southeast Asia. *Doritis* is an important parent in breeding with *Phalaenopsis. Doritis* contributes its long flowering season, compact growth, and often an upright inflorescence to hybrids. Primary hybrids with *Doritis* as one parent usually have an inflorescence that grows ahead for many months, opening flowers over a long season.

Disa *Vetchii* (Disa racemosa *X* Disa uniflora) *has rose-pink flowers.*

One charming dwarf hybrid with miniature flowers is *Doriella* Tiny, a cross of *Doritis pulcherrima* with *Kingiella philippinensis* (syn. *Kingidium deliciosum*). Although I have seen *Doritis* thriving as a terrestrial in well-drained garden beds at the Singapore Botanical Gardens, it is usually treated as an epiphyte when grown in pots. Hybrids with *Phalaenopsis,* called *Doritaenopsis,* thrive with the same intermediate to warm temperatures and epiphyte potting mixes that phalaenopsis receive. *Doritis* and its hybrids will accept stronger light than *Phalaenopsis.*

Dracula (DRA-kew-la) is a new genus name for a group long known as *Masdevallia* but recently separated because of slight differences in flower form. *Dracula* species crossed with *Masdevallia* species make the genus *Dracuvallia*. Most popular species in the *Dracula* group come from high up in the Colombian and Ecuadorian Andes. Plants can grow indoors in small pots of unmilled sphagnum moss with diffuse light, high humidity, good air circulation, and cool temperatures. They also succeed under fluorescent lamps. *Dracula chimaera* (maroon and yellow, white hairs) and *Dracula vampira* (white, with heavy black-brown lines) are popular species in specialists' collections. (See also *Masdevallia*.)

Dracula chimaera (*syn.* Masdevallia chimaera) *is typical of many rare orchids from Andean jungles.*

Epidendrum (ep-ee-DEN-drum) is a large genus of about a thousand species which range from North Carolina (*Epi. conopseum*) through Florida, Mexico, Central America, and throughout the New World tropics. The name stems from the Greek meaning "upon a tree," referring to those epiphytic species that cling to trees. Some epidendrums, such as *Epi. radicans,* are ground-dwelling terrestrials that live with roots in sharply drained humus, or ramble over grass and shrubs. Most of the forty to fifty species popular in cultivation are epiphytes.

Some of these tough pseudobulbous epiphytes have been transferred by taxonomists to the genus *Encyclia,* but most catalogs list them by the horticulturally accepted genus name of *Epidendrum.* Within the group botanically separated as *Encyclia* (en-SIK-lee-ah) are several famous species such as *Epidendrum atropurpureum* (syn. *Encyclia atropurpurea*), and the south Florida "Butterfly Orchid" *Epi. tampense.*

Epidendrums are wonderful plants because they are so adaptable and floriferous, as well as usually being compact and fragrant. Excellent hybrids between epidendrums and related genera, such as *Cattleya (Epicattleya)*, offer larger flowers than straight *Epidendrum* species, and in greater color variations. Of the pure species, *Epi. atropurpureum* is a rewarding spring bloomer with erect spikes of 2- to 3-inch brownish-yellow flowers with brilliant magenta lips and a rich spice fragrance. Some types have almost pure white flowers.

Epidendrum fragrans and *Epi. radiatum* are species most appreciated for fragrant flowers produced on short sprays during the summer months. The creamy-white flowers are similar and have purple lines inside. *Epi. tampense* is found in subtropical Florida, with some forms on Caribbean islands. The golden-brown white-lipped flowers have a honey scent. The flowers, when crossed with cattleyas and other epidendrums, create dwarf offspring with sprays of small- to medium-sized flowers.

Culture: Pot epidendrums in well-drained containers with tree fern or bark mix. Provide very strong light for the species with hard pseudobulbs such as *Epi. atropurpureum.* Furnish bright diffuse light for those species with longer, softer pseudobulbs and thinner leaves, such as *Epi. fragrans.* All types benefit from fertilizer every other watering while they are making new growth. Keep slightly dry when not growing.

Many species adapt to dry seasons lasting several months so roots are likely to rot if inactive plants are kept too moist. Nights of 55° to 65° F. are ideal, but epidendrums accept higher temperatures when grown with bright light. Hybrids inherit compact growth, multiple-flowered spikes, fragrance, and adaptability.

Some of the smaller species do well when mounted on slabs of cork bark or hard tree fern. Hardwood logs, such as oak or sassafras, are also suitable supports.

Reed-stem epidendrums are worth growing for their brilliant orange to red flowers (see color photograph of *Epi. radicans*) in long-blooming clusters. Since their growth habit is tall and vine-like, with many thin aerial roots, it is necessary to provide a support for their stems. Outdoors in the tropics, these orchids thrive in raised beds with poles, mesh, or tree fern logs as support. Indoors, use tree fern poles or a wire cylinder stuffed with coconut fiber or unmilled sphagnum moss.

Propagation is easy from plantlets that form on the stems. Terrestrial types that are mainly reed-stem hybrids need strong light to thrive. However, one hybrid, *Epiphronitis* Veitchii, a cross with *Sophronitis coccinea*

Epidendrum pseudepidendrum *has thin stems up to 36 inches tall and green flowers with orange lips.*

(syn. *grandiflora*), matures at 6 to 8 inches tall and can grow in bright diffuse light or under fluorescent lamps. *Ephs.* Veitchii has a constant succession of red flowers with yellow in the lips.

Epicattleya hybrids with pseudobulbous species have compact growth and larger flowers than epidendrums. *Kirchara* is a man-made genus combining *Epidendrum, Laelia, Cattleya,* and *Sophronitis.* Most Kircharas have deep lavender, magenta to red flowers (see color photograph of *Kirchara* Kulowe).

Eria (EAR-ee-a) is a genus of more than five hundred pseudobulbous species from tropical Asia. I have found some, such as *Eria javanica,* growing as terrestrials on well-drained lava-flow slopes with intermediate to warm temperatures. Other species such as *Eria coronaria* grow more frequently as epiphytes. Eria flowers are produced on erect and then arching spikes, and they usually have a pleasant fragrance. Species should be potted in well-drained containers with plain tree fern, osmunda, or bark with unmilled sphagnum.

After new growths are complete, keep roots slightly dry between waterings. Erias will bloom in diffuse light but make more compact growth in bright diffuse sun or under broad-spectrum fluorescents. Suit temperatures to each species, giving high-altitude types 50° to 55° F. nights and other species 55° to 65° F. nights. Good intermediate types include *Eria coronaria,* with 4- to 6-inch pseudobulbs, leathery foliage 6 to 8 inches long, and shiny 2-inch white fragrant flowers marked purple and yellow; and *Eria javanica,* with egg-shaped pseudobulbs, leathery foliage, and 1- to 2-foot spikes of lemon-scented yellow to cream flowers. Let erias form clumps for best flower show.

Eulophia (you-LOH-fee-a) is a genus of about three hundred terrestrial species, with most popular types coming from tropical Africa. These are robust species, forming leathery leaves and 2- to 6-foot spikes of flowers resembling *Phaius.* Pot eulophias in a terrestrial mix, and provide bright diffuse light and frequent dilute fertilizer when growing. After growths are complete, cut back on watering and stop all fertilizer. Permit clumps to remain inactive until growth resumes.

A reasonably compact species is *Eulophia streptopetala,* which can be grown in an 8- to 12-inch pot. Its flowers are 1½ to 2 inches across, yellowish-brown with brighter yellow lip. *Eulophia alta* is found in southern Florida and can be grown under cool conditions.

Eulophidium (yew-loh-FID-ee-um) *maculatum,* a rare terrestrial species found in tropical Africa and Brazil, is worth growing for the leathery 4- to 6-inch-long dark-green and silver-marked foliage alone, but I also enjoy the small waxy flowers which appear on erect 12-inch spikes. Flowers are about ¾-inch size, and are creamy-white with red and brown markings. (This species is now classified as *Oeceoclades maculata.*)

Plants will thrive in a terrestrial mix permitted to dry slightly between waterings. Nights at 60° to 65° F. and diffuse light produce attractive foliage and flowers in the fall, then often again in late winter. Pot in a 3- to 4-inch container with thick roots well into the mix but with plump pseudobulbs at the surface.

Eulophiella (yew-loh-fee-EL-lah) is a genus from Madagascar where its several species live as epiphytes on pandanus trees under warm humid conditions. Eulophiellas have vigorous creeping rhizomes and so plants are best grown in shallow well-drained containers or rafts with coarse sphagnum moss and tree fern or plain osmunda. Provide bright light and 65° to 70° F. nights.

If you have the space, try *Eul. roemplerana,* which has 6- to 10-inch pseudobulbs, 3- to 4-foot-long leaves, and branched erect inflorescences 2 to 4 feet tall with fragrant 3- to 4-inch dark-pink flowers. These flowers open over a period of weeks, like cymbidiums. This species received a First Class Certificate from the Royal Horticultural Society in 1898.

Eulophiella roemplerana (*syn.* Eul.
peetersiana) *has very tall spikes
with pink flowers.*

Eurychone rothschildiana *is a rare miniature epiphyte from Uganda.*

Eurychone (yoo-ree-KOH-nee) *rothschildiana* is a rare miniature epiphyte from tropical Africa, and it reminds me of a small phalaenopsis.
Grow this species on a chunk of tree fern or cork bark with 65° to 70° F.
nights, diffuse light, and high humidity. Small white flowers open on short
stems close to the leaves.

Gastrochilus (gas-tro-KYE-lus) species are dwarf monopodial epiphytes from tropical Asia. The flowers are waxy, fragrant, ½ to 1 inch across, and are produced in tight clusters close to the thick foliage. These are excellent compact orchids for light gardens, where they thrive 3 to 6 inches under broad-spectrum lamps. Species can be mounted on tree fern or cork slabs, or potted in small containers of charcoal and tree fern. Provide bright diffuse light, 60° to 65° F. nights, and 60 to 70 per cent humidity.

Gastrochilus bellinus is a 2- to 3-inch-tall species from Southeast Asia. The 1½-inch yellow and brown flowers have white lips. *Gastrochilus dasypogon* has tight clusters of fragrant ½-inch yellow flowers, spotted red. *Gastrochilus* is crossed with *Ascocenda* to make *Eastonara,* which are lovely dwarf hybrids that usually bloom several times each year. *Gastrochilus* crossed with *Sarcochilus* makes a similar dwarf genus *Gastrosarcochilus.*

Eastonara *Advancement* (Gastrochilus monticolus *X* Ascocenda *Jim Wilkins*) *is a dwarf epiphytic orchid with red-orange flowers.*

Gomesa (go-MEE-sa), related to *Oncidium,* contains about ten species of dwarf Brazilian epiphytes, all with densely packed, arching to pendulous spikes of fragrant flowers. These are adaptable orchids suited to a windowsill, light garden, or greenhouse with a 60° to 70° F. night range. I have grown small clumps of gomesas on tree fern slabs but find that the plants are easier to care for in relatively small baskets or pots filled with tree fern or bark mix. Flower colors are rather plain cream to greenish-yellow, but their shape is intricate and their fragrance is pleasant. *Gomesa* is crossed with *Oncidium* to make *Oncidesa.*

Gongora (gon-GOR-ah) has about twenty epiphytic species from Mexico to South America. The plants are compact, with attractive broad leathery leaves and ribbed pseudobulbs. Pendulous spikes of fragrant flowers appear two or three times a year on most species. In the jungle, gongoras thrive with diffuse light, often with moss around the roots. During a trip to the Peruvian Amazon, I found *Gongora quinquenervis* growing in dim light with dwarf *Anthurium gracile.*

Indoors, gongoras do well with 60° to 70° F. nights. They look nice on a stout tree fern log or in small baskets so the pendulous spikes of creamy-tan to yellow flowers can be appreciated. *Gongora* is related to *Coryanthes* and *Stanhopea,* and needs similar care.

Goodyeara (good-YER-ah) *pubescens* is the hardy "Jewel Orchid" so often seen in woodland terrariums. As a cold-hardy species it does best with 50° to 55° F. nights. Tropical species thrive with the same care given *Anoectochilus* and do well in terrariums.

Grammangis (gram-MANG-giss) contains several robust epiphytes from tropical Madagascar and Southeast Asia. They thrive in big baskets or pots with plain tree fern over a sharp drainage of charcoal. Provide bright diffuse light, 65° to 70° F. nights, and 60 to 70 per cent humidity in order for the plants to form big clumps of flowers.

Summer-blooming *Grammangis ellisii* has 6-inch-tall pseudobulbs, thick flexible foliage 15 to 24 inches long, and an arching spike which springs from the current growth. At least twenty fragrant 3- to 4-inch yellow and reddish-brown glossy flowers with white lips open over a period of weeks. These plants are suitable for a spacious greenhouse.

Grammatophyllum (gram-ma-toe-FILL-um) species are like giant *Grammangis,* yet some rare species can be grown in the space needed for common cymbidiums. *Gram. elegans* has 1½- to 2-inch yellow-green flowers marked with purple on an upright and then arching spike. *Gram. fenzlianum* grows up to 2 feet tall and has greenish flowers marked with brown bars. Grow these in bright light with warm nights and high humidity. Give frequent applications of dilute fertilizer. Tree fern and bark mixes, and coconut husk, are suitable.

Gram. speciosum is grown in raised beds under full tropical sun throughout Southeast Asia where this giant produces spikes 5 to 10 feet tall. The heavy reddish-brown flowers open over a long period of time. This species is definitely for outdoor growing since pseudobulbs can tower up to 25 feet, making this orchid the world's tallest.

Habenaria (hab-e-NAH-ree-ah) is a genus of more than five hundred terrestrial species found in temperate and tropical regions throughout the world. All plants have swollen tuberous roots, some are cold-hardy, and others come from tropical climates. Cultivated species include pure white-flowered *Habenaria radiata* (syn. *Pecteilis radiata*), a cool-growing species, and *Habenaria rhodocheila* from tropical Southeast Asia, a species which can have 1½-inch red or yellow flowers on an upright 10-inch spike. Grow these in a well-drained terrestrial mix. Add oak leaf mold or coarse sphagnum peat moss if your water is alkaline.

When foliage dies back, rest the tubers in a pot with 50° to 55° F. nights until sprouts appear, then move to 60° to 65° F. conditions (55° to 60° F. for cool growers). Provide bright diffuse light and even moisture at the roots. Repot or divide when they have lost all their foliage. However, keep them dry, just short of shrinking, until new roots begin. *Habenaria* species can also be grown in pure, coarse sphagnum moss.

Hexisea (hex-ISS-ee-a) *bidentata* is an adaptable Latin American epiphyte with loosely arranged 1-foot jointed pseudobulbs. It has clusters of brilliant orange-red, ½- to 1-inch flowers from the junction of its top leaf and stem. Flowers appear several times each year when hexiseas are given bright light and fertilizer. Provide hexiseas with 55°–65° F. nights and an epiphyte mix. They can also be mounted on a tree fern slab.

Hexisea bidentata *is an epiphyte from Latin America with orange-red flowers.*

Huntleya (HUNT-lee-a) is a genus of several species from Central and South America but only Brazilian *Hya. meleagris* is common in collections. I have seen huntleyas growing as terrestrials on steep gravelly slopes in the Colombian Andes, but in containers they thrive with a tree fern or bark mix over gravel and hardwood charcoal. If you choose a clay pot, add some sphagnum moss around the stem. Huntleyas have no water-storing pseudobulbs. Keep roots evenly moist as new leaves are forming, and only slightly drier at other times. Provide diffuse light, 50° to 60° F. nights, 60 to 70 per cent humidity, and good air circulation. The waxy fragrant 4- to 5-inch flowers are brown, orange, and white, and last several weeks. Costa Rican *Hya. burtii,* considered only a variety by some taxonomists, has yellow in its flowers and a good round shape.

Huntleya meleagris *is a fragrant species from Colombia.*

Ionopsis (eye-o-NOP-sis) is a small genus of dwarf, creeping epiphytes with airy sprays of white to lilac flowers, and short leathery 3- to 5-inch leaves. *Ionopsis utricularoides* grows from southern Florida to Mexico to South America. Ionopsis do best on tree fern chunks or in small clay pots of coarse sphagnum. Grow with bright light, high humidity, good air circulation, and 55° to 65° F. nights. Many growers report that plants decline after a few years, even with good culture. This short life when being grown indoors also appears in the related genus *Rodriguezia,* but plants on slabs have the best chance to survive longer.

Isabelia (iz-a-BELL-ee-a) *virginalis,* a miniature epiphyte from Brazil, is unique for its netted pseudobulbs. Its flowers are ½ inch, pure white with a red column, and its leaves resemble pine needles. The best *Isabelia* I've ever seen was grown by Phil Jesup, an expert in miniature orchids, who grew *Isabelia virginalis* on an oak log. Provide good air circulation, 60° to 65° F. nights, high humidity, and bright diffuse light. This plant is a good miniature for a light garden.

Isabelia virginalis, *a miniature epiphyte from Brazil, has pure-white flowers.*

Jumellea (joo-MELL-ee-a) is a genus of monopodial epiphytes related to *Angraecum* and *Aeranthes.* Its flowers are white to green, and very fragrant. These species thrive with the same care given dwarf angraecums and aeranthes—basically, 60° to 65° F. nights, high humidity, and bright diffuse light. *Jumellea fragrans* from the Mascarene Islands near Madagascar was once harvested for its leaves which were used for tea. Recently

Jumellea has been crossed with *Angraecum* to make *Angramellea* and with *Aeranthes* to create *Jumanthes.* These unusual dwarf hybrids are hard to find but a few orchid specialists offer them.

Kingiella (king-ee-EL-a) *philippinensis* is a dwarf phalaenopsis relative from the Philippines. Botanically, this *Kingiella* is called *Kingidium deliciosum.* It is used to make dwarf-growing small-flowered hybrids with *Phalaenopsis* (*Phaliella*) and with *Doritis* (*Doriella*). Compact *Kingiella* and its hybrids are good choices for a light garden. All thrive with the same culture as *Phalaenopsis.* In my orchid collection, dwarf *Phaliella* Speck O' Gold (a cross with *Phal. cornu-cervi*) grows on a slab of tree fern under fluorescent lamps.

Laelia (LAY-lee-a) is often used in hybridizing with related genera such as *Brassavola* and *Cattleya.* White flowers with deep-purple lips are often bred from *L. purpurata,* and glowing yellow multiflowered sprays are bred from *L. flava.* Bronze colors are inherited from *L. tenebrosa* and red-toned flowers on dwarf plants have come from *L. milleri.*

About seventy-five *Laelia* species, all from the Central American and South American tropics, are recognized. Some taxonomists classify *Schomburgkia* species with *Laelia,* but horticulturally the genera are quite different. Laelias are epiphytes, adapted to live on trees and rocks, and have pseudobulbs with a single leaf and flowers on an erect spike.

Plant size varies from *L. pumila,* a 3-inch dwarf from Brazil with 3- to 4-inch lavender flowers in very round form, to 12- to 24-inch *L. purpurata* (the national flower of Brazil) and *L. tenebrosa* which look very much like Cattleyas. These two tall species have a single broad leaf, and 6- to 8-inch flowers, lavender-purple in *L. purpurata* and bronze in *L. tenebrosa.*

Some other species are *L. flava* (yellow) and *L. cinnabarina* (orange) which grow 1 to 2 feet tall and have slender compact-growing pseudobulbs. *L. anceps* from Mexico and Central America has tightly clustered, four-sided, waxy-coated, 6-inch pseudobulbs and a flower spike that can reach 3 feet tall. *L. anceps* usually has lavender-pink flowers in midwinter but white types are also seen.

Culture: Laelias prosper with intermediate temperatures. Species from warm lowland habitats, such as *L. gloriosa, L. purpurata,* and *L. tenebrosa,* do well with 65° F. nights. Species from cooler habitats, such as *L. albida, L. anceps,* and *L. rubescens,* survive outside in semi-tropics where they can endure an occasional night in the 30s. These cool growers are good choices for a sunporch or greenhouse where nights drop to 50° F.

The shorter waxy-leaved laelias such as *L. anceps* and *L. rubescens* will accept almost full sun, but taller species with softer leaves, such as *L. purpurata,* need protection from direct midday sun and thrive with the same light intensity as cattleyas. Some of my hybrids bred from Brazilian *L. cinnabarina* and *L. flava* do well under broad-spectrum fluorescent lamps, but smaller types are easier to manage because tall flower spikes are difficult to accommodate in a light garden.

Dwarf *L. milleri* (red-orange), *L. pumila* (lavender), and *L. rubescens* (white to pink) fit well under fluorescent lamps but bloom only if light intensity is high, such as with four 40-watt tubes several inches above the foliage. These are all good choices for windowsill gardens since they will tolerate lower humidity than most orchids, except for *L. pumila* which needs 50 to 60 per cent humidity to thrive.

Potting: Grow laelias in an epiphyte mix, as for cattleyas. Small-growing species do well on chunks of tree fern or cork. Species such as *L. anceps* and *L. rubescens* can go many weeks without being soaked but should be watered regularly when they are making new pseudobulbs. All laelias respond well to fertilizer.

Laelia crispa *from Brazil has 4- to 5-inch fragrant white to light-pink flowers with dark-purple, white, and yellow lips.*

Lepanthes (lee-PAN-theez) species are miniature Latin American epiphytes related to *Masdevallia* and *Pleurothallis*. They grow under cool, humid conditions with diffuse light. Mount them on tree fern or keep in small pots of sphagnum moss. *Lepanthes* succeed with the same environment as *Stelis* and *Pleurothallis* and so they are good companions in a collection of miniatures. Keep a magnifying glass handy to appreciate their flowers.

Leptodes (lep-TOH-deez) species are dwarf epiphytes from Brazil and Paraguay. They look like tiny *Brassavola nodosa* clumps and thrive on tree fern slabs or hardwood branches. You can also grow them in small clay pots with a bark or tree fern mix, but they look best when mounted, since flowers are close to the stem and sometimes droop down. *Leptodes bicolor* has 3- to 5-inch leaves, and 1- to 2-inch fragrant rose-pink flowers that are marked purple. *Lpt. unicolor* is similar but its flowers are pure lavender. Both thrive with intermediate temperatures and bright diffuse sun, and they grow into impressive clumps.

Lockhartia (lok-HART-ee-a) species are worth growing for their unusual braided leaves. The small yellow flowers are attractive and can make a good show when plants form a clump of blooming stems. Grow these epiphytes in small pots of tree fern and sphagnum moss, or on slabs of tree fern. Provide 60° to 65° F. nights, diffuse light, and even moisture at the roots. The Central American *Lockhartia oerstedii* blooms several times a year and thrives under fluorescent lights or in a greenhouse. I fertilize my growing clumps by misting the foliage with dilute fertilizer.

Ludisia (loo-DIS-ee-a) *discolor* is a tropical terrestrial "Jewel Orchid" long known as *Haemaria discolor*. Tropical Southeast Asia is the habitat of this low-creeping foliage orchid, which prospers with 65° to 70° F. nights, high humidity, and diffuse light. Well-grown clumps will produce erect spikes of ¾-inch fringed white flowers with yellow anther caps. Its flowers are showy but *Haemaria* is grown mainly for deep maroon-red leaves veined in silvery pink. Pot in well-drained shallow containers with terrestrial mix or prepared houseplant soil, such as Jungle Growth or Jiffy Mix, combined with ⅓ fine fir bark. This is also a good orchid for medium to large terrariums, and is perfect in light gardens.

Lycaste (lie-KASS-tee) is a genus of about thirty-five species from tropical Latin America. All species have unusual triangular, heavy-substanced, long-lived fragrant flowers. Lycastes are treated as epiphytes indoors although they may live as semi-terrestrials in well-drained ground. Their pseudobulbs are like large eggs topped with broad palm-like leaves which fall after the pseudobulbs complete their growth. This deciduous habit lets species survive dry seasons.

Choose cool growers if your nights are 50° to 60° F., intermediate-growing species for warmer conditions. The hybrids adapt to a wide temperature range if they are derived from a combination of cool- to warm-growing types.

Lyc. aromatica has 2½-inch fragrant yellow flowers on a 4- to 6-inch-tall spike from the base of each pseudobulb. A well-grown specimen will have several spikes from each pseudobulb, usually in winter. This is a cool to intermediate grower from Central America. *Lyc. deppei,* from similar habitats in Mexico and Guatemala, has green and white flowers with yellow lips. *Lyc. macrophylla,* a winter to spring bloomer from Peru, thrives with 55° to 65° F. nights. It has 3- to 4-inch fragrant flowers which vary in color but are usually greenish-brown with white lips sometimes spotted red. *Lyc. skinneri* (syn. *Lyc. virginalis*) is the pink- to white-flowered national flower of Guatemala. This delightfully fragrant 4- to 6-inch flower appears in winter on plants which do best with 50° to 55° F. nights.

Hybrids between species are worthwhile as are intergeneric crosses. *Lycaste* is crossed with *Anguloa* to make *Angulocaste* and with *Bifrenaria* to create *Lycastenaria*.

Culture: All species need vigorous air circulation and bright diffuse light. Several species in my collection grow under a greenhouse bench with a combination of diffuse sun and fluorescent light. Resting clumps, usually without leaves, require less water and light than active plants.

In their tropical habitats, lycastes live in trees, pockets of humus on rocks, or sometimes in moss on well-drained ground. When potted, they thrive in an epiphyte mix with unmilled sphagnum moss or coconut fiber. Paul Gripp, professional orchid grower of the Santa Barbara Orchid Estate, uses a mix of 2 parts fine fir bark, 1 part medium fir bark, and about ½ part sphagnum moss, dampened with water before use.

Lycaste roots should never dry out as thoroughly as cattleyas. Use fertilizer every other watering for growing lycastes. Avoid rot by keeping water out of tightly folded new growths. Lycaste leaves are 3 to 5 inches broad and may reach 3 feet long, so mature lycastes need much more space than more formal upright-growing genera such as cattleyas.

Lycaste macrophylla 'Kiyoshi', grown by Chester Kawakami, is the recipient of a Judges Certificate from the American Orchid Society. This is a clone with olive-green sepals, white petals, and pink lips.

The giant greenish-brown flowers of Lycaste denningiana *are admired by Maria de Barahona, who collected the flowering orchid in the Ecuadorian Andes, 2,400 meters in elevation.*

Masdevallia (maz-de-VAH-lee-a) is a South American genus of miniature to dwarf epiphytes. More than three hundred species are recognized but only about thirty are commonly offered in catalogs. Dr. José Masdevall, an eighteenth-century Spanish botanist-physician, is honored by the genus name. In the nineteenth century several hybrids were grown.

Presently it is difficult to locate hybrids but the species are well worth growing. These are ideal companions to Pleurothallis and Stelis, well suited to growing in large glass cases where one can design a miniature cloud-forest habitat, providing a constant moist atmosphere.

Masdevallias are mature when they are 3 to 8 inches tall. A clump of leaves in a 3-inch pot may be nearly hidden with flowers, produced one to three per spike. Plants only need limited space to grow. Leaves grow from the top of thin stalks above a fine root system.

Masdevallias survive without pseudobulbs because their cloud-forest habitats are cool and very humid, but a few species store water in unusually thick succulent foliage. I recall seeing *Masd. pachyantha* (yellow and red flowers) 9,000 feet above sea level, on rocky hills in the Colombian Andes, but most species are found on mossy tree branches or sharply drained banks of moss between 7,000 and 12,000 feet in altitude.

Culture: Nights 50° to 55° F. are suitable, with daytime highs in the 70s. In summer the species will endure higher temperatures if the humidity is kept above 60 per cent and the sun is diffuse. In regions where nights seldom drop below 35° F., masdevallias can be grown outdoors all year round. Masdevallias may be grown with diffuse sun or fluorescent light.

Professional growers who specialize in masdevallias grow a comprehensive collection of species in mixtures of chopped osmunda and sphagnum moss, or well-drained combinations of tree fern and coarse perlite. Roots must stay lightly moist but never soggy. Use small clay or plastic pots with gravel in the bottom for drainage. Live sphagnum moss is a good mulch.

In Colombia I grew several species outdoors on a terrace at over 9,000 feet in altitude. The orchids did well in pure sphagnum loosely packed in shallow clay containers. Indoors, the foliage should be misted on sunny mornings and furnished with brisk air circulation to guard against fungus on the foliage. Repot and divide as new growth starts, usually between March and September, allowing at least three stems plus an active lead per division.

Masdevallia morenoi 'J & L', a white-flowered
miniature, is shown growing on a cork slab. This
plant was awarded a Certificate of Horticultural
Merit by the American Orchid Society.

Masdevallia veitchiana 'Prince de Gaule' has red flowers with a purple blush. The American Orchid Society presented it with an Award of Merit.

Selections: Masd. caudata has 6- to 8-inch yellow flowers marked red. Some species long known as *Masdevallia* have been transferred into the genus *Dracula,* but horticulturally the requirements are the same. *Masd. ignea* (syn. *Masd. militaris*) from Colombia has red flowers from winter to spring. *Masd. coccinea* is similar but its color varies from rose to magenta. *Masd. tovarensis* of Venezuela has 4- to 6-inch-tall spikes with two or three white flowers on each. This species will tolerate warmer temperatures. *Masd. veitchiana* from the Peruvian Andes has spectacular red-pink flowers, 5 to 6 inches long, on 8-inch-tall plants.

Maxillaria (max-il-LAR-ee-a) is a genus of pseudobulbous epiphytes from Latin America, sometimes grown for their colorful but usually small flowers or unusual fragrance. Creeping *Max. tenuifolia* has 1½- to 2-inch red and yellow flowers which smell just like toasted coconut. Most species are sprawling, with several inches between pseudobulbs, but even these can be controlled by growing the plants on tree fern poles or slabs.

Cultivated species thrive with 55° to 65° F. nights and bright diffuse sun or broad-spectrum fluorescents. Since the more than three hundred species range in their temperature preferences, individual plants should be grown in microclimates according to their original habitats. The "Coconut Orchid" *Max. tenuifolia* is a fine plant to have in your collection. A large-flowered species is Ecuadorian *Max. sanderiana,* with fragrant red-spotted white flowers about 5 inches across. Plants are about 1 foot tall and thrive with 55° to 60° F. nights.

Maxillaria grandiflora *'Puyo', AM/AOS, is a white-flowered, fragrant species from Ecuador.*

Meiracyllium (my-ra-SIL-ee-um) *trinasutum* and *Meiracyllium wendlandi* are dwarf, creeping epiphytes with waxy 1¼-inch purple flowers held close to thick 1- to 2-inch-long leaves. This epiphytic species grows on bare bark in bright light under rather dry conditions throughout Mexico and Central America. Indoors, plants should be mounted on tree fern slabs. Provide 60° to 65° F. nights for growing plants and slightly cooler temperatures when new growths are complete. These are charming miniatures in a light garden.

Miltonia (mil-TONE-ee-a) has about twenty species throughout Central America, Panama, the Colombian Andes, Ecuador, and Peru. Several medium-sized species live in Brazil in warmer habitats. "Pansy Orchid," a popular name, refers to the flat flower form seen in the large-flowered, cool- to intermediate-growing Andean types.

Miltonias have 2- to 4-inch pseudobulbs, partially covered by thin foliage. Their leaves are usually light green and mature when 8 to 12 inches long. Andean types are compact with growths close together, while warmer-growing Brazilian species have longer rhizomes and tend to sprawl.

Culture: Provide nights in the 60s for Brazilian species and their hybrids. Large-flowered Andean types will live in intermediate temperatures but do better with nights in the mid-50s. Maintain humidity at 50 to 60 per cent. Low humidity or uneven watering for growing plants often causes foliage to buckle and grow in a crinkled fashion. Thin graceful miltonia leaves are easily spotted by fungus so be sure that foliage is dry by night and keep air circulating with a fan.

Light: Andean species and their large-flowered hybrids do best with bright diffuse sun (1,000 to 1,500 footcandles) but need protection from the hot sun. Broad-spectrum fluorescent lamps are also suitable light for Andean and Brazilian types. The species from Brazil thrive with the same light intensity given cattleyas, but shade them during the summer if their leaves get too yellow. All respond well to fertilizer when light is bright and plants are active.

Since miltonias have fine roots, they need a medium- to fine-textured epiphyte mix. I find that Andean types accept a finer, moister mix than Brazilian types. Plastic pots are ideal because they help maintain even moisture. Provide sharp drainage so the mix will never be soggy. Let miltonias grow into clumps for the best display. Repot and divide when active plants have new growths 2 to 4 inches tall with roots just starting.

Flowers: Miltonias have one or two spikes next to new pseudobulbs. Andean selections bred from *Milt. roezlii* and *Milt. vexillaria* have 3- to 4-inch flowers which last several weeks on the plant but droop when picked. Brazilian species such as *Milt. spectabilis* and *Milt. clowesii* have 1- to 3-inch flowers, usually white to yellow with dark markings, on thin spikes 10 to 15 inches tall. These flowers last well when cut, as do some of the hybrids between Andean and Brazilian types. *Milt. warscewiczii,* which grows at intermediate temperatures, has curly, fragrant, 2-inch, reddish flowers. It is an excellent parent for hybrids with long-lasting ruffled flowers and an adaptable habit.

Miltonias are crossed with related genera to make hybrids with new forms and different colors. *Miltassias* are hybrids of *Miltonia* with *Brassia; Miltonidium* is made by crossing *Miltonia* with *Oncidium.* Spray-flowered *Colmanara* is an adaptable genus combining *Miltonia, Odontoglossum,* and *Oncidium. Miltonia* and its hybrids can be propagated with modern cloning techniques.

Miltonia vexillaria, *with light-pink flowers, thrives in a basket on the* *porch of a country home in Colombia.*

Miltonia *Limelight 'Imogene Smith', AM/AOS, is an Andean red-and-* *white hybrid. It received a Certificate of Cultural Merit when grown* *into this impressive clump by Don Richardson of the J. H. Whitney* *estate.*

Mormodes (more-MOE-dez) is a genus of about twenty epiphytes, related to Catasetum, which have horn-shaped pseudobulbs and thin deciduous foliage. Mormodes are lovely plants with fragrant yellow, cream, or maroon flowers and an adaptable growth habit. The species are all interesting and worth space in your collection. *Mormodes colossus* from tropical Central America has 12- to 24-inch arching spikes with long-lasting yellow to brownish-orange 3-inch flowers, which remind me of birds in flight.

Grow *Mormodes* with 60° to 68° F. nights and bright diffuse light. Inactive clumps need much less water than growing plants. I find that mormodes do best in well-drained clay pots with bark or tree fern mix. *Mormodes* crossed with *Catasetum* makes the hybrid *Catamodes,* and with *Cycnoches* to create the hybrid *Cycnodes.*

Cycnodes *Ginger Snap* (Cycnoches chlorochilon *X* Mormodes colossus) *has orange-tan flowers.*

Mystacidium (miss-ta-SID-ee-um) are dwarf monopodial epiphytes from tropical Africa. These plants thrive with the same care as *Angraecum* and *Aerangis.* They are well suited to light gardens and thrive on tree fern slabs. *Mystacidium distichum* (syn. *Angraecum*) is a 4- to 6-inch dwarf with tightly braided short leaves, and tiny white fragrant flowers which appear during the year. Grow this species in a small pot or on a tree fern slab with 65° to 70° F. nights and diffuse light. *Mystacidium capense* looks like a tiny phalaenopsis plant and has 4- to 6-inch-long spikes of 1-inch fragrant white flowers. The species thrives with 60° to 65° F. nights, high humidity, and bright diffuse light.

Nageliella (nay-gell-i-EL-a) *angustifolia* and *Nageliella purpurea* are dwarf, creeping epiphytes with succulent leaves that are spotted brown. These are adaptable to lower humidity and so are good choices for windowsill growing. Bright purple flowers are only ½ inch but they are waxy and long-lasting. These flowers appear on short branches from a thin 10- to 12-inch arching inflorescence. The spike blooms for several years, so avoid cutting it off. I grow nageliellas on cork slabs with miniature *Tillandsia* species, just as the orchid grows with bromeliads in the Guatemalan habitat. Night temperatures of 55° to 60° F. are ideal. The plants' foliage is more compact if bright light is given, but diffuse light is also acceptable.

Neofinetia (nee-o-fin-ET-ee-ah) *falcata* from subtropical Japan and Korea looks like a dwarf 6- to 8-inch-tall succulent *Angraecum*. It thrives with 60° to 65° F. nights and bright diffuse light or fluorescents. *Neofinetia* can grow in tree fern or bark mix. Its pure-white 1-inch flowers have the fragrance of vanilla and will perfume a whole room or greenhouse.

Neofinetia is crossed with *Ascocentrum* to make *Ascofinetia,* dwarf hybrids which bloom several times a year. *Nakamotoara* is created with *Neofinetia, Vanda,* and *Ascocentrum. Neofinetia* contributes dwarf growth and flower shape to its hybrids but its delicious perfume is not always passed on. Some rare Japanese clones have white variegated foliage.

Notylia (no-TILL-ee-a) species are dwarf epiphytes from Mexico into northern South America. Plants thrive on tree fern slabs and grow 3 to 6 inches tall. Looking like small succulent oncidiums, notylias produce 6- to 12-inch pendulous spikes of many ½- to 1-inch yellowish-green flowers, often spotted purple. Grow notylias in diffuse light, high humidity, and with 60° to 65° F. nights. I have found these orchids growing on shrubs in humid jungles near Tikal, Guatemala.

Odontoglossum (oh-dont-oh-GLOSS-um) species range from Mexico through Central America into Andean South America. Popular species are epiphytes which do well with 50° to 55° F. nights. New hybrids come from crosses with warmer-growing genera such as *Aspasia* and *Brassia,* so they adapt well to 60° to 65° F. nights. However, pure Andean types need cool nights to do their best.

Odontoglossums have an arching inflorescence which grows from the base of plump pseudobulbs. Each spike grows 1 to 3 feet tall and may carry more than twenty flowers. These flowers are usually round, and white or cream to yellow, with darker spots or blotches. Species most often grown are found on trees, moss-covered rocks, or on very well-drained slopes among low shrubs.

Culture: Odontoglossums do best in small pots with excellent drainage and an epiphyte mix that retains moisture without getting soggy. Some of my odontoglossum hybrids thrive in small clay pots with pure unmilled sphagnum moss over gravel and hardwood charcoal. They can also be grown in a mixture of equal parts of fine fir bark, peat moss, and fine pea gravel. Repot every two or three years but always into small containers.

Provide plants with bright diffuse sun or fluorescent light and 50 to 60 per cent humidity. Night temperatures should be 55° to 60° F. for hybrids with warmer-growing species, and 50° to 60° F. for pure Andean types bred from *Odm. crispum.*

Selections: Odm. crispum from the Colombian Andes is the foundation for large modern hybrids. It has round flowers about 3 inches across, white-spotted, dark red-brown with a sparkling texture. Hybrids with *Cochlioda (Odontioda)* and *Miltonia (Odontonia)* often have contrasting calico patterns on a red or yellow to white background. Hybrids with *Aspasia (Aspoglossum)* are waxy and long-lasting, often in red or yellow tones.

More popular than plain *Odontoglossum* species are hybrids with related genera because these often have a more adaptable nature, better flower form, and unusual colors. *Vuylstekeara* Cambria 'Plush' is a good example since it combines the genera *Odontoglossum, Cochlioda,* and *Miltonia* in an adaptable hybrid now available as meristem plantlets. This hybrid clone, which thrives under intermediate temperature conditions, has red flowers with white lips about 4 inches across. It has received a First Class Certificate from the Royal Horticultural Society. Another excellent combination is *Colmanara (Miltonia, Odontoglossum,* and *Oncidium)*, which has arching sprays of bright flowers and compact growth.

This cool-growing hybrid of Odontoglossum *Yukon Harbor and* Odm. triumphans *has yellow- and cream-colored flowers and was raised under fluorescent lights.*

Odm. bictoniense from Mexico and Central America is a cool to intermediate grower with stiff erect spikes of 1½-inch white and pink flowers. Its hybrids inherit upright spikes which are sometimes branched. *Odm. grande* is an easy-to-grow species from Mexico and Guatemala. Although it thrives with intermediate temperatures when making new growth it must have a cool dry rest (50° F. nights) to produce its shiny heavy-substanced 4- to 6-inch yellow and brown flowers. *Odontonia* Tiger Cub (*Odm. grande* X *Odtna.* Wonder), an unusual hybrid with pink lips and yellow petals, is easier to flower than *Odm. grande.*

Odm. pulchellum, the "Lily of the Valley" orchid, has fragrant white to pink-blushed flowers. It is a cool- to intermediate-growing species native to Mexico and Central America. Some showy hybrids made from intermediate-growing Mexican species include *Odm.* George Day (*Odm. rossii* X *Odm. crispum*) with white, pink, and brown 3-inch flowers, and *Odm.* California (*Odm. johnsonorum* X *Odm.* Olinda) with eight to twelve white and brown flowers on each spike.

Oncidium (on-SID-ee-um) is a genus with more than 750 species which range from southern Florida to the Caribbean, Mexico through Central America, and South America. Oncidiums are often bred with related genera such as *Brassia, Miltonia,* and *Odontoglossum.* The *Oncidium* genus name is from a classic Greek word meaning "tumor" or "swelling," referring to warty calluses on the lips of all oncidiums.

These epiphytes do best with sharp drainage and excellent air circulation. Species differ in temperature requirements according to their original habitats. Those from high altitudes need 50° to 60° F. nights. Warm-preference species from low altitudes do well with a 60° to 70° F. range. Most of the cultivated oncidiums with bright flowers thrive with nights in the 60° to 65° F. range, an intermediate temperature suitable for hundreds of other orchids. Bright light is needed for species with thick succulent foliage, and diffuse sun is needed for species with thin leaves. All medium to large species grow well in pots of epiphyte mix, but small types are best suited to tree fern or cork slabs.

Onc. triquetrum, from the Caribbean islands and Jamaica, grows 3 inches tall and lives on shrub or tree twigs. Plants need bright light and warm temperatures to thrive. *Onc. sphacelatum,* from Central America, does well with high humidity and even moisture. It forms plump 6-inch pseudobulbs and a 4- to 6-foot arching spike of yellow flowers. Oncidiums with long spikes can be grown in limited space if one trains the developing inflorescence around a wire hoop, gently holding it in place with plastic-covered wire or thick string.

The smallest popular hybrids of *Oncidium* are called *equitant,* bred from hand-sized succulent Caribbean species. These thrive on tree fern slabs and produce spikes of ¼- to 1-inch flowers on 6- to 24-inch sprays in many different color combinations.

Oncidium lanceanum *is a long-lasting, fragrant species with yellow-brown flowers with purple-pink lips.*

Large succulent oncidiums are called "Mule Ear" types because the 4- to 8-inch leaves look like big ears. In this group are *Onc. lanceanum*, with fragrant yellow and red-brown flowers, and *Onc. splendidum*, with yellow waxy flowers. Hybrids with thick-leaved species are usually compact and endure lower humidity than most orchids. They should dry out between soakings.

In the group with thin foliage one can find compact species or tall growers. *Onc. ampliatum* var. *majus* has arching branched sprays of ½- to 1-inch yellow flowers in the spring. It thrives in a clay pot or on a big slab of tree fern. *Onc. kramerianum* and *Onc. papilio* or the hybrid between these two, *Onc.* Kahili, have 2- to 3-inch flowers resembling a butterfly face, which are yellow with brown markings. The flowers open one at a time at the tip of a 10- to 15-inch inflorescence. Protect the spikes since they produce blooms at the growing tip for many years. Another nice compact selection is *Onc. ornithorhynchum*, which produces 12- to 20-inch sprays of fragrant pink flowers in the winter and thrives under fluorescent lights.

Onc. sphacelatum can develop into a big clump with multiple spikes arching 4 to 5 feet and creating a cloud of yellow. Its hybrid with *Onc. flexuosum* (*Onc. Goldiana*) is easy to grow in a 6- to 8-inch pot and has sprays of yellow flowers that are marked brown from the spring into the summer. Check catalogs for meristem propagations of select clones, including awarded species and hybrids.

Ornithocephalus (or-ni-tho-SEFF-ah-lus) is a genus of about thirty-five dwarf succulent epiphytes from Mexico, Central America, and Brazil. The flowers are delightful when studied under a magnifying glass. The tiny cream to yellow-green fuzzy flowers are only ¼ to ¾ inch across but many of them open on 2- to 4-inch-long spikes, often several spikes from a single 3- to 6-inch plant. Provide plants with diffuse light, 60° to 65° F. nights, high humidity, and even moisture at the roots. These plants are succulent but have no pseudobulbs. Give growing plants half-strength fertilizer every other watering.

Peristeria (per-is-TER-ee-a) *elata,* the "Holy Ghost" orchid, and the national flower of Panama, is grown for its waxy, fragrant white flowers. This terrestrial thrives in a well-drained mixture of houseplant soil with ⅓ to ½ fine fir bark or any mixture that grows satisfactory paphiopedilums. Provide plants with diffuse light, 60° to 65° F. nights, and even moisture at the roots while the plants are growing. Then they should be kept much drier for a period of weeks until new growth is again under way. Permit clumps to form and apply frequent dilute fertilizer to growing plants.

Phaius (FAY-us) species are robust Asian terrestrials with broad palm-like leaves and upright spikes of fragrant flowers opening over a period of weeks. Most popular is the "Nun Orchid," *Phaius grandifolius* (syn. *Phaius tancarvillae*). I have found this species growing in full sun on lava-flow slopes in Java. Throughout the tropics it thrives outdoors, and it is often grown in gardens where clumps prosper with a humus-rich soil and rotted manure.

In containers, phaius needs a well-drained terrestrial mix, 55° to 65° F. nights, and bright diffuse light. Its flowers are 3 to 4 inches across, brown with a maroon to magenta lip, and white petals on the reverse. *Phaius* is crossed with *Calanthe* to make the rare *Phaiocalanthe* hybrids.

Phaius occasionally forms plantlets at the nodes on an inflorescence. To encourage these propagations, cut the whole spike at ground level after the flowers fall. Dust the wound with Rootone. Place the spike on moist sphagnum moss in diffuse light. Pot the plantlets after the roots are several inches long.

Phragmipedium (frag-mi-PEE-de-um) species resemble *Paphiopedilum* plants but their flowers are different, often with long twisted petals. *Phragmipedium* has about twelve species which range from Mexico through Panama into South America. Some grow as epiphytes with moss around the roots; others are terrestrials. In containers they thrive with well-drained terrestrial mixes. Provide bright diffuse sun (slightly brighter than given paphiopedilums), nights 55° to 60° F., and even moisture at the roots. Fertilize every few weeks when new growths are forming.

Phragmipedium *Grande* (Phrag. caudatum X Phrag. longifolium) *has brown, green, and white flowers.*

Flowers appear on upright spikes, often with several open at one time. *Phrag. caudatum* has green and tan flowers with petals that can trail 15 to 20 inches. *Phrag. boissierianum* has 6-inch green and cream flowers with wavy-margined petals.

Pleione (play-OH-nee) is a genus of terrestrial or rarely epiphytic species from India and Southeast Asia. Plants grow from round pseudobulbs which resemble crocus corms. Pot in a well-drained terrestrial compost using bulb pans or similar shallow containers. Provide plants with bright diffuse light, 50° to 60° F. nights, and even moisture as plants make new growth. They should be kept much drier when their leaves drop. Flowers appear after the leafless pseudobulbs have rested. When flowers fade, repot the pseudobulbs, planting several to each container. Resume watering when new roots appear and apply fertilizer solution every few waterings to active plants. *Pln. praecox* from the Himalayas is especially lovely for its 3-inch fragrant rose-pink flowers in the fall.

Pleurothallis (plur-o-THAL-is) is a genus of more than a thousand species, mainly small-flowered dwarf to miniature epiphytes with thin stems and a clumping growth habit. I have seen some Andean species grow 20 inches tall but most popular types are dwarf or miniature and mature in 1- to 2-inch pots. The species' habitats vary from chilly mountain slopes to hot Amazonian lowlands, so one must fit temperatures to individual plants. Intermediate- to warm-growing *Pleurothallis grobyi,* with its many sprays of yellow flowers, is an excellent plant which will fill a 2-inch pot with flowering growths.

Grow pleurothallis in small clay pots of fine tree fern with sphagnum moss or pure coarse sphagnum moss over hardwood charcoal, or mounted on chunks of tree fern. Provide plants with diffuse light. Some direct sun early in the morning is good, but never at midday. Maintain high humidity and even moisture, and apply dilute fertilizer every few waterings. Permit plants to develop clumps. These do well under fluorescent lamps.

Polyrrhiza (poly-RYE-za) species are rare leafless epiphytes with fragrant white flowers and odd gray-green roots which function like leaves to manufacture food. The two species occasionally found in orchid collections are *Polyrrhiza funalis,* from Cuba and Jamaica, and *Polyrrhiza lindeni,* which lives on cypress trees in south Florida and also grows in Cuba. Grow these plants by tightly tying them to tree fern slabs or hardwood logs. Mist polyrrhizas frequently and give them a half-strength fertilizer solution every month. Provide plants with 60° to 68° F. nights, diffuse light, and good air circulation. The white fragrant flowers of *P. funalis* are 2 inches long; *P. lindeni's* flowers are 4 to 5 inches long.

Polystachya (poly-STAK-ee-a) is a genus with almost two hundred species of epiphytic small-flowered orchids, mainly from tropical Africa. However, one species, *Pol. flavescens* (syn. *Pol. luteola*) is found in Florida, tropical Latin America, and the Asian tropics. Such a wide geographical distribution of orchid species is rare. Polystachyas grow with a 60° to 70° F. temperature range, bright diffuse light, and 50 to 60 per cent humidity. Pot them in small clay containers with tree fern or bark

Polystachya phalax *'Spring Hill', recipient of a Certificate of Botanical Merit from the American Orchid Society, has fragrant 1-inch white flowers.*

mix, or mount them on tree fern slabs. Robust clumps form when active plants are given frequent dilute fertilizer.

Greenish-yellow *Pol. grandiflora* from Africa, with 1½-inch flowers, is one of the largest species. *Pol. flavescens* is an easy-to-grow species with branched spikes of fragrant ¼-inch greenish-cream flowers. Plants usually bloom several times each year.

Promenaea (pro-men-EYE-a) is a genus of about fifteen Brazilian epiphytes, all with compact growth. Flowers, which are 1½ to 2 inches, grow on short spikes which stick out at the base of plump 1-inch pseudobulbs. These are excellent dwarf orchids and are easy to grow in small pots of chopped sphagnum moss with tree fern, or on cork slabs where humidity is 60 to 70 per cent. Provide plants with 60° to 68° F. nights and diffuse light with direct sun early each day, or broad-spectrum fluorescent lamps.

Promenaea xanthina has 2-inch yellow fragrant flowers on 1- to 2-inch-tall plants. *Prom. stapellioides* has round 2-inch maroon flowers with dark purple-black lips. *Promenaea* Crawshayana is the hybrid between these two species and has purple-spotted yellow flowers.

Renanthera (ren-ANN-ther-a) is a genus of monopodial *Vanda* relatives from tropical Asia. Four or five species are commonly cultivated for their long-branched sprays of scarlet, long-lasting flowers. In tropical regions, especially Southeast Asia, these plants are grown outside in raised beds or on well-drained slopes with charcoal, coconut husks, and sometimes rotted manure. Aerial roots are thick and will grip support poles. These epiphytes need excellent drainage, bright light, and high humidity.

Renanthera monachica, which is 1 to 2 feet tall, is the most compact species. It can be grown in a 6- to 8-inch clay pot with charcoal, pebbles, and tree fern chunks. Flowers, which are 1½ inches, are yellow with numerous red spots. Other species grow 3 to 15 feet tall and are best grown in a sunny greenhouse or an outdoor tropical garden.

Hybrids with smaller genera are useful in light gardens or windowsill growing areas. For example, renantheras are crossed with phalaenopsis to make *Renanthopsis,* 1- to 2-foot-tall plants. *Renanthopsis* have the flower shape and plant habit like the *Phalaenopsis* parent; but they inherit their color from *Renanthera,* producing well-formed flowers in peach, yellow, pink, or other combinations, often with fine dots in darker tones.

Renanstylis Queen Emma is a hybrid of *Ren. storiei* (red flowers, 15- to 20-foot stems) with the compact *Rhynchostylis gigantea.* The *Renanstylis* combines beauty from both parents, producing branched sprays of red flowers much shorter than pure renantheras. *Renanthera* crossed with *Ascocentrum* makes *Renancentrum,* an adaptable genus growing 2 to 3 feet tall.

Renantheras thrive with the same care that vandas receive (see Chapter 11). Hybrids with other genera often need less intense light. *Renanthopsis,* for example, thrive with cattleya light conditions, and even do well under broad-spectrum fluorescent light.

Rhynchostylis (rink-oh-STY-lis) contains four species, which are monopodial epiphytes from tropical Asia. This genus was formerly referred to as *Saccolabium.* Thailand is the habitat of the most famous species, *Rhy. gigantea.* Intergeneric hybrids using *Rhynchostylis* as a parent are also popular in Southeast Asia. An outstanding example is *Opsistylis,* which combines *Rhynchostylis* with *Vandopsis.*

"Fox Tail Orchid" is a popular name for *Rhynchostylis* because the upright to pendulous spikes are bushy, with a multitude of closely packed 1½-inch fragrant flowers. Plants mature and bloom when they are 6 to 8 inches tall; eventually they reach 12 to 15 inches in height. Flowers on my *Rhy. gigantea* are brilliant magenta and last at least thirty days. Reddish clones have been crossed to make the internationally famous Sagarik's Strain, now available as seedlings and a few outstanding clones as vegetative propagations. A white form of *Rhy. gigantea* is also popular.

Rhynchostylis coelestis has ¾-inch white and indigo blue flowers, densely packed on upright spikes. Frequently several spikes appear at once on healthy plants. *Rhy. retusa,* from India, Thailand, the Malay Peninsula, the Philippines, Borneo, and Java, has pendulous inflorescences of white flowers which are heavily spotted with purple. *Rhy. violacea* is similar but with less-packed spikes. Foliage on all species is thick, often blushed purple in bright light. Yellowish stripes are normal on leaves.

Roots are stiff, thick, and quite at home hanging free in the air. Slat baskets are excellent containers for this genus.

Culture: Intermediate to warm 65° to 70° F. nights and bright light are ideal. Maintain a minimum relative humidity of 60 per cent. Mist roots and foliage on bright mornings and fertilize active plants every few waterings. *Rhy. gigantea* in my collection grows in a 6-inch clear-plastic pot with a mix of hardwood charcoal, coconut fiber, and broken crocks, but several of the thick roots are sticking out into the air. Compact *Rhy. coelestis* does well in shallow bulb pans or slat baskets; it also blooms under broad-spectrum fluorescents.

Keep roots evenly moist but never soggy. Slight drying between soakings is acceptable. Dry healthy roots are silvery white; damp roots are gray-green. Best bloom occurs on established clumps, so avoid disturbing the roots. If the potting media rots, wash or pluck it out from around the thick roots, then add fresh material. Potting with inorganic or long-lasting materials is best.

Hybrids: Hybrids with other vandaceous genera are usually compact, floriferous, and often fragrant. One of my favorites is 8-inch-tall *Rhynchocentrum* Sagarik (*Rhy. coelestis* X *Ascocentrum curvifolium*), a golden-yellow flower with blue lips on upright to slightly arching spikes which bloom two or three times each year. *Opsistylis* (*Rhynchostylis* X *Vandopsis*) hybrids are a delightful blending of dwarf plant habit. They inherited the many flowers of *Rhynchostylis* with the better flower form and size of *Vandopsis*. Excellent examples include *Opst.* Lanna Thai (*Vdps. parishii* X *Rhy. gigantea*) with burgundy flowers and *Opst.* Memoria Mary Nattrass (*Vdps. gigantea* X *Rhy. gigantea*) with white flowers, heavily marked pink to magenta. Since different parental clones are used to create these hybrids, offspring can vary in color. Check current catalogs for details about the strains offered.

Rodriguezia (rod-ree-GEEZ-ee-a) is a Latin American genus of about thirty epiphytes related to *Ionopsis* and *Oncidium*. These are compact 4- to 8-inch-tall orchids but they have a creeping habit that makes them difficult to keep in pots. I grow them on slabs of tree fern or in a pot with a tree fern pole for the rhizomes to climb. Nights at 60–70° F. are satisfactory. Provide bright diffuse light and 50 to 60 per cent relative humidity.

Deep-pink *Rdza. secunda* has 1-inch flowers on 8- to 12-inch arching spikes several times each year. *Rdza. venusta* (syn. *Rdza. bracteata*) has fragrant white flowers. Hybrids with *Comparettia* (*Rodrettia*) and *Oncidium* (*Rodricidium*) are compact, floriferous, and nice in light gardens.

Saccolabium (sak-oh-LAB-ee-um) is a genus of tropical Asian epiphytes related to *Gastrochilus*. These plants are worth growing for their dwarf habit and tight clusters of long-lasting, waxy, fragrant flowers. *Saccolabium quisumbingii* (syn. *Tuberolabium kotoense*) from the Philippines thrives on a chunk of tree fern or in a small pot of tree fern with sphagnum moss. Plants have short spikes of creamy-white fragrant flowers dotted purple. This species crossed with *Angraecum philippinense* makes the dwarf hybrid *Tubaecum* Snow Gem. Grow saccolabiums with bright diffuse sun or strong fluorescent light and warm temperatures.

Saccolabium quisumbingii (*syn.* Tuberolabium kotoense),
a 6- to 8-inch-tall plant, has whtie flowers with red markings.

Sarcochilus (sar-KOK-i-lus) is a genus of dwarf monopodial epiphytes from tropical Asia and Australia. These thrive with 60° to 65° F. nights and bright diffuse sun. Plants grow well on slabs of tree fern. *Sarco. falcatus* is a favorite for its 3- to 6-inch compact habit and tight clusters of white fragrant waxy flowers.

Schomburgkia (shom-BERG-key-a) species are robust epiphytes from Mexico, the West Indies, and parts of South America. I have seen them growing on rocks in full sun and on bare trees in swamps, often in areas of limited rainfall during certain months but always with good humidity. *Schomburgkia* flowers look like ruffled laelias or cattleyas but plants have hollow pseudobulbs and longer inflorescences. Some adaptable tall-flowered hybrids are created by crossing schomburgkias with cattleyas.

In the tropics, ants often live inside schomburgkia pseudobulbs, a relationship also seen in *Diacrium* (syn. *Caularthron*). Some taxonomists classify *Schomburgkia* in the genus *Laelia,* but horticulturally the genera are distinct.

Culture: Grow *schomburgkia* species like cattleyas, but provide as much bright light as plants can accept without burning. The best flowering and compact growth occurs with almost full sun. The hybrids with other genera thrive under cattleya conditions. Epiphyte mixes over hardwood charcoal or big slabs of tree fern are suitable supports. Let plants dry out between waterings. Schomburgkias often rest for a month or so each year at which time they require much less water.

Selections: The smallest-growing species, most practical indoors, is *Schom. thomsoniana* from Cuba and the Cayman Islands, with a mature height of 6 to 8 inches but a typical tall spike is 4 feet long! The ruffled flowers are golden-yellow blushed bronze, with deep-purple lips. An excellent primary hybrid is *Schombocattleya* Trudy Fennell, the cross with fragrant *Cattleya granulosa.*

Schomburgkia thomsoniana *usually has creamy-buff flowers with a purple lip, but this clone has almost white flowers.*

Schom. humboldtii from Venezuela has 3-inch, fragrant, pale-lilac flowers, but a pure-white variety with yellow lip is also in cultivation. This species has a 3- to 4-foot-long spike, and usually has flowers during the summer. *Schom. tibicinis* of Mexico and Central America has 15- to 24-inch hollow pseudobulbs topped by two or three 1-foot-long leaves. The magenta to purple-brown 2- to 3-inch flowers have yellow and purple lips, and open on tall spikes over a period of weeks.

Schom. undulata from Colombia and Venezuela looks like *Schom. tibicinis* but grows slightly smaller and has 2½-inch shiny brownish-purple flowers in big clusters on top of 2- to 5-foot spikes. *Schombodiacrium* Orchidglade is an interesting adaptable hybrid of *Schom. undulata* and *Diacrium bicornutum.*

Scuticaria (skoo-ti-KAR-ee-a) is a genus of several pendulous epiphytes from Brazil, the Guianas, and Venezuela. The fragrant, heavy-substanced, 3-inch flowers are produced one at a time on a short spike from the base of each clump. Rounded succulent leaves trail to 4 feet long in *Scuticaria steelii.* Mount scuticarias on slabs of tree fern or hang them in a humid bright location with 65° to 70° F. nights. These grow quite well with cattleyas.

Sobralia (so-BRAL-ee-a) is a Latin American genus of tall-growing terrestrials with broad thin leaves, slender stems, and large cattleya-shaped flowers. These succeed in 8- to 15-inch pots where they form impressive clumps 3 to 8 feet tall. Since the flowers are short-lived and plants get so tall, sobralias are best suited for tropical gardens or spacious conservatories.

Indoors, provide sobralias with a cymbidium-type terrestrial mix, 60° to 68° F. nights, bright sun, and even moisture at their roots. Plants should receive frequent applications of a water-soluble fertilizer while they are growing, but no fertilizer and less water after their stems reach maximum height. Permit sobralias to form clumps for best flower production.

Sob. macrantha has fragrant 6- to 10-inch flowers in rose-pink or white, produced at the top of 6- to 8-foot stems. *Arundina* is the Asian relative of *Sobralia* and has similar growth habits but smaller flowers.

Sophronitis (sof-roe-NYE-tiss) are dwarf epiphytes from Brazil. The best known of the six to eight species is brilliant-orange- to red-flowered *Soph. coccinea* (syn. *Soph. grandiflora*). Although the pure species are charming, the genus is most famous as a parent in breeding red cattleya hybrids. The two most popular species are deep-scarlet forms of *Soph. coccinea* and orange-flowered *Soph. cernua,* both of which will succeed under humid intermediate conditions with broad-spectrum fluorescent lamps or bright diffuse sun.

I have found *Soph. cernua* in Brazil at lower elevations growing on trees with lichens and bromeliads. Most popular forms of *Soph. coccinea* come from higher elevations where nights are cooler and humidity is high because of frequent mists. Growing sophronitis species on hardwood logs or tree fern slabs permits one to mist them and provide high humidity without the clumps ever getting too soggy. *Soph. cernua* may be inactive for a few weeks each year while *Soph. coccinea* clones tend to continue growth, a habit transferred to its hybrids which often bloom several times each year as new growths mature.

Hybrids with a *Sophronitis* species as one parent are mature when they are 4 to 8 inches tall. They usually have brightly colored orange to red flowers. An excellent hybrid, originally registered in 1902 but since remade by several modern breeders, is *Sophrolaelia Psyche* (*L. cinnabarina* X *Soph. coccinea*), a deep orange-red-flowered hybrid that thrives under fluorescent lamps and blooms several times each year. *Epiphronitis* Veitchii (*Epidendrum ibaguense* X *Soph. coccinea*), also an old hybrid, has bushy 8- to 10-inch stems like a miniature reed-stem epidendrum. Clusters of glowing red-fringed flowers with yellow lips are almost always in bloom.

Soph. violacea is a Brazilian species sometimes called *Sophronitella*. It has compact growth but is taller than the creeping sophronitis species. The 1-inch flowers are violet-lavender. Plants do well on tree fern slabs with 65° to 70° F. nights, high humidity, and diffuse sun or broad-spectrum fluorescents. Let *Soph. violacea* form clumps for best flower show.

Spathoglottis (spath-oh-GLOT-is) species are tropical terrestrials from Asia and New Guinea where they are often grown as garden plants in raised beds or big urns around homes and temples. Indoors, pot pseudobulbs at ground level with a terrestrial mix over gravel and hardwood charcoal. Grow with 40 to 60 per cent humidity, with 55° to 65° F. nights, and bright light.

Some popular species, such as yellow-flowered *Spa. affinis,* lose leaves each year so they require much less water until new growth sprouts. *Spa. plicata* grows 15 to 24 inches tall and has an erect spike slightly taller than the leaves. Its 1½-inch purple flowers are marked yellow in the center and open over a long period. Several color variations occur.

Stanhopea (stan-HOPE-ee-a) is a genus of epiphytes from Mexico, Central America, and South America. Several species are popular in collections for their large, waxy, fragrant flowers which appear on sharply pendulous spikes. I have found stanhopeas in tropical jungles growing on lower tree trunks where the flower spikes have freedom to develop directly below the clumps of round pseudobulbs and broad leaves. Indoors, stanhopeas must be grown in slat baskets or on rafts so the spikes can develop normally.

Culture: Pot stanhopeas in a basket with ½- to 1-inch mesh or slat raft with osmunda, sphagnum moss, or coconut fiber. Tree fern slabs are also

A Spathoglottis plicata *flower is shown here with the same species coated with 24-carat gold in Thailand.*

suitable. Provide 60° to 65° F. nights, up to 70° F. for active plants from warm lowlands, high humidity, and good air circulation. Diffuse sun or fluorescent lamps are satisfactory light. I hang stanhopeas under cattleyas in my greenhouse. Even with relatively dim light, they grow and bloom well.

Selections: Any species you can find is worth growing since all have fragrant waxy flowers of intricate design. *Stan. eburnea* is a white-flowered, fall-blooming species from warm areas. *Stan. ecornuta* from Central America has 5-inch creamy-yellow flowers marked with maroon dots and orange lips. *Stan. oculata* from Mexico and Central America has five to eight flowers that are up to 5 inches across and are scented like chocolate. Flowers are usually yellow or white with purple markings. *Stan. wardii* is a similar species.

Stelis (stel-IS) is a genus of miniature epiphytes from Central and South America. Of the more than three hundred species, only a few are available in collections but they are worth having if you enjoy diminutive orchids. Like their relatives, *Pleurothallis,* the flowers are best appreciated with a magnifying glass. Individual blooms are usually ¼ inch, but many of them appear on slender upright spikes so a clump of *Stelis* can be showy. These orchids thrive in small clay pots with sphagnum moss or can be mounted on medium to soft tree fern. They thrive side by side

Cycnoches chlorochilon.

Epidendrum radicans.

Kirchara *Kulowe 'Talisman Cove'* is a complex dwarf hybrid (Slc. *Estella Jewell* and Epi. atropurpureum).

Masdevallia caudata, *a cool-growing species from the Colombian Andes.*

Miltonia *Bremen 'Talisman Cove' grown under fluorescent lights. This is an Andean-type hybrid* (Milt. *Limelight and* Milt. *Herrenhausen*).

Odontioda *Cheer crossed with* Cochlioda noetzliana, *a red-flowered, cool-growing Peruvian species, produced this glowing* Odontioda *which I grew in the basement under lights.*

Aliceara *Maury Island 'Vashon', AM/AOS, is an intermediate growing hybrid* (Miltassia *Vino X* Oncidium marshallianum).

Sophrolaelia *Psyche 'Talisman Cove', a dwarf hybrid* (Laelia cinnabarina *X* Sophronitis coccinea).

with pleurothallis and need 60° to 65° F. nights and diffuse light. Because *Stelis* are so tiny, they are ideal in light gardens or even airy terrariums.

Trichocentrum (trik-o-SEN-trum) is a genus of about eighteen dwarf epiphytes from Central and South America. The plants look like small succulent oncidiums and thrive when mounted on cork or tree fern slabs, or in small clay pots. Grow with strong diffuse light, 60° to 65° F. nights, and 50 to 60 per cent humidity. I have good luck with these in a light garden, too.

Trichocentrum albopurpureum (syn. *albococcineum*) and *Trctm. tigrinum* are species with the largest flowers, which are yellow with brown spots and big white lips marked purple. Hybrids with *Oncidium* are also 4 to 6 inches tall but have large fragrant flowers and adaptable habits. *Trichocidium* Elvena (*Trctm. albopurpureum* X *Onc. lanceanum*) and *Trcdm.* Honduras (*Onc. splendidum* X *Trctm. tigrinum*) are excellent choices; they are resistant to low humidity.

Trichoceros (try-koe-SER-os) is a genus of Andean epiphytes with small pseudobulbs, thick leaves, and thin erect inflorescences with ¾- to 1-inch yellow and brown flowers. The center of each flower looks like an insect. Grow these on tree fern slabs with bright diffuse light and 55° to 65° F. nights.

Trichoglottis (trik-o-GLOTT-is) is a genus of about thirty monopodial *Vanda* relatives from tropical Southeast Asia. These require bright light and conditions similar to vandas. A compact sort, suitable for the average greenhouse, is *Trgl. sagarikii* from Thailand. This species, which is mature at 12 inches, has yellow and brown flowers, and white lips that are marked magenta. It is best to grow larger species outside in raised beds or in bright light, with a tree fern pole for support. Hybrids are made with related genera including *Vanda* (*Trichovanda*) and *Renanthera* (*Renaglottis*).

Trichopilia (try-koe-PIL-ee-ah) species are pseudobulbous epiphytes from Latin America related to *Miltonia* and *Oncidium*. I have found trichopilias growing as epiphytes in bright diffuse light, often near waterfalls or streams. Indoors, pot them in small containers with bark or tree fern mix topped with coarse sphagnum moss, or mount plants on tree fern slabs. Mist these every bright morning.

Trpla. fragrans grows 6 to 8 inches tall and has an 8- to 12-inch arching inflorescence with white, fragrant, 4-inch flowers with yellow marking inside. *Trpla. suavis,* blooming in the spring, has 4-inch fragrant creamy-white flowers spotted pink. These are good under lights where they thrive with cattleya hybrids but need less intensity. Divide and repot container-grown clumps every two or three years as new growth begins.

Trichopilia suavis *has clusters of fragrant 3- to 4-inch flowers with pink lips.*

Vandopsis (van-DOP-siss) is a tropical Asian genus of about twelve monopodial epiphytes related to vandas and thriving with the same care. *Vandopsis lissochiloides* (syn. *Vanda batemannii*) should be grown outdoors because it matures at 4 to 6 feet tall. This species has thick 3-inch fragrant yellow flowers that are spotted purple. *Vdps. parishii* (bot. syn. *Hygrochilus parishii*) from Thailand is suitable for growing indoors. This dwarf species can be grown on a tree fern slab, raft, or in a 6-inch clay pot. Its flowers are round, waxy, fragrant, and 2½ inches across. Their color is yellow, dotted red, with a magenta lip. Hybrids with *Rhynchostylis,* such as *Opsistylis* Lanna Thai, are outstanding dwarf orchids with thick-substanced fragrant flowers, usually deep purple-red.

Vanilla (va-NIL-lah) is a genus of succulent vines. Well-known species are *Vanilla planifolia,* with greenish-yellow flowers, and *Vanilla pompona,* which furnishes the seedpods used for vanilla flavoring. In a greenhouse or outdoors in the tropics, these thrive on tree fern poles with well-drained terrestrial compost at the base. Their flowers are small and last only a day or two. *Vanilla imperialis* from Africa is more beautiful than the commercial species. It has short spikes of frilly yellow-green flowers with purple lips.

All vanillas need a support on which to twine, so a sturdy tree fern log or pole is best anchored in a clay pot with gravel. Then add terrestrial compost around the vanilla roots. The stem will soon sprout roots to grip the tree fern. Propagate by chopping off a 10- to 15-inch-tip cutting.

Vanilla planifolia *in Papeete, Tahiti.*

Zygopetalum (zye-go-PET-a-lum) is a genus of fragrant flowered pseudobulbous species from Central and South America. Cultivated species and their hybrids are grown in terrestrial composts although some may occasionally be found as epiphytes in moist tropical jungles. Popular in cultivation are *Z. crinitum, Z. intermedium,* and *Z. mackayi,* all with upright spikes of 2- to 3-inch long-lasting yellow-green fragrant flowers. These are blotched brown, with broad white lips heavily lined with purple. Provide bright diffuse light, good air circulation, and 60° to 65° F. nights. Avoid getting water in new growths. Spray with Benlate if the foliage develops fungus spots. It is normal for older leaves to fall after new growth has begun.

Zygopetalum crinitum, *var.* coeruleum *'Gleneyrie', has received a Certificate of Botanical Merit from the American Orchid Society.*

13. Propagation Techniques

NEW ORCHID HYBRIDS and fine species are often reproduced sexually from seed. Even easier than seed propagation is increasing orchids by vegetative means, from divisions and offsets. The fastest way to propagate your favorite orchids is to divide them once plants form mature clumps. Each technique will be explained in this chapter.

BACKBULB GROWTH

Orchids with pseudobulbs are easy to propagate by division. Older pseudobulbs behind the main growth (backbulbs) often have dormant buds which will begin to grow when the backbulbs are cut away from the active sprout or lead.

An arrow shows where to cut through the rhizome for dividing or to encourage backbulbs to sprout leads.

A useful technique to encourage backbulb sprouting before a clump is ready for repotting or division is to cut through the rhizome halfway with a sterile sharp knife. Dust the cut with a fungicide or Rootone powder. This partial injury to the rhizome connecting the lead with older pseudobulbs usually prompts backbulbs to sprout. If this does not occur in two months, cut the rhizome through but leave the clump in place. Having an established root system encourages the new buds to make sturdy progress.

To propagate a multi-lead plant, divide the clump into sections of three to four pseudobulbs, each with an active lead. The live buds in leftover backbulbs, now free from the leads, will sprout in a month or two. To discourage rot from starting in fresh cuts, dust the wounds with Rootone powder—a root-stimulating hormone with fungicide to discourage disease.

The point of the arrow shows where to cut through the rhizome for division of four healthy pseudobulbs plus active lead (left).

DIVISION

Dividing plants at repotting time is convenient but the main consideration is to do the surgery during the orchid's active growth. From spring into summer is a good time for most genera, but each plant should be treated individually. If you have a species that begins new growth and roots in October, then fall is a good time to divide it. Orchids disturbed for repotting or dividing when they are relatively inactive take longer to recover.

This is a cattleya hybrid division with new growth. Some older roots are growing into the hardwood charcoal chunk. Plastic-covered wire (top) holds the pseudobulbs neatly together.

This division of an orchid hybrid has just been repotted in a clay pot. Old backbulbs (right) may sprout and then bloom in one to three years.

POTTING PAPHIOPEDILUMS

(pages 188–90)

The paphiopedilum at the right should not be divided until it has finished flowering. The plant at the left has finished flowering so it can be divided and repotted now.

The arrow shows where this clump can be pulled apart to form two plants.

Gently tap the pot to loosen the root ball, then lift the plant out. If the plant doesn't move, turn the pot upside down and knock the rim on the edge of a table.

Trim away dead or broken roots with a sterile tool.

Cuts on the rhizome of the divided plant should be dusted with fungicide or, as shown here, sprayed with tree-pruning paint to discourage rot.

Orchids with rhizomes, such as epidendrums and cattleyas, usually need to be cut apart with sharp sterile shears, although some types can be gently pulled apart without damaging the plant. Sometimes the connecting stem between active portions of a mature clump will rot so that division can be accomplished with a gentle twist at repotting time. Tough orchids such as cymbidiums will first have to be twisted to expose the rhizome, then cut through with a long sharp knife.

Paphiopedilums should be left to form a clump of six to eight growths. A clump with good roots will produce better-quality flowers than smaller divisions. (See the photographs on pages 188–90 for a step-by-step procedure for potting paphiopedilums.) This technique also works with close-growing fine-rooted orchids such as miltonias and pleurothallis.

After Division Put newly divided plants in a bright humid location with 65° to 68° F. nights. Water these orchids with a transplanting solution of lukewarm water plus a root-stimulating hormone, such as SUPER-thrive or Tender Leaf Plant Starter. Let the pots drain thoroughly. Epiphytes require no water at the roots until new roots start; however, you

From an overgrown clump of Trichocidium *Elvena (above), there were produced five divisions, each with one to three active leads.*

should mist the pot's surface on bright mornings, or every morning for plants grown under fluorescent lamps. Terrestrials need high humidity and evenly moist compost, but slightly less damp than for established plants. A slightly dry potting medium encourages vigorous new roots.

In extreme cases of root loss where a valuable plant's roots have rotted or been otherwise removed, put the whole plant inside a clear-plastic bag. Keep the bag on until new roots have begun to grow, then gradually remove the bag, opening it slightly more each day over a period of seven to ten days. Soaking the potting mix of a rootless orchid encourages rot but keeping the whole plant in a very humid atmosphere will encourage roots to form while drastically reducing water loss from the plant tissues.

Dusting cuts with a combination of rooting hormone and fungicide (such as Rootone) further helps divisions establish. Another technique, unnecessary for sturdy plants but useful for weak orchids, is a sugar feeding. Mix 1 tablespoon of table sugar with a gallon of warm water until the sugar is dissolved. Add to this several drops of SUPERthrive, Dexol Tender Leaf Plant Starter, or similar liquid with B1 and hormones.

Put the solution in a plastic plant-mister and spray the foliage each bright morning, or once for plants to be kept under plastic. If the orchid has some live roots, let the solution drip down on them but avoid saturation. This solution is also excellent for newly imported orchids that have been through the shock of long-distance international shipment.

Cymbidium *pseudobulbs offered at a commercial nursery for low prices are often from costly clones of excellent quality.*

A healthy dormant bud sprouted on the backbulb of this Oncidium splendidum *after two months.*

Sturdy new growth has started from backbulbs of
Miltassia *Charles M. Fitch after several months on*
moist sphagnum moss.

PROPAGATION BY OFFSETS

Genera without pseudobulbs, such as Angraecums, Phalaenopsis types, and Vandas, occasionally form offsets at the base of larger plants. Genera without pseudobulbs cannot be divided until they have at least two main growing points, comparable to leads in sympodial orchids. Many phalaenopsis never have more than one growing point; they simply grow ahead each year from the same active bud. Angraecums and ascocentrums are more generous in forming offsets or keikis. These offsets are the best way to propagate such orchids at home.

Once an offset has several sturdy roots, it can be twisted from the main plant. Dust the open wounds with Rootone, then pot the offset in a suitable mix and a small container. If you wish to have a specimen plant with several growing points, pot the offsets around the edge of a larger specimen, or just leave the offsets alone, attached to the mature plant. Eventually they all will bloom.

Renantanda *Seminole* (*top*) *has outgrown its pot and will be cut
down, then repotted. The same plant* (*below*) *had its lower stem cut
off and the main plant with offshoots was potted in fresh potting mix.
A mature offshoot on the right will be potted separately.*

FLOWER STEM PLANTLETS

Phalaenopsis and related hybrids may form plantlets on the inflorescence. Some species do this more often than others. For example, *Phal. lueddemanniana* frequently forms flowers *and* plantlets on an inflorescence, sometimes forming arching fountains of keikis with flowers. Plantlets on the inflorescence can be removed once a few roots have formed. Pack coconut fiber or sphagnum moss around the forming roots. Hold the slightly moist wad of rooting material together with a plastic-covered plant wire, or fasten the inflorescence against a small plastic pot in which the plantlet can establish. Once the keiki has grown some roots in the new pot (after about two months), you can cut the new plant away from its parent.

Doritaenopsis *Purple Gem produced two plantlets on old inflorescences. The plantlet on the left can be cut off just below its roots in order to be potted. The plantlet on the right was potted while still attached to the mother plant and can now be cut from the flower spike at the arrow's point.*

To encourage plantlet formation on the dormant buds of *Phalaenopsis* inflorescences, apply some hormone paste. (Consult the American Orchid Society *Bulletin* for suppliers.) The hormone stimulates keikis to form from dormant buds. Sometimes the keikis grow but no roots form. If this happens, apply some rooting powder such as Rootone or Hormodin to the keiki base. Barring a rare mutation, the plantlets removed from an inflorescence will be identical to the parent plants, as are offsets from around the base of a plant.

Dendrobium nobile and its hybrids usually produce flowers directly from the pseudobulbs. When mature plants are given cool (50° F.) nights as their pseudobulbs near completion, flower buds form along the upper sections. If the mature plants are kept warm upon completion of the growths, usually fall into early winter, the pseudobulbs will sprout keikis instead of flower buds. These plantlets will soon form roots, at which point they can be cut or twisted off for propagation.

Since this is another form of vegetative propagation, the keikis will be identical to the parent plants. Orchid growers sometimes offer keikis of superior clones at very reasonable prices. With good culture the keikis grow into flowering plants in two seasons.

CLONING

What is a *clone?* "An individual plant raised from a single seed, with all its subsequent vegetative propagations," according to the American Orchid Society's *An Orchidist's Glossary.* Each plant that grows from a seed is unique; although there may be others that are similar, *no other* is a precise duplicate. When an individual orchid is multiplied by vegetative propagation (i.e., division, offsets, or tissue culture), all the resulting plants are considered the same clone. They are biologically identical.

The main value of cloning is to reproduce great quantities of plants identical to a certain superior parent plant. Plant tissues are reasonably stable during the first meristeming process but the more times a given culture (mass of tissue from a single meristem excision) is divided, the greater the risk of unusual mutations. Sometimes mutated plants produce flowers superior even to the select donor clone but other times the mutations are not an advantage. For the most part, meristem plantlets are genetically identical to the plant from which the tissue was removed, although there may be occasional variations. Of course, culture can influence flower form and color, apart from any possible genetic change. This is why even gross division propagations may seem to be different from the original orchid one may see pictured in a catalog or magazine.

Superior clones are reproduced by meristem tissue culture, a popular form of cloning originally developed to obtain virus-free plants from select clones that had contracted debilitating virus infections. Food crops such as potatoes were the first to be commercially cloned. Other crops such as carnations, where virus had infected the popular superior clones, soon followed as subjects for tissue culture.

Meristem tissue culture is accomplished in the following manner. A $\frac{1}{10}$ to $\frac{1}{2}$mm section of the apical meristem tissue is cut from the center of a growing bud tip of an orchid. (Clones can be propagated from inflorescence buds, shoot tips, even roots.) The orchid tissue is placed in a liquid or agar base sterile solution and sealed in a container, which must be given a suitable rhythm for proper cell growth. Some genera grow best with a vibrating shake; others thrive with a gyrating rattle; and still others proliferate when rolled in a rotator at regular intervals.

The process is not simple, although one can learn how to proceed after a few weeks of hands-on instruction from an expert. For example, a precise understanding of the correct culture media is necessary since each genus requires a slightly different medium composition. Some precise formulas can be found in advanced scientific texts such as *Orchid Biology,* edited by Joseph Arditti (see Bibliography). Researchers and commercial growers are continually working to improve methods of producing the best-quality meristem orchids in the most efficient manner.

Mericlones Orchid clones elected for tissue culture are called mericlones. Most modern commercial firms offer a selection of mericlones at prices close to those of sexually produced seedlings. Mericlones are identical to the plants from which they are derived so one knows what to expect when mericlone plantlets mature. This does not offer the same suspense as waiting for a seedling to bloom, with the hope that your $10 investment will flower as an award-quality $100 clone. However, mericlones are the most practical way of adding proven superior clones to a collection.

Commercially, mericlones are important because they let a grower know just what type of flowers will be produced. One can tailor a specific crop to periods of peak demand. Even in a home collection it is an advantage to collect orchids with known blooming seasons.

To date, it is possible to buy mericlones of cattleya hybrids, oncidiums, vandaceous types, dendrobiums, phalaenopsis, in fact most of the popular orchids with the exception of *Paphiopedilum,* which is propagated by division and seed.

SEED PRODUCTION

Orchids reproduce sexually by producing seed, usually the result of two different plants combining sex cells with the aid of an animal pollinator. Birds, bees, flies, bats, moths, butterflies are pollinators of orchids. The creatures search for sweet nectar, or male insects may copulate with orchid flowers, believing them to be females of the same bee or fly species. The flower pollen (pollinia) comes off the bloom and sticks to the creature, as its body rubs the flower parts. When the next bloom is visited, pollen grains usually catch on sticky fluid in the stigma, thus pollinating the bloom. Some orchid flowers have physical structures to grasp pollen stuck on the pollinator; other orchids have delicate triggers which, when hit, cause pollen to eject, quickly sticking to the pollinator.

An anther cap is being removed from a cattleya hybrid. Pollinia are seen inside, below the tip of the needle.

Waxy pollen masses removed from the anther cap can be picked up with a pin for placement on the stigma of the female parent.

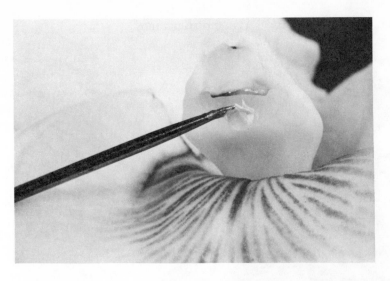

A pollen mass is placed into the sticky fluid on the stigma, inside the flower.

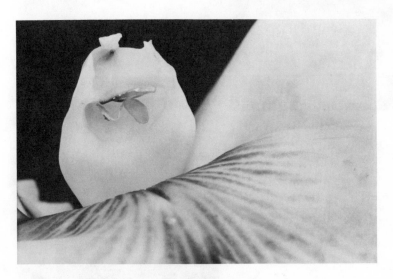

This view into the underside of the plant shows the pollen mass attached to the sticky stigma.

If all goes well, pollen grains sprout on the stigma, sending a long tube down into the ovary where sperm are released to complete fertilization by combining with female cells. Seeds then begin to develop in the ovary.

Orchid pollination is also accomplished by hybridizers who select parents with specific characteristics in mind. A hybridizer may attempt to change the flower form, color, flowering season, or size of specific species.

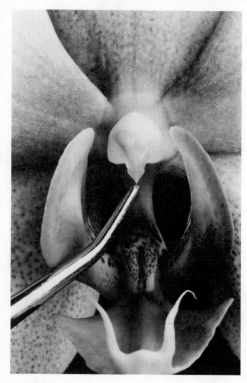

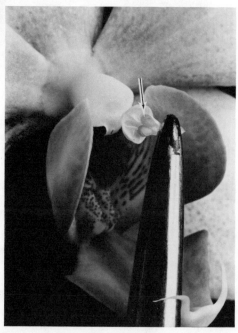

To collect pollen from an orchid, such as this phalaenopsis, gently remove the anther cap with a needle or delicate tweezers. Hold a card or your hand below the flower in case a pollen mass drops. The photo on the right is a close-up view of the pollen masses inside a Phalaenopsis *anther cap.*

Sexual reproduction with seed combines genes from each parent, producing a multitude of variations in offspring. Crossing a hybrid with its own pollen also breeds offspring with varied characteristics, although they are given the same hybrid name (grex name) for international registration. Crossing a pure species with itself, or another plant of the same species, results in only minor variations, although each of many seedlings grows from a single seed.

After pollination, an orchid flower may need up to 400 days before the seedpod is ripe. Not all orchids need the same number of days to mature seed. Famous hybridizer W. W. G. Moir reports that his hybrids with small equitant variegata oncidiums vary in the period they need to ripen seed, from 65 days to 350 days. Even within a genus, variations are common. For example, *Aspasia principissa* will take 400 days while *Asp. lunata* needs only 150 to 170 days. The male parent may also cause a given female to ripen seed sooner or later than another. Orchid pods first form seed toward the base, then gradually expand, forming more seed farther out toward the pod tip until mature.

When orchids with different chromosome counts are crossed, a full seedpod with quantities of viable seed may not form if the pod is left to ripen fully, so hybridizers pick the immature pod, then immediately sow the seed to obtain even a few seedlings. This technique is called *green pod culture.*

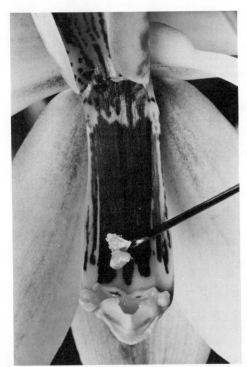

To pollinate orchids such as this cymbidium, push the pollen mass into the sticky liquid on the underside of the column. To avoid having the flower pollinate itself, remove the anther cap and pollinia from the female parent before it is pollinated.

Seedpods are forming on this Cattleya aurantiaca *hybrid.*
Old flowers still cling to the pods as ovaries swell with seed.

This is a plump but still un-
ripe pod of Eulophidium
maculata (*syn.* Oeceoclades
maculata).

With some unusual crosses, viable seed occurs in the first period of development but may die before the whole pod matures, so green pod culture has saved many unique hybrids. Green pod culture has one other advantage. Orchid seed must be sterilized before being sown if it is from an open pod. While the pod is unbroken, the seed within is free from pathogens such as fungus that can quickly kill seedlings in a closed flask.

A green pod can be sterilized with a strong solution such as a 50 per cent Clorox wash and even though parts of the pod tissue are damaged, the seed inside remains untouched. The pod is then cut open with a sterile tool inside of the clean-air sterile sowing box. Seed is sown directly without having been subjected to a strong sterilizing solution.

Some orchid firms, such as Jones and Scully, offer a green pod seed sowing service. Here are their recommendations for harvesting seedpods:

Aerides   90 days
Brassavola   90 to 100 days
Broughtonia   30 to 45 days
Cattleya bifoliate types   90 days
Cattleya unifoliate types   120 to 135 days
Dendrobium nobile hybrids   90 to 100 days
Dendrobiums other than nobile   60 to 75 days
Doritaenopsis hybrids   90 to 100 days
Epidendrum   150 to 165 days
Oncidium   60 to 75 days
Phalaenopsis   90 to 100 days
Vanda   90 to 120 days

Following these guidelines, you could harvest an *Epidendrum* pod 150 to 165 days after it had begun to form. An orchid may have millions of seed in a single pod. *Catasetum* and *Cycnoches* are very generous with seed, producing between two and four million seeds per pod. In the wild, only a few of these dust-like seed germinate, even fewer reach maturity.

When the orchid seedpod ripens and splits open, seed is disbursed by the slightest breeze. Some seed even drops around the parent plant, often starting colonies of seedlings on moss or even moss-covered rocks nearby. Rain further distributes the fine seed and some seed may even be carried away on the feet of birds.

Orchid seed contains a small embryo made up of several types of cells, mainly fat and starch storage cells. In the wild, a fungus invades the cells, then converts some of the starch to sugar. The sugar permits the seed to germinate completely, forming roots and green tissue for photosynthesis. Without sugar, orchid seed may turn green but will not continue to grow. In the wild, a microscopic fungus is required for the orchid seed to develop correctly.

SEED SOWING

The scientist most responsible for commercial success in growing orchids from seed was plant physiologist Lewis Knudson. Dr. Knudson experimented with sowing orchid seed on sterile mixtures of agar with various nutrients, including sugar. When he succeeded in obtaining healthy orchid seedlings with this totally asymbiotic (without fungus contribution) method, he published his findings, first in Spanish in 1922, then the following year in English.

Commercial firms were quick to realize the value of growing orchid species and hybrids on nutrient agar under controlled conditions. Until Dr. Knudson's popularization of the asymbiotic method, orchid seed had been sown on moss, often around the base of a mature plant. The early hybrids produced by English growers were from seed sown at the base of orchids in greenhouse collections. Naturally only a few of the seeds grew into mature plants. Many sowings were unsuccessful.

These orchid seedlings on nutrient agar are ready for transplanting to another flask or to community pots.

Tiny seedlings are planted directly from flasks into a fine seedling mix.

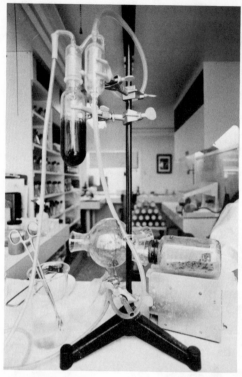

In this orchid propagation laboratory, orchid seed can be sown, flasks can be transplanted, and meristem cultures can be made without contamination if the worker is precise.

Paphiopedilum seedlings are being transplanted from one flask to another. Between them is a McEwen flask in which air is blown over potassium permanganate to kill bacteria. Transplanting is done with a delicate sterilized tool.

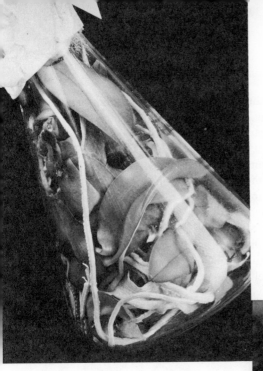

These phalaenopsis seedlings are in their second flask since being grown from seed. The flask will be broken to get the plants for repotting since they are too large to be removed through the flask's mouth.

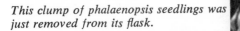

This clump of phalaenopsis seedlings was just removed from its flask.

The seedlings are then washed in a warm solution of Physan. All agar should be washed free from the roots or else mold may develop.

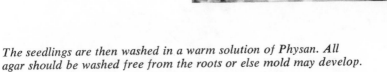

Now the seedling orchids you buy are all grown on nutrient agar. Once seedlings are an inch or two long, they are transplanted into larger flasks with a fresh batch of nutrient agar. Some orchids may go through several flaskings before being planted into community pots. The typical process for cattleyas takes two years from sowing to a community pot, then four to six years more before most of the seedlings bloom.

Growing orchids from seed is not for the average orchidist. Even if some of the flasks become contaminated with fungus, one will end up with hundreds of seedlings. There is a fascination to hybridizing.

If you want to grow orchids from seed but do not wish to sow the seed yourself, contact a commercial grower or lab that offers a flasking service. You can then make crosses or self-pollinate superior clones, but send the seedpod to a professional for sowing. A local orchid society will appreciate some of the extra seedlings if you have picked the parents carefully. Growing orchids from seed is such a long process that only seed from excellent parents or rare species should be sown.

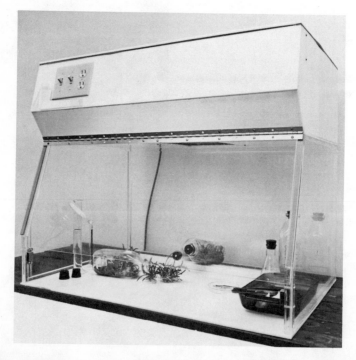

This Clean*Air flasking station contains orchid seedlings ready to be transplanted to another flask with fresh agar medium. The unit is equipped with a built-in fluorescent light fixture and blower fan to filter out dirt particles in the air. (Photo by Martin Aronow, courtesy of Clean*Air Work Stations, Inc.)

14. Keeping Your Orchids Healthy

WHEN ORCHIDS are kept healthy by good culture, serious problems seldom occur. One will have an occasional leaf rot or buds may blast when the air is polluted, but major problems are fortunately rare. Keep on guard against pests. Avoid serious infestations of aphids, mealybugs, and spider mites by catching the first few that show up. The best technique for keeping orchids in good condition is to combine good culture with constant grooming.

GROOMING

Keeping orchids tidy helps prevent disease and keeps away pests by eliminating their hiding or breeding places. Well-groomed orchids are much more attractive than plants that are not cared for. Standard grooming starts with keeping foliage free from dust. An occasional overhead shower on a bright warm morning will cleanse the leaves. When leaves become disfigured by mechanical injury, sunburn, or common leaf-tip dieback, cut away the dead leaf tip or injured section with a sharp clean knife or scissors.

When trimming dead parts, cut slightly into the healthy tissue. Dust any large wounds with a fungicide powder. Sterilize your cutting tool over a flame between each plant.

Occasionally orchids carry a serious virus which may not show up as an obvious symptom. A seemingly healthy plant can be infected with a virus and transmit the virus in its sap. Orchid viruses are spread from plant to plant by insects and on unsterilized cutting tools.

If a large leaf is only injured in one small area, by a sun scald or other noninfectious means, there is no reason why the leaf needs to be cut. For example, a large flat cattleya leaf with an inch or so of burned tissue in the center will still function as a healthy leaf, providing the plant with food for growth. Injuries on the tips of leaves can be cut away since most of the healthy tissue will still be intact.

Trim off old flower spikes with a sterile tool.

Cutting Off Old Flower Spikes After flowers fade, they usually fall. A few orchids hold their flowers on an inflorescence until they dry. However, it is best to remove and throw away faded flowers. Dead flowers are good places for fungus to grow. Except for a few orchids such as *Onc. kramerianum* types, old flower spikes should be cut off, level with the pseudobulb or main growth. In cattleya hybrids, the old flower stem may be several inches long, often accompanied by a dead sheath. Cut off the sheath and flower spike just above the pseudobulb.

Phalaenopsis inflorescences sometimes continue to grow at the tip after the main flush of flowers fades. If you let the tip grow, it may produce more flowers, or even a plantlet. However, there is more chance of a full second flowering if you cut back the phalaenopsis inflorescence until just above the second or third node, counting from the plant center. This will leave a short spike about 6 to 10 inches long. Often one of the dormant buds (nodes) will sprout to form a secondary inflorescence. On established healthy plants, one can have several spikes flowering at once.

Thick *Cymbidium* stalks may have to be cut with sturdy garden clippers. Wait until the inflorescence has dropped all the flowers, then cut the spike as close to the ground as possible. If you want cut-flower orchids, this same sort of cut is made while the spike has a crop of ripe flowers. Orchid blooms, however, last longer on the plant than when cut.

*Some orchids, especially yellow cattleya hybrids,
occasionally produce an odd inflorescence. The sheath
of this* Blc. *Tambourine had to be split so that the
odd stem could expand.*

The tropical orchids we grow indoors are never cut back after flowering. The only parts that one cuts away are old flower spikes, dead leaves, rotted roots, and older pseudobulbs without leaves. Vandaceous orchids will eventually get so tall that they may have to be cut above the compost but below healthy roots. Pot the plants lower, to be more manageable indoors.

Vandas and their relatives grown outdoors in the tropics are frequently propagated by stem tip cuttings. Those hybrids with terete vandas in their background are easy to propagate in this way. A new growing tip usually sprouts below the cut. All of these cuts are for propagation or repotting. Such procedures are different from the cutting back or pruning commonly practiced on overgrown coleus, geraniums, gardenias, and similar houseplants. When your orchids finish flowering, the only parts that require cutting are old flower stems.

Cattleya hybrids that bloom several months after pseudobulbs are mature may have dry sheaths. Here, flowers from an older growth are having difficulty growing from a dry sheath. By tearing open the sheath, the flowers have room to expand.

Cycnoches chlorochilon will soon lose all its leaves now that its flowers are faded. The old inflorescence (right) can be cut off, but the leaves should be allowed to fall naturally.

Top-heavy Angraecum *Ol Tukai should have its stem shortened so that it can be repotted lower. The top vigorous portion of the plant, with healthy new roots, is then repotted with its offshoot in order to get more flowers in less space.*

PSEUDOBULB CARE

Orchids which form pseudobulbs grow ahead each year, with new pseudobulbs forming from the rhizome or horizontal stem. The growth of cattleya orchids is typical of cultivated pseudobulbous genera. Some orchids produce pseudobulbs very close together, as seen in *Brassavola nodosa,* while others may have several inches between each growth, a habit seen in some bulbophyllums and oncidiums.

Keeping the most recent pseudobulb healthy is necessary in order to grow floriferous orchids. The old pseudobulbs without leaves should be cut off at repotting time, but two to four younger pseudobulbs with leaves should be left with each active division. Cattleya hybrids and some other orchids have a thin membrane around developing pseudobulbs. This skin-like tissue eventually dies, turning a light brown. There is no reason to pull this off growths made in the last year. In fact, the membrane is usually quite firmly attached to the pseudobulb until at least a season has passed. Pulling off this membrane prematurely can injure the outer layer of pseudobulb tissue.

Once the membrane dries and begins to separate from the live tissue it can safely be removed as you groom each plant. Wetting the tissue makes it easier to remove. Older growths with dead membranes can become a breeding ground for mealybugs or scales, so there is a good reason to clean off the membrane once it is dead. If part of the membrane adheres to a recent growth, leave it there until it becomes naturally dry and separates easily from the live tissue. If you prefer to leave the pseudobulbs covered with this membrane, even after it turns brown, no harm will come to the orchid; just be extra vigilant in looking for signs of pests.

Old pseudobulbs of this Colmanara *hybrid have rotted (left) but not before sprouting new growth (right). Now is the time to cut off the dead part of the plant and repot the new growth in a small pot.*

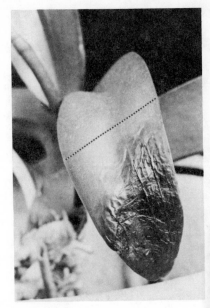

This phalaenopsis leaf froze when it touched a glass pane during the winter. Cut off the damaged part plus a small portion of the healthy tissue, as shown by the dotted line.

Variation in water supply or temperature extremes may cause uneven growth on Dendrobium nobile *hybrids.*

TRAINING STEMS

Orchid stems and pseudobulbs frequently need to be guided as they grow, if one wishes a symmetrical compact plant. A cattleya left to its own habitats under greenhouse or windowsill conditions may take up much more space than necessary. If you gently tie up pseudobulbs as they form, an orchid can be trained to look nicer and take up less space.

New growth on orchids follows the brightest source of light. This cattleya hybrid received light from below when on display in a living room. A new lead developed at the same time and reached for the fluorescent light that was used to illuminate the flowers.

Tall stems on *Dendrobium* and *Vanda* may need to be tied to a stake or encouraged to grip a tree fern pole if they have aerial roots. Use plastic-covered wire or soft twine to guide stems. Paper-covered wire, often used on outdoor plants, soon loses its protective paper covering under warm wet conditions, and then the wire could injure orchid stems. I find that plastic-covered wire lasts five to six years and it is available at many local garden stores.

DISEASES

Even with good culture, orchids sometimes become infected with a fungus or bacterial disease. Modern sprays and drenches (water solutions for soaking) are able to control the common diseases. For precise diagnosis of any disease, submit a specimen to the nearest agricultural extension agent (consult your local telephone directory). Some botanical gardens and universities also offer diagnosis of ornamental plant diseases for a small fee. If no local source of individual help is available, contact the American Orchid Society.

It is important to know which disease one is confronting because the various fungi and bacteria are controlled by different preparations. Several organisms can attack an orchid plant at once. Following are descriptions and photos showing the symptoms of some of the most common diseases and how to treat and control them.

Anthracnose, caused by *Colletotrichum* and *Gloeosporium* fungi, usually attacks a plant's leaves, causing brown rings and sunken spots. Control anthracnose with benomyl spray (1 tablespoon per gallon of lukewarm water) to which you add 8 to 10 drops of a wetting agent such as Triton B-1956 spreader-sticker liquid.

Black rot, caused by *Phytophthora cactorum* and *Pythium ultimum* fungi, is favored by high humidity during cool weather and is spread by splashing water. Symptoms include soft-rotted areas on leaves, usually brownish-purple turning black. The rotting spreads into the pseudobulb and plants eventually die if the fungus is not controlled. Treat by drenching orchids with Truban (½ tablespoon per gallon of water) or use Banrot (1 tablespoon per gallon of water) to fight fusarium wilt at the same time.

Fusarium wilt, *Fusarium oxysporum cattleyae,* usually attacks orchids through injured tissue such as damaged roots or cut rhizomes. Leaves shrink and wilt since roots rot. Control the disease by cutting away all infected parts of the plant (which are easily seen by the discolored tissue) with a flame-sterilized knife or shears. Slice about ¼ inch into healthy tis-

This Cattleytonia *has been attacked by the anthracnose fungus* (Gloeosporium).

sue as you remove the infected section. Dust all wounds with Fermate to prevent secondary fungus invasion. Spray the plant with benomyl (Benlate), 1 tablespoon per gallon of room-temperature water. To eliminate the possible source of reinfection, throw out all present potting materials from infected plants, wash pots thoroughly, and repot plants in a fresh mix. Mist plants with a solution of root stimulant plus Physan every few days to encourage new roots and discourage fungus.

Leaf spot, caused by *Cercospora* species bacteria, disfigures foliage with brown spots, often spreading rapidly to kill the whole leaf. To control leaf spot, remove all infected parts of the plant, spray the orchid with benomyl (1 tablespoon per gallon of water) plus a few drops of wetting agent such as Triton B-1956. Spray all plants in the vicinity for best control, then repeat the spray three more times, at fifteen-day intervals.

Brown spot, caused by *Pseudomonas cattleyae* bacteria, can be a big problem on *Phalaenopsis*. This type of leaf spot appears as a soft watery lesion surrounded with yellowing tissue. Dead tissue turns brown, then black. This bacteria is spread by splashing water, so avoid overhead watering if this problem occurs in your collection. Control by cutting away the infected tissue and dusting the cuts with Fermate or Benlate made into a paste. Then spray the plants with a Physan solution (½ tablespoon to 1 gallon of water). Spray all plants in the area with Physan as a safeguard against the spread of this disease.

Potinara *Fortunes Peak shows petal-spotting due to* Botrytis cinerea *fungus. Mist the buds and flowers in the morning with a room-temperature solution of Physan, ½ teaspoon per gallon of water. Avoid spraying in direct sunlight and be sure the plants are dry by evening.*

Rust, caused by several different genera of fungus, occurs on many types of orchids as orange to brown pustules (raised infected tissue spots). The disease usually shows up on the undersides of leaves but can progress to their top surfaces as well. Control by spraying your plants with Fermate (Ferbam) or Captan in a solution with a wetting agent. Cut away severely infected foliage to prevent the spread of the spores. Treat cuts with Captan or Ferbam.

Snow mold, caused by *Ptychogaster* fungi species, lives as a saprophyte on organic potting media. Using highly acid redwood bark as part of a mix will help to control this fungus. Snow mold forms an almost waterproof film of white fuzz through the potting mix, soon covering the roots and lower stems. Since the fungus stops orchids from absorbing water, the plants suffer, even though the fungus is not a parasite.

Control snow mold with Shield-10%, mixed 1 ounce (2 tablespoons) per 4 gallons of water, as a soak for the infested potting mix. For lightly infested plants, a drenching spray may be effective, but the best treatment is to repot the orchids in a fresh mix after washing the roots with the Shield solution.

Plant pathologist Harry C. Burnett reports that an acid drench of vinegar solution will often control snow mold. Mix 20 parts of water with 1 part cider vinegar, then drench the potting mix. The acid solution discourages snow mold fungus, as does redwood bark or fiber in the potting mix.

Southern blight, caused by *Sclerotium rolfsii* fungus, moves rapidly through orchids, causing rotted roots, pseudobulbs, and leaves. Sometimes the disease starts at the base of a cane or stem and then works its way up the plant. Other times a leaf becomes infected and soon collapses as its tissues die. Since this is a serious, fast-moving infectious disease, the best control starts with the destruction of badly infected plants. Throw infected orchids into a plastic bag, seal it well and put it in the trash. Or you can burn the badly infected plant.

Disinfect the area where the plants were growing with a solution of 4 per cent formalin or a drenching spray of Natriphene. Lightly infected orchids which you wish to save can be treated as follows: Cut away all infected parts, slicing into healthy tissue ½ inch as you operate. Dust cuts with Fermate or Benlate to prevent secondary fungus invasion. Soak the whole plant in a solution of Natriphene 1:2,000 solution for one hour. Repot the plants in a fresh mix and isolate from the rest of your collection until you are sure that the disease is controlled.

Virus diseases attack orchids but are rare in well-kept commercial collections. Infected orchids may have flowers with odd off-color blotching (color break) and foliage with sunken brown spots. Cymbidium mosaic virus and tobacco mosaic virus are common orchid viral strains. The same virus strain can cause different symptoms in the same orchid type.

Some orchids can be infected without showing any dramatic symptoms. Once a virus becomes well established in the plant, it loses vigor and is more susceptible to other diseases.

Avoid buying orchids that have brown-spotted foliage or flowers with odd-colored breaks such as ugly white areas in a random pattern. Thoroughly sterilize your cutting tools between their use on each plant. There is no cure for virus so it is important to avoid spreading the disease. In fact, since any of the diseases mentioned above can be spread easily, be sure to wash your hands often, especially between handling sick plants and healthy orchids.

Southern blight stem rot causes the stem on this dendrobium to collapse as its tissues die.

ROTS ON NEW GROWTH

Sometimes a new growth will develop a rot which turns the tips of new foliage brown or black, then the rot proceeds down the growth until reaching the pseudobulb. Often the rot stops at this point. If this happens, check that you are providing a suitable healthy environment. Fresh air and adequate light are especially important. To stop the advance of this new growth rot, spray with Truban, 1 teaspoon per gallon of water in the

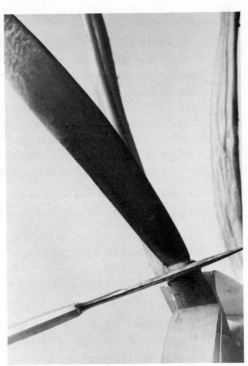

The photo on the left shows rot on the new growth of a cattleya hybrid. A sterile knife is used to cut off the rotted portion after the membrane has been pulled back to expose the dead tissue. Dust the cuts with fungicide.

morning. In two weeks, repeat the spray. Cut away any black rotted portions, dust the open cut with a fungicide like Banrot, and restrain from overhead watering until the rot is controlled. Remember, overcrowding, high humidity, low light, and weak growths are most conducive to rot.

FUNGICIDES AND BACTERICIDES

Fungicides and bactericides are modern preparations to control fungus and bacteria. They are offered in some garden stores and in most large orchid catalogs. Recommendations for use of fungicides and bactericides are given in this section. If package directions mention orchids, follow their instructions, unless otherwise instructed by a plant pathologist.

Banrot is a blend of Truban fungicide with a fungicide similar to benomyl. Banrot works to control many troublesome orchid diseases, excluding bacteria. This powder can be used as a drench, spray, or paste applied to wounds after rotted tisssue is cut away.

Benomyl 50 is a wettable powder often offered as Benlate 50W in catalogs and garden stores. Benomyl is a broad-spectrum systemic fungicide that is absorbed by plants. Harry C. Burnett, orchid specialist and plant pathologist with the Florida Department of Agriculture, conducted tests with this material and determined that orchids are best protected when treated with a concentration of 1 tablespoon of benomyl per gallon of water, stronger than listed on the package. For better coverage, add 8 drops of a wetting agent per gallon of spray. I use Benlate to control leaf spot that often attacks in moist weather and in overcrowded places.

Captan is a fungicide used mainly to control rust. Mix 3⅓ tablespoons per gallon of water or apply as a paste to the infected tissue.

Ferbam, often offered as the black powder Fermate, is useful to control some rusts and to dust cuts as a preventative against fungus attacks. Before the availability of benomyl, Ferbam was a favorite material to control leaf spot. It is still used in the outdoor garden to control black spot on roses.

Natriphene is a powerful preparation for controlling Southern blight (*Sclerotium rolfsii*). Dissolve the Natriphene powder to make a 1:2,000 solution, ¾ teaspooon per gallon of water or 1 tablespoon per 4 gallons. Soak infected orchids in the solution for one hour. Natriphene fungicide-bactericide is useful mainly as a soak for hard-to-conquer fungus on orchids, but I use it occasionally as a heavy mist to control damping-off. Add 6 to 8 drops of wetting agent per gallon of solution to improve effectiveness.

Physan, once known as Consan, is a liquid concentrate which is mixed with water, then sprayed to control a wide range of fungus and bacteria. The manufacturers of Physan also recommend the product to control algae. The concentration of Physan solution varies according to the treatment desired. For example, ½ teaspoon per gallon can be used to wash off orchid seedlings being transplanted from flasks; 2 teaspoons per gallon should be used as a preventative spray on seedlings to stop damp-off fungus, a devastating fungus that can kill seedlings in two or three days. I use Physan on all types of orchids and have never had the product damage orchids when used as directed.

Shield is a preparation useful in controlling snow mold. Mix 2 tablespoons of Shield-10% in 4 gallons of water. Use this solution as a soak bath for the lower half of orchids invaded by snow mold.

Truban is a wettable powder used to control black rot. Mix ½ tablespoon of Truban powder with 1 gallon of water as a drench. Since the effective ingredient of Truban is already incorporated into the fungicide Banrot, there is no need to use Truban for fungus problems if Banrot is already available.

BUD BLAST

When buds turn yellow and drop off, or partially open and then stop developing, this is known as "bud blast." The most common cause of this condition is ethylene air pollution. *Dendrobium, Cattleya,* and *Phalaenopsis* are genera most often affected, but other genera and plant families can be affected as well.

Ethylene is an ingredient in smog and causes serious problems to commercial cut-flower growers in regions where the air is frequently polluted. Some commercial growers are even breeding orchids to be especially resistant to polluted air. (Certain hybrids do resist ethylene pollution better than others and occasionally a catalog identifies such selections, but more often than not, one must rely on information from personal experience or friends who grow orchids.)

Ethylene is produced when garden refuse or fallen leaves are burned. Gasoline-powered vehicles also give off ethylene in their exhaust. Another source of ethylene gas is ripe or ripening fruit. A basket of ripe apples or other fruit in a small greenhouse can cause quite a problem with orchid flowers although the quantity of ethylene produced will not kill plants.

Polluted air caused this cattleya's flowers to close in a day or two.

The best solution to ethylene pollution is to keep orchids away from polluted air and to select resistant plants that can open flowers with slight air pollution. Some years you may notice no problem and other times many buds may blast, especially in the fall and spring.

If you have open-burner nonvented gas heaters in your sunporch or greenhouse, the gas must burn thoroughly. Even with correctly adjusted flames, a slight quantity of gas and ethylene escapes as the heater turns on. Gas heaters that burn outside, sending only hot air into the greenhouse or sunporch, are much safer.

INSECTS AND OTHER SMALL PESTS

Some insects, slugs, snails, and mites enjoy eating orchids so you may have to control them from time to time. It is best to check over orchids before buying them, whenever possible, or at least before placing new plants in your main collection. Despite regular spray programs used by commercial growers, it is still common to receive a few free mealybugs or snails with an orchid order.

Examine the plants' roots and potting mix for signs of snails and slugs. Then put the pot in a waterproof tray and pour a solution of snail killer through the potting mix. An alternative preventative step is to sprinkle a snail bait into the mix.

These mealybugs were discovered in new foliage of Catasetum pileatum.

Mealybugs are usually easy to find when an infestation is serious, but small mealybugs deep inside new growths are often impossible to see. To safeguard a healthy collection, spray all new orchids with an insecticide such as Isotox or diazinon, used according to directions. It also is a good idea to isolate new orchids for a few weeks. Check them carefully after this period to be sure no pests have hatched in the interim.

After snails and mealybugs, the next most common pests are red spider mites and related mite species. These are almost microscopic spider relatives that suck plants' sap, causing leaf and flower damage. Thin-leaved orchids such as cymbidiums and catasetums are especially susceptible to mite attack, but certain mites also attack *Phalaenopsis, Dendrobium,* and similar genera with tough leaves. Mites are so tiny that they are difficult to see without a magnifying glass. Keep a small magnifier handy to make your search effective.

Seriously infested orchids will show damaged leaves, and some mites will form a fine network of webbing. However, strive to stop mites before these symptoms occur. Mites are resistant to some insecticides. Isotox is a spray that contains a mixture of insecticides including Kelthane, a specific poison for mites. An alternative is to mix a miticide such as malathion with a few drops of a wetting agent in the hopes of also killing mealybugs.

Honey fungus may form on the sweet sap exuded by healthy, fast-growing orchids. Wipe off the fungus. Then spray with a Physan solution. Honey fungus will not harm the orchid but it looks unsightly.

Although scale insects do not afflict orchids as often as other pests, it is wise to be aware of possible symptoms on your plants. An infestation of scale insects is easy to see since the white or brown sucking creatures cling to pseudobulbs and foliage. Scales are difficult to eradicate once they start in a collection.

Malathion and diazinon sprays will kill young crawling scale insects of any species, including soft brown scale. Black scale, which are tougher to control, and species covered with a hard waxy shield are resistant to insecticides as adults. These tough scales must be scrubbed off first. After you have washed off as many as possible, spray your plants with malathion or diazinon. The insecticide spray must be repeated 4 times at three- to four-week intervals. The warmer the temperature, the faster the scales reproduce. One must repeat the spraying to catch the scale insects at their vulnerable crawling stage. Scales can also come on fruit so keep it away from your orchids.

Other pests that attack orchids are easier to see than mites or scale. Beetles and weevils may eat parts of your plants but are quickly controlled with insecticides. During the summer, or anytime in the tropics, caterpillars may be a problem, but these too succumb to commonly available insecticides. Aphids sometimes attack orchid buds. They can be con-

The arrows point to brown scale on a Boston fern. Young crawling scales are seen as white dots on the fern fronds.

trolled by washing them off your plant, but use an insecticide if aphids are abundant. Otherwise, damaged flowers will be the result.

Another common outdoor pest, thrips, occasionally attack orchid flower buds. Thrips are killed with diazinon or malathion used according to directions. As a preventive measure, spray all new plants and inspect your orchids as you care for them.

Hobbyists with indoor collections should use pesticides on their plants only if they discover pests on them. Commercial growers and orchidists who grow their orchids outdoors must be more cautious and spray their plants regularly to keep them pest-free. In any collection, it is most important to make careful, frequent observations of your plants to see that they are well-groomed and healthy.

This Blc. hybrid flower has been attacked by a weevil.

PEST CONTROL

The most common orchid pests, the damage they do to plants, and how to control them, are outlined here.

Ants carry mealybugs and other pests to plants and make nests in the potting mix. Ants can be controlled with ant bait traps. Their nests in the ground can be sprayed with a drench of diazinon. Spray your plants with a weaker solution of diazinon if the ants are abundant.

Aphids suck sap from a plant's new growth and distort its flowers. Wash off pests. For a serious infestation, spray with diazinon or malathion. Orthene biodegradable insect spray is also effective.

Beetles eat buds and sometimes leaves. Remove beetles from plants when you find them. Sevin spray will control serious invasions.

Caterpillars eat a plant's buds and leaves. Thuricide spray is safe but takes a while to be effective. Isotox and Ortho Orthene, a systemic insecticide, are useful for fast action.

Cockroaches eat a plant's roots, stems, and buds. Diazinon spray on benches and the floor will help control them. I have also found that fine cayenne pepper sprinkled along shelves and around pots will discourage roaches.

Mealybugs suck sap and distort the growth of plants. Cygon spray is effective and safe for cattleyas but may injure other genera. Isotox, Orthene, and malathion are safe for any orchid.

Mites suck orchids' sap, as well as killing their leaves and disfiguring their buds. Pentac or Kelthane sprays will control mites, especially if applied to the undersides of leaves. Follow package directions.

This odd inflorescence on a Slc. Night Lights *seedling is genetic. However, other distortions of orchid buds may be caused by insect pests or wide variations in temperature or very low humidity.*

Scale insects suck a plant's sap and weaken its growth. Control scales with malathion or diazinon used one month between applications, 3 times minimum.

Slugs eat new plant growths, buds, and flower spikes, thus weakening and killing plants. Place slug bait near your orchids' pots and sprinkle granules on the potting mix. Slug-It spray is also helpful.

Snails eat root tips and weaken plants. Spray potting mix and the area around the pots with Slug-It or a similar metaldehyde snail killer. Q.U.E. Bane is a granular form of metaldehyde that can be sprinkled on a potting mix without causing plant damage.

Thrips suck a plant's sap and cause distorted flowers. Spray with Orthene, malathion, or diazinon.

Whiteflies suck sap and weaken plants. Spray plants with insecticide containing resmethrin, such as Pratts Whitefly Spray or Dexol Whitefly and Mealybug Spray.

MICE, RATS

A mouse can be one of the most destructive creatures in an orchid collection. If a field mouse gets into a greenhouse it could eat orchid buds, root tips, and, worst of all, new growths. To prevent mice from getting in, keep the doors and windows of your greenhouse screened. This includes using small mesh wire over vents and vent pipes for stoves.

Rats are a bigger problem because they knock down pots, pull seedlings into corners to line nests, and also break off new growths. Several alternatives are to use a live trap which catches the creature unharmed (such as Havahart), an old-fashioned rat trap, or a rat bait in your greenhouse or basement light garden.

CARE OF ORCHIDS WHILE YOU'RE AWAY

How can you be sure that your orchids will stay healthy while you are away? Whether or not your orchids stay healthy during your absence depends on the type of plants you are growing (epiphytes or terrestrials), the stage of growth the plants are in (resting or active), and their usual environment.

In a modern greenhouse with automatic controls for ventilation, heating, and humidification, one can leave well-watered epiphytic orchids alone for two weeks during some seasons of the year and the plants will continue to thrive. In fact, if you normally tend to overwater, the orchids will appreciate the brief vacation from soggy roots. Terrestrials such as cymbidiums and paphiopedilums will survive at least a full week if left fully watered, then kept in a humid atmosphere.

Reducing the light intensity will reduce the orchid's need for water, thus helping them to survive longer before water is needed. In a window garden, pull light curtains across the window. In a light garden, reduce the light hours to eight hours per day. In a greenhouse, provide more shading. Fill all humidity trays with water to keep the atmosphere moist. If you usually keep the environment warm (for example, 68° to 70° F. at night), then reduce the minimum night temperature to 60° F. to slow down plant growth. These steps will keep orchids healthy under most conditions for up to two weeks. For longer periods of time, have a friend water your plants once each week, or hire a professional gardener who understands orchids.

Do not put orchids in plastic bags where they will sit in direct sun. The sun will heat the air enough to harm plants sealed in bags. Plants grown under fluorescent lights can be kept in plastic bags without danger of being damaged by heat but one must guard against fungus. Water the

Uneven water supplies may cause thin-leaved orchids, such as this Miltonia *hybrid, to grow crinkled leaves.*

plants thoroughly, then let them dry at least twenty-four hours before enclosing them in clear-plastic bags. Use bamboo or wire stakes to hold the plastic off the foliage. The plastic around these plants will form a barrier to water loss so orchids can go many days without needing water but never are too wet.

Usual growing conditions of 50 per cent relative humidity or higher must be maintained if you expect your orchids to remain healthy for more than a few days. In some situations one can use a clear-plastic sheet to hold humidity in a given area, as in a sunroom or window greenhouse. Terrestrial orchids have a moist compost to sustain them and pots can be placed on moist gravel as well, or even on a soaked bath towel. Epiphytic orchids must not be soggy at the roots but those with pseudobulbs will endure many days without water. Some of the pseudobulbous epidendrums from Central America live through five months of rainless season, as do the deciduous genera such as *Catasetum*.

If you leave your collection during warm weather, it is safe to put the orchids outdoors under high shade, hanging on racks or placed on a raised bench. With the orchids outdoors in freely circulating air and relatively bright light, a neighbor can water them once a week and mist them on sunny mornings without the usual risk that you will return to drowned plants.

If you only have a small orchid collection in your home or apartment, you can put a few soaking-wet bath towels in your bathtub and then set your orchid pots on the moist cloth. If you will be gone more than a few days, the orchids must be given some light. In that case, you should buy a 40-watt fluorescent fixture to hang above the orchids (see Chapter 4). Connect the fixture to an automatic timer set to give eight hours of light per day. The type of lamps you select for this brief period does not matter; any household fluorescent tubes will do.

If you plan to leave your orchids during very cold weather it is wise to have a friend check for minimum temperatures every few days. A power failure is bad enough when one is home, but if you are away when the heat fails, you may return home to frozen flowers. Remember that a maximum/minimum thermometer is part of every well-run orchid collection. Keep it near your plants and ask a friend to check for safe minimum temperatures every few days. Leave the phone number of your heating company for reference in the rare event that something does go wrong while you are away.

If you are a frequent traveler, I suggest that you instruct someone how to care for your orchids by leaving "cue cards" with special care instructions next to individual plants. For example, one cue card above a greenhouse bench could read: "Mist on sunny mornings. Full watering every 3 to 4 sunny days." Another card may say: "Just potted; mist only." By using this system and providing a brief outline about the basic care of your orchid collection, a trained person can keep your collection in perfect condition for months at a time.

If you have favorite insecticides and fungicides for orchid problems, be sure to list these in your notes and have an adequate supply on hand before leaving. If you are planning to be away a very long time, think about giving away most of your collection and then buying new orchids upon your return. For example, I once left my plants for more than two years, but in kindness to my tolerant friends who volunteered to care for some plants, I only let them "plant-sit" a few special clones. All the rest were donated to a local orchid society auction or sent to a professional greenhouse where they lived until my return, running up a rather high rent bill. All things considered, it is usually less expensive to give away plants and repurchase later than to have orchids boarded at a professional greenhouse for more than a few months.

15. Fun with Orchids

HAVING FUN with orchids is an important part of being an orchidist, and many hobbies and interests, such as creating cut-flower arrangements with orchids or participating in orchid competition, fit naturally with the raising of these outstanding exotics. Some growers spend many happy hours capturing their flowers on film; others create paintings, cast orchid flowers in silver or gold, patiently translate orchid blooms into needlepoint designs, even make ceramics based on orchids. Of course, the most universal use of orchids still remains decoration with orchid flowers.

This arrangement of Lc. Bill P. Fitch, a yellow orchid with red lips, is in a dining-table candle holder.

ORCHIDS AS CUT FLOWERS

Orchids are very popular as cut flowers, especially for flower arrangement and corsages. Popular hybrids last at least a week when kept in water. The longest-lasting are cymbidiums (three weeks or more) and many vanda hybrids. Paphiopedilums also look lovely for weeks. Orchid hybrid strains developed with the cut-flower market in mind are especially good for floral arrangements because they were bred to be long-lasting. Some examples include the spray-flowered dendrobiums, vanda hybrids, and cattleya hybrids.

For the longest cut-flower life, orchids must be fully ripe before they are cut. Cattleyas will ripen two to three days after the buds open. A good test is to sniff for fragrance. If an orchid variety has fragrance, then the flower is ripe. Paphiopedilums ripen in three to four days. Cymbidiums start opening buds at the bottom of the spike and may not have their topmost flowers open for several weeks after the first blooms are ripe. However, you can pick the lower flowers three or four days after they have expanded fully. Wait until all buds have opened if you want to pick the entire spike.

A few orchids do not last well when cut. Among the popular types that are not good as cut flowers are cool-growing, large-flowered Miltonias from the Andes. Hybrids of cool-growing species, such as *Milt. vexillaria* and *Milt. roezlii,* last weeks on the plant but wilt soon after they are picked. Hybrids between smaller-flowered warm-growing Brazilian species and cool-growing Andean species have flowers which endure as cut flowers, as do the flowers from pure Brazilian species such as *Milt. rengelli.* All orchid blooms usually close if pollen is disturbed and cymbidiums may change color.

Supplies   Some simple florist's supplies will help you to make professional-looking corsages and arrangements. These items can often be found in large orchid catalogs and local garden stores:

Thin florist's wire, preferably green, to stiffen or form stems
Florist's tape to cover stem tips
Small glass tubes with rubber caps to hold flowers
Chunks of Styrofoam in which you can stick glass or plastic orchid tubes
Cotton-tipped swabs to clean off any spots from flowers
Clear-plastic corsage boxes with lids to protect corsages
Shredded wax paper to cushion corsages
Assorted bud vases for displaying single flowers or small sprays
Foil in various colors
Large pins

Cutting Techniques Cut orchid flowers when they are cool, early in the morning or in the evening. Use a clean knife, razor, or clippers. Put the stem into water immediately. Refer to the series of step-by-step photos on pages 235–37 which show how to make a corsage with an orchid flower.

If you are cutting blooms from several different plants, sterilize the cutting tool between uses, to prevent the spread of disease. Viruses can be spread on contaminated cutting tools.

If you plan to make a floral arrangement, consider waiting until a whole spike or spray of orchids is open and ripe before cutting. Pick an entire inflorescence with as long a stem as possible. This will help to make your flower arrangement even more dramatic.

This series of photos shows the steps in cutting orchid flowers and making a basic corsage. Here, a sheath of Lc. Gift of Spring *is split so that the flower can easily be cut.*

Use a sterile knife to cut the stem.

Put the cut stem in water at once. Orchid flowers can be kept in various-sized tubes.

Squeeze excess water from a wet piece of cotton, then wrap the base of the stem in a small wad to preserve the orchid.

Cut a length of florist's tape to wrap around the moist cotton.

The tape will hold the cotton in contact
with the stem.

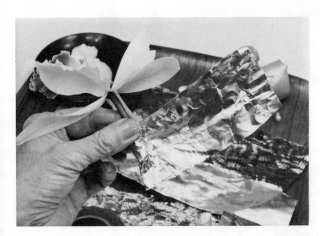

Cover the tape with foil.

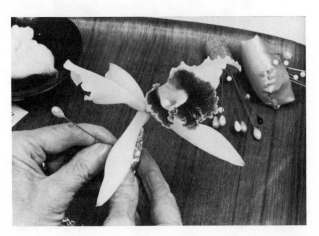

Select a large pin so that the orchid can be held on clothing.

Corsage flowers also need some stem so that you can position the flower attractively. The usual corsage orchids, such as cattleyas and paphiopedilums, have long stems. Others, such as some phalaenopsis and dendrobiums, may not have a very long stem when only one flower is used. A thin section of florist's wire or pipe cleaner will serve to form a longer artificial stem to help in making a corsage.

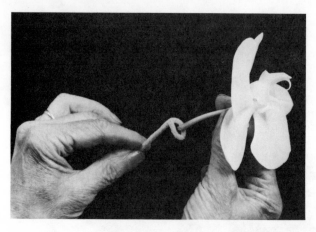

To make a stronger or longer stem for a corsage, twist a pipe cleaner around the orchid stem. Thin florist's wire can also be used.

Gently wrap the flexible pipe cleaner around the stem.

Conditioning Let the cut orchids stay with their stems in water as long as possible. Add 1 teaspoon of Physan per gallon of water to retard rot for cut orchids that will be kept in water on display. If you want the flower to last several days before it is used, leave the stem in about an inch of water and put the flower in the warmest section of the refrigerator. Temperatures of 45° to 50° F. are ideal. Keep the cut orchids away from ripe fruit. Ethylene gas given off by ripe fruit will reduce the life of blooms.

Putting the cut orchid bloom gently inside a lightweight plastic bag is a good way to protect the delicate flower while it is in the refrigerator. Blow into the bag to get it fully open, put the flower inside, and tie the bag end closed. A fresh-cut orchid flower will last a week or so with this treatment, a good way to preserve a corsage for future occasions.

DECORATING WITH ORCHIDS

One of the best means to enjoy orchids is by incorporating them into the living space in your home—on a coffee table in your living room, on a shelf in your study, on your dining-room table—where their beauty can be appreciated by you, your family, and guests who come to visit.

To get a double impression of your orchid flowers, place the vase containing the blooms in front of a mirror. In my home I have a shelf on a living-room wall, lined with a mirror, on which small statues from around the world share space with orchid flowers. This creates an unusual arrangement that changes according to the season.

Create intriguing designs with contrasting sizes and shapes of flowers. I love to display the smallest phalaenopsis flowers next to large white

Cymbidium *Madrid 'Forest King'*, *HCC/AOS, a green flower with red lip, is on display in an English Georgian pitcher.*

hybrids, and to combine deeply colored pink- or apricot-flowered clones with pristine whites. With cattleyas you can make dramatic arrangements of white flowers accented with one or two true-red types. Sprays of *Dendrobium phalaenopsis* hybrids are most striking when seen as a group of several sprays lit by a direct spotlight.

For a centerpiece, consider using a chunk of coral set in a low water-filled dish. Float cut orchids around the sides, with a few colorful blooms on the coral "island." If an important dinner is planned, decorate the salad dishes or dessert with washed golden oncidiums, or other diminutive orchid flowers in contrasting colors.

A few flat vandas or phalaenopsis might even be quick-frozen in clear ice for a punch bowl decoration. Single cut flowers at each place bring joy to all during the dinner, and are welcome favors for friends to take home later. Wrap the stems in moist cotton and colorful foil so that the flowers will last.

Orchid blooms, even short sprays with multiple flowers, can be pushed into water-filled tubes, then set among green houseplants such as ferns. I have one clump of 'Fluffy Ruffles' Boston fern that provides a delicate background for small individual flowers that look lost if set in a vase alone. Brighten your desk, vanity, or office reception area with a fresh-cut orchid every few days. A flower with its stem in water will last at least a week.

A blue Wedgwood vase is harmonious with creamy-white, lavender-splashed Blc. *Pride of Salem 'Talisman Cove'.*

Entire sprays of cut orchids blend well with other cut flowers if their colors are carefully selected. Whites blend with any color. Yellows look nice with blues, lavenders with greens or golds.

Orchids for dining-table decorations should not have a strong perfume. Strongly scented orchids interfere with the sense of taste and could spoil one's enjoyment of a meal. For example, a *Cycnoches* or heavily perfumed *Brassocattleya* hybrid on a table could make you think that you are eating a tropical fruit salad although the dish might be roast beef.

ORCHID SOCIETIES

The American Orchid Society has more than 330 affiliated societies around the world, dedicated to helping their members enjoy orchid growing. Most of the large orchid societies outside the United States participate in an exchange of publications, slide programs, and similar activities with the American Orchid Society. Local groups usually have a regular meeting time and place, and frequently welcome visitors. Information about orchid groups is listed in the American Orchid Society *Bulletin* and in the A.O.S. *Yearbook.*

Going to orchid society meetings can be a rewarding activity because programs often feature practical culture information. This is also an opportunity to meet other orchidists with whom you can discuss your own orchid collection. If growing orchids is a new hobby for you, these meetings can be especially helpful.

By joining the American Orchid Society, you will receive the monthly color-illustrated A.O.S. *Bulletin,* which contains interesting articles, advertisements from professional growers and supply companies, and information about orchid shows.

AMERICAN ORCHID SOCIETY JUDGING

The A.O.S. sponsors monthly orchid judging at 18 different locations in the United States, including Hawaii. Trained judges evaluate orchid plants and flowers and then award official A.O.S. commendations to those that are the most outstanding.

Anyone may enter an orchid plant or cut orchid bloom for the judging. Most regional centers request a small donation, but no official entry fee is charged. One must fill out an entry form for each orchid to be shown. It is most important to fill out the information clearly, especially the plant names. The owner's name and address go on the back of each entry form. The completed form is put with the appropriate entry.

During judging, a judge or clerk will read the front of the form so that all judges understand the name of the orchid entered. If one of the judges thinks that the flower or species is outstanding, it will be nominated for an award. Awards are granted on the basis of minimum total point scores based on the judges' evaluations. Each entry is judged independently by a minimum of three judges who fill out their evaluation forms according to an official point score system. A discussion of an entry's merits may be held before the judges fill out their forms.

At the regional judging centers where orchids are submitted each month, the judging is according to the merit of each entry. At special orchid shows, held regionally by various local orchid groups, the judging may also include evaluation of whole displays, as well as the usual awards for individual orchids.

Complete details regarding the A.O.S. system for judging are available in a publication offered by the society, *Handbook on Judging and Exhibition*. The official A.O.S. system has been adopted by most of the affiliated orchid societies around the world.

A.O.S. judges must go through a lengthy training period, then enter a probation period before being voted a full judge. Most of the regional judging centers permit entrants to watch the judging procedure.

Official Point Scores   The most popular genera are included in an official Composite Score Sheet for Flower Quality Awards. Within the points possible, judges view each plant according to type and breeding, thus giving judges some freedom to interpret the points awarded under each characteristic. The official form is shown on the facing page.

The division of points varies slightly between genera, according to what the Committee on Awards feels is most important in each type of flower. In all cases the judges must be knowledgeable about the orchids shown. To assist the judging team, local clerks maintain a file of the *Awards Quarterly* magazines (in which most awarded orchids are pictured and all are fully described), reference books about species, and photographs of orchids awarded at other regional centers.

Award Categories   The American Orchid Society judging criteria are designed to encourage the raising of top-quality orchids. Special certificates and medals are occasionally given for outstanding achievements in the field of breeding orchids or service to the orchid world. At the monthly regional judging, cultural and flower awards are frequently granted to the best plants or blooms on display.

Presently the most granted A.O.S. awards are:

First Class Certificate (F.C.C.) for 90 points or more;
Award of Merit (A.M.) for 80 to 89 points;
Highly Commended Certificate (H.C.C.) for species or hybrids ". . . of unusual distinctiveness . . ." with a score of at least 75 points;
Certificate of Botanical Recognition (C.B.R.) given by unanimous con-

AMERICAN ORCHID SOCIETY

Composite Score Sheet for Flower Quality Awards

Date _____ Place _____ Show _____

Name of Plant _____ Cultivar _____

Parentage _____

ENTRY NUMBER _____ Draw Vertical Line Through Point Scale Used

Award _____

Average Score _____

Point Scale Used: No. _____

	1. General	2. Cattleya	3. Cymbidium	4. Paphiopedilum	5. Dendrobium	6. Miltonia	7. Odontoglossum	8. Phalaenopsis	9. Vanda	Points Scored
FLOWER FORM	30	30	30	40	30	30	30	30	30	
General Form		15	15	20	15	15	15	15	15	
Sepals		5	5	10	5	6	5	5	7	
Petals		5	5	5	5		5	6	5	
Labellum (*Pouch)		5	5	5*	5	9	5	4	3	
COLOR OF FLOWER	30	30	30	40	30	30	30	30	30	
General Color		15	15	20	15	15	15	15	15	
Sepals		7	8	10	5	6	5	10	7	
Petals				5	5		5		5	
Labellum (*Pouch)		8	7	5*	5	9	5	5	3	
OTHER CHARACTERISTICS	40	40	40	20	40	40	40	40	40	
Size of Flower	10	10	10	10	10	10	10	10	10	
Substance and Texture	10	20	10	5	10	10	10	10	10	
Habit and Arrangement of Inflorescence	10		10		10	10	10	10	10	
Floriferousness	10		10		10	10	10	10	10	
Floriferousness and Stem		10								
Stem				5						
								Total Points		

DESCRIPTION and COMMENTS – please print or write legibly. Use other side if necessary.

_____
Signature of Judge

sent of the judging team to species or natural hybrids deemed worthy because of rarity, novelty, and educational value;

Certificate of Cultural Merit (C.C.M.) given for 80 or more points awarded to a specimen plant with robust health and an unusually large number of flowers;

Certificate of Horticultural Merit (C.H.M.) awarded to well-grown and -flowered species or natural hybrids which receive at least 80 points based on aesthetic appeal, educational interest, and outstanding characteristics of the entry.

Owners of awarded orchids pay a fee to cover the cost of the certificate, photographs, and related expenses. Eventually the exhibitor will receive a printed award certificate and a color slide of his awarded orchid. Awarded entries are described in the A.O.S. *Awards Quarterly* in terms of measurements, flower count, points received, judges on the team, and the name and address of the entry owner. Most orchids are also pictured.

LOCAL SHOW JUDGING

Local garden groups welcome orchid entries for seasonal garden shows. These events frequently include a section for cut-flower arrangements and other sections for various plants, grouped according to their family, size, use in horticulture, and other categories, such as orchids grown under lights or at a windowsill. Some of the better-organized shows have a complete program with details about each class—and there may be more than a hundred classes. Sometimes these are not official A.O.S. events, so judging may be less formal than the strict A.O.S. point score system.

Regional orchid societies often have a monthly show table. Some local groups have a panel of experienced orchidists who agree to discuss each orchid, then grant awards according to the general merit of each plant. Sometimes ribbons or colored stickers are given to winners. These events are fun to attend and one can often learn from the comments made as each orchid is discussed. Many of these local awards are separate from the internationally recognized American Orchid Society awards.

WORLD ORCHID CONFERENCES

Every three years, orchidists from around the world gather at the World Orchid Conference. Here they discuss orchids, attend presentations made by distinguished speakers from many countries, and learn about the latest in orchid research. Past World Orchid Conferences have been held in such differing locations as Australia, California, Colombia, England, Germany, Hawaii, Singapore, and Thailand. The 1978 W.O.C. in Thailand was a favorite of mine because so many outstanding orchids come from that beautiful country.

Attending a World Orchid Conference is an exciting way to meet friendly orchid growers from many different countries. Besides the official program of lectures, local host groups plan excursions, such as visits to commercial orchid nurseries, homes of orchid growers, and orchid habitats. After each World Orchid Conference, the proceedings are published in book form and may be ordered from orchid societies.

PHOTOGRAPHING ORCHIDS

Orchid growing and photography are natural companions. You will enjoy capturing orchids on film to record favorite flowers, show friends your plants, document progress in your collection, make personal greeting cards, create striking enlargements for decoration. Photography is an important part of official orchid judging around the world since all awarded orchids must be photographed in color to faithfully record their characteristics.

Botanical institutions use photographs to supplement their libraries and herbarium specimens. Habitat photos of orchids in their tropical homes are desired, along with close-ups of the plants and flowers, for a full record of each species.

Commercial growers must have color photographs of their flowering orchids for catalogs. Orchid societies use color slides for educational programs and several orchid magazines need professional-quality orchid photos to illustrate articles. Even if you do not plan on creating slide programs, catalogs, or articles, you will still enjoy having your own orchid flowers captured on color film for pleasure long after the flowers fade. This outline will help you to obtain top-quality orchid photographs.

Equipment The most precise artistic orchid photographs are taken with cameras that let the photographer see just what the film will record. A single-lens reflex camera design permits one to look directly through the camera lens, compose and focus, even check depth of field (zone of acceptable sharpness) before taking the photo. A modern 35mm single-lens reflex camera is a most versatile camera, perfectly suited to taking excellent orchid portraits.

Close-ups Most people have no problem taking medium to wide views. Landscapes, groups of friends, beds of flowering plants, even big specimen orchids can be captured with a normal lens. Creating dramatic close-up photos of medium- to small-sized subjects, such as a cattleya flower, involves more attention to lens selection and photographic techniques.

Screw-in close-up lenses permit you to focus the camera lens closer than usual. With a single-lens reflex, there is no problem about focusing or composing precisely. Screw-in close-up lenses look like clear filters and do not require increased exposure. When a camera lens is used at a small iris opening (f/stop) such as f/11 to f/32, the sharpness will be acceptable. At larger f/stops, the edges may be soft. Of course, how sharp a photograph should be is a matter of personal choice.

Close-focusing Lenses The best results in close-focusing lenses are obtained with lenses designed for extreme close-up use. These lenses are called *macro* lenses. A number of companies offer macro lenses to fit popular 35mm SLRs. A well-designed macro will yield excellent results at faraway distances too, but it will surpass normal lenses in the close-focusing area.

If you plan on doing lots of close-up work with orchids, a macro lens is a wise investment. Using a 100 to 105mm macro lens lets you work at double the distance of the 50 to 55mm lens but still gives you the same size enlargement on film. One of my favorite macro lenses for orchid portraits is a 105mm f/4 "Micro Nikkor." I can fill the frame with a 2½-inch flower when the lens is 8 to 9 inches away, thus leaving adequate room for lighting, reflectors, and causing fewer problems with shadows cast by equipment. Since the semi-telephoto 105mm macro has a narrower angle of view than the 55mm macro, one can use a smaller background, too.

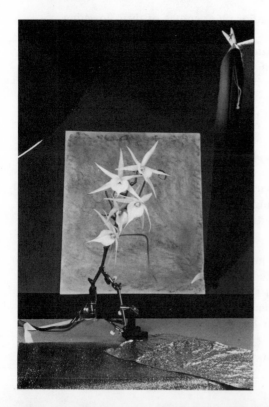

To photograph these flowers of
Angraecum *Ol Tukai, I held*
the inflorescence with a weighted
workbench grip. A hand-painted
background is behind the flowers.
Light from a diffuse electronic
strobe is bounced back into the
photo by reflector foil.

Extension Tubes A third way to focus close is by using extension tubes between the lens and the camera. By moving the lens away from the film, one can focus much closer. The disadvantage of an extension tube, or series of extension tubes, is that the focusing range is restricted, not continuous as in a close-focusing macro lens.

Bellows For maximum enlargement of small subjects, use a bellows. A normal lens can be reversed on a bellows but longer lenses, such as a 105mm, will give a better working range, even when reversed. Bellows attachments are made by camera manufacturers and independent firms to fit various lens mounts. A bellows can be used with any lens but most common for flower photographs is a bellows with 100 to 135mm range lens. If a normal lens is used, it should be reversed for best quality.

Accessories The most important addition to a camera system is a sturdy tripod that permits quick adjustment of height and vertical/horizontal tilt controls. A tripod is required for slow exposures, so camera movement does not blur the picture. Having a camera ridged is also helpful in composing and for making several identical photos with slightly different exposures, a professional technique called bracketing.

Cases Protect your camera with a case. If you only have one camera and lens, an ever-ready case made for your camera is suitable. If you have several lenses and perhaps more than one camera body, a separate camera bag is more convenient. For work indoors, the sort of case that opens like a suitcase or attaché is handy, since one can see all the equipment and choose what is needed quickly. In the field, a shoulder bag is easier to use.

In the field, a small tripod is useful when one uses a long telephoto lens. Here on an Andean slope, I'm taking photos of a distant orchid with a 200mm lens.

Small Flash Units A portable electronic flash is useful for photography at orchid shows, in the field, and other places where one can't arrange more elaborate lighting. Modern electronic flash units, sometimes called "strobes," will function on disposable batteries, rechargeable cells, or household current. Choose a model that has a dual current feature if you plan to use it with electricity in various countries.

Lights at Home When you have the freedom to set up lights just for orchid photography, you will have more control over the photos. By using a reflector or more than one light, you will often get more pleasing results than with small portable single-flash photography. Photoflood lamps are the least expensive way to light flowers and see just what the lights are doing. With small electronic flash units one does not have a way to preview the actual flash with any degree of precision. Sometimes the flash will make a shadow that is not wanted. Larger studio electronic flash units have built-in focusing lamps, often called modeling lamps, so one can preview the flash effect.

Purchase an electronic flash with built-in focusing light if you have the funds. The moderately priced units have light, flash tube, and power pack in one compact case, designed to fit on a stand. For several hundred dollars, one can buy a smaller studio-type electronic flash with built-in focusing light. Most modern units also have a special holder for an umbrella, since soft-surround umbrella lighting is a favorite with fashion photographers. I often use umbrella lighting for orchid photos.

Daylight Sun is perfect for orchid photography but direct rays are too harsh for most tastes. Diffusing the sun with colorless diffusion material will soften the strong sun, turning it into a pleasing light. Plastic diffusion material is offered at photo stores and by some mail-order firms.

Backgrounds Pleasant orchid photos can be taken in a greenhouse without special backgrounds but you must use the depth of field carefully to avoid having distracting background matter come out in sharp focus. Remember that at small f/stops, depth of field increases, while with wider open f/stops, the depth of field becomes progressively shallow. By taking the photograph at a moderate- to well-open f/stop, you can throw the background out of focus. To preview this effect, push in the camera depth-of-field button. This stops down the lens aperture to the f/stop that will be used as the picture is taken, thus giving you a preview of the actual depth of field to appear on the film. Lenses also have depth-of-field scales on the mounts but it is easier to judge the effect by looking through a stopped-down lens.

Artificial backgrounds give you much more control over the final effect. For the least distracting background, as might be desired in award or scientific photographs, hang a sheet of black velvet several feet behind the flowers. The black will be so underexposed that it looks pure black. If too much light hits the black, it may come out with texture or even dark gray, so use care to keep light off the background and place the flowers well in front of the material.

Film Choice If you plan on showing slides, select a quality color reversal film. You can obtain slides from color negatives and color negatives from slides, but it is most economical to select the film according to your primary needs—prints or slides.

OTHER HOBBIES FOR ORCHIDISTS

Collecting living plants is the most challenging way to enjoy orchids, but you can increase your orchid pleasure with orchid paintings, prints, books, sculpture, and sparkling gold orchid flowers. Another enjoyable hobby is collecting orchid postage stamps issued by tropical countries in order to show their native species. Specialized stamp publications list offerings of flower stamps, including orchid issues. Also, a few countries have included orchid flowers on currency and at least one airline uses the orchid as its symbol of friendly superior service.

This attractive original design of an orchid, Phal. cornu-cervi, *was stitched on a shirt in Indonesia.*

Perfect gold castings of orchid flowers are unusual and you can find some lovely examples at reasonable prices by consulting orchid society magazines. Orchids cast in gold are a durable fascinating addition to your daily enjoyment of living flowers. Gold orchids are also perfect gifts for special events.

Gold orchids are a popular buy in tropical countries where they are made, including Malaysia, Singapore, and Thailand. These charming life-size castings, in 22- to 24-carat gold, are not inexpensive but they will retain aesthetic and monetary value for generations.

This brass-toned phalaenopsis belt buckle was made from a mold formed around a live flower.

16. Sources of Orchids and Supplies

COMMERCIAL ORCHID firms are accustomed to sending living plants through the mails and by air to other countries. If you live in a temperate climate, order orchids by mail anytime *except* during the coldest months when plants are liable to freeze. When I order orchids for delivery at my New York address they are sent until December, then not until spring arrives, usually late March. Orchids sent to me in midwinter have been frozen, even when packaged carefully and boxes marked "Keep Above Freezing—Living Plants."

It is rewarding to visit a nursery, and especially helpful if you are just starting a collection. By seeing what is in bloom every month or two, you can create your own personally selected collection of orchids that always has flowers.

Before visiting larger nurseries, obtain their catalogs, study what is offered, make notes about those plants you wish to see, and ask questions. Ordering orchids from firms in your own country requires no special paper work, just a clear listing of what you want and correct payment. Buying orchids from overseas firms requires more planning.

SHIPMENTS FROM ABROAD

It is safe to order orchids from established firms in other countries if you deal with firms of good reputation, usually those that advertise in major orchid society publications or that have been personally recommended by other orchidists. For any order coming into the United States one must have an import permit from the United States Department of Agriculture. To obtain a free permit, send a letter listing the country from which you plan to order orchids. Mention the port of entry if you know it and the method by which the orchids will be imported (airfreight, airmail, in personal baggage). Send your request to:

Permit Unit, U. S. Dept. of Agriculture
APHIS, PPQ, Federal Bldg., Room 368
Hyattsville, Md. 20782

You will be sent a permit and some mailing labels. When you order orchids from another country, send the permit number (not the permit itself) and a few of the labels. The orchid nursery will ship the orchids to the U.S.D.A. inspection station as listed on the mailing labels. After inspection, the orchids will be forwarded to you if it is a mail shipment or released for your pickup if they were sent by airfreight.

Orchids are listed under the Endangered Species Act. Any orchid coming into the United States (and most other countries) must be accompanied by a certificate of origin which complies with the complicated regulations of international law. Most commercial firms will obtain this document for you and include the required paper work in the plant parcel. You may have to pay an extra fee for this.

Careful packing helps orchids travel long distances without being damaged.

SHIPPING METHODS

If you are ordering a few orchids and wish to have them delivered to your address, specify shipment by *Air Parcel Post* or other direct door-to-door mail service. Plants sent by Air Parcel Post (and other mail service) are first inspected by the U.S.D.A. at the port of entry, then promptly sent on to your address by mail at no extra charge. This is the most efficient way to receive small shipments. The total value must be under $250, otherwise you must pay a special broker's fee to have a formal customs declaration made, or go to the port of entry to do this yourself. Orders valued under $250 go directly ahead. If any customs duty is required, you can pay it at your local post office.

Having orchids imported by other than regular mail service involves considerably more paper work and time. For example, Air Freight and Air Express are not international mail services but are private firms that deliver parcels for a specific charge. When orchids arrive by Air Freight or Air Express, an agent must be appointed to deliver the parcel for U.S.D.A. inspection. Most of the major airlines will do this for a small fee but it is the importer's responsibility to be sure that a parcel will be delivered for inspection.

After agricultural inspection, the orchids must be shown to a U. S. Customs agent and the value declared. If the total value is under $250, an informal entry can be arranged and any required duty paid in cash or by check to a customs inspector at the port of entry. Unless you are ready to hire a broker at the port of entry, or to go personally to the port of entry for retrieval of the orchids, avoid receiving plants by Air Freight or Air Express.

Complete up-to-date details about importing orchids can be obtained from the U.S.D.A. APHIS office at the address listed earlier. If you plan to order orchids from overseas, obtain the latest printing of the free government publication, "Plant Importing Procedures and Responsibilities of Plant Importers." Federal regulations are subject to frequent revision.

Air Freight or Express? In some countries the mail service is not as reliable as professional privately owned Air Express and Air Freight firms. Commercial orchid growers may find it more efficient to develop friendly working relationships with officials at private shipping locations, in contrast to the postal service. Often shipments are better treated and well insured when sent with private freight or express firms, such as the major international airlines.

Using Air Freight or Air Express for large shipments is a safe practical method of importing orchids. Commercial orchid growers frequently use Air Freight because the value and size of their orders make this the most efficient means of importation. However, because of the procedures involved, necessitating attention of the importer or paid broker, small orders are much easier to receive via the mail service.

I have received orchids from Africa, South America, and Asia by Air Parcel Post with good results. Shipments have also come to me by Air Freight but the drive to John F. Kennedy Airport, all the time required to complete the required forms, and extra fees for parcel transportation are not worth the bother when satisfactory results can be had with a direct airmail shipment.

SOURCE LIST

Here are some of the many firms across the country and around the world from which you can order orchid plants and supplies by mail.

Alberts and Merkel Bros., Inc.
2210 S. Federal Hwy.
Boynton Beach, FL 33435

Orchid hybrids and species. Catalog ($1) is free to A.O.S. members.

American Louver Co.
7700 Austin Ave.
Skokie, IL 60076

Free bulletins about paracube louvers used to hide fluorescent tubes.

The Angraecum House
P.O. Box 1859
Grass Valley, CA 95945

Free list of rare species and primary hybrids.

Ann Mann's Orchids
Route 3, Box 202
Orlando, FL 32811

Coconut fiber potting material. Catalog ($1) lists orchids and supplies.

Armacost and Royston
P.O. Box 385
3376 Foothill Rd.
Carpinteria, CA 93013

Free catalog features cattleya and paphiopedilum hybrids, outstanding clones.

Barrington Industries
P.O. Box 133
Barrington, IL 60010

Catalog ($2) of potting mixes, growing supplies, greenhouse equipment and insulation.

The Beall Co.
Vashon Island, WA 98070

Free lists of unusual hybrids, intergeneric types, select species.

W. Atlee Burpee Co.
Warminster, PA 18974

Free catalog lists growing supplies, seeds of other plants.

Carter and Holmes Orchids
P.O. Box 491
Newberry, SC 29108

Free catalog of orchids.

Chula Orchids
230 Chula Vista St.
Chula Vista, CA 92010

Orchids and hoyas, plus
greenhouse supplies. Free catalog.

Clean*Air Work Stations, Inc.
P.O. Box 50
Commack, NY 11725

Free folder about seed
sowing/flasking cabinets.

The Coes' Orchid Acres
4647 Winding Way
Sacramento, CA 95841

Free folder about special indoor
growing chamber.

Consan Pacific Inc.
P.O. Box 208
Whittier, CA 90608

Free folder on Physan applications.

Cork Textures Inc.
Box 1271
Morristown, NJ 07960

Cork bark. Free list.

Day's
4725 N.W. 36th Ave.
Miami, FL 33142

Free folder about unique
galvanized orchid racks, patio tiers.

J. T. Dimmick Forest Co.
P.O. Box 310
Garberville, CA 95440

Redwood bark potting media. Free
sample packet and price list.

Finck Floral Co.
9848 Kimker Lane
St. Louis, MO 63127

Free list of orchids.

Floralite Co.
4124 East Oakwood Rd.
Oak Creek, WI 53154

Free list of fluorescent light
fixtures, stands.

Fogg-It Nozzle Co.
P.O. Box 16053
San Francisco, CA 94116

Watering nozzles. Pot waterer and
mist nozzle combo, 14- or 24-inch
size. Free folder.

Grass Roots
RD 3, Box 38
Rhinebeck, NY 12572

Sets of small hand-blown bud vases. Free catalog.

Great Lake Orchids
P.O. Box 1114
Monroe, MI 48161

Species specialist. Free catalog.

The Green House
9515 Flower St.
Bellflower, CA 90706

Free brochure about light garden stands.

GTE Sylvania
Danvers, MA 01923

Bulletins related to fluorescent tubes.

Indoor Gardening Supplies
P.O. Box 40567
Detroit, MI 48240

Free catalog with selection of light garden supplies and lamps.

J & L Orchids
20 Sherwood Rd.
Easton, CT 06612

Free list of rare South American orchids.

Jones and Scully Inc.
2200 N.W. 33rd Ave.
Miami, FL 33142

Free catalog. Visitors welcome at the nursery.

Kasem Boonchoo Nursery
109/3 Phaholyotin Soi 15
Sapan Kwai
Bangkok 4, Thailand

Many Asian orchid hybrids. Color catalog ($1).

Kensington Orchids Inc.
3301 Plyers Mill Rd.
Kensington, MD 20795

Free list.

Lauray of Salisbury
Undermountain Rd., Rte. 41
Salisbury, CT 06068

Catalog ($1) lists some orchids, plus many companion houseplants.

A. M. Leonard Inc.
6665 Spiker Rd.
Piqua, OH 45356

Free catalog of tools, fertilizer, shade cloth, watering devices.

Robert Lester Orchids
280 W. 4th St.
New York, NY 11014

Custom-designed orchid
collections, rare species, including
miniatures.

Lord and Burnham Co.
Irvington, NY 10533

Free folder of greenhouses,
greenhouse equipment.

Maka Koa Corp.
Box 411
Haleiwa, HI 96712

New hybrids and select mericlones.
Color catalog ($2).

Marko
94 Porete Ave.
North Arlington, NJ 07032

Self-contained wall garden units
with three lamps and wedged
louver. Free folder.

Mary Noble McQuerry
5700 W. Salerno Rd.
Jacksonville, FL 32210

Rare orchid books and A.O.S.
Register of Awards.

Mayfair Orchids
P.O. Box 627
Oyster Bay, NY 11771

Free list includes unusual
phalaenopsis hybrids.

Rod McLellan Co.
1450 El Camino Real
South San Francisco, CA 94080

Catalog ($1) lists many hybrids,
species. Visitors welcome to
extensive greenhouses.

Mellinger's
2310 West South Range Rd.
North Lima, OH 44452

Free catalog filled with growing
supplies, including potting
materials.

The Natriphene Co.
P.O. Box 1126
Midland, MI 48640

Free folder about use of
Natriphene fungicide.

Old Dutch Materials Co.
350 Pfingsten Rd.
Northbrook, IL 60062

StoneScaping materials, including
stone aggregates that look like
bark. Free folder.

Orchid Plant Food Co.
1699 Sage Ave.
Los Osos, CA 93402

Free list of fertilizers and
snail/slug baits.

Orchids by Hausermann, Inc.
P.O. Box 363
Elmhurst, IL 60126

Color catalog ($1.25) includes
mericlones, species, new hybrids,
supplies.

Orchids by Kelly
11295 S.W. 93rd St.
Miami, FL 33176

Unusual meristems and new
hybrids in many genera.

Pacific Coast Greenhouse Mfg. Co.
8260 Industrial Ave.
Cotati, CA 94928

Catalog of redwood greenhouses
and greenhouse supplies.

George W. Park Seed Co.
P.O. Box 31
Greenwood, SC 29647

Free catalog includes many
growing supplies, some orchids.

Robert B. Peters Co.
2833 Pennsylvania St.
Allentown, PA 18104

Free folder about various chemical
fertilizers.

Plantation Garden Products
P.O. Box 127
Boynton Beach, FL 33435

Catalog lists potting media, other
supplies.

The Pro Lab Inc.
1200 W. Mississippi
Denver, CO 80223

Special diffusion screens. Free
folder.

R. J. Rands Orchids
15322 Mulholland Dr.
Los Angeles, CA 90024

Paphiopedilums, their primary
hybrids. Free catalog lists pure
species, culture notes.

Peter Reimuller Greenhouses
980 17th Ave.
Santa Cruz, CA 95062

Free catalog of greenhouses with
redwood frames.

Rosco Laboratories, Inc.
36 Bush Ave.
Port Chester, NY 10573 *or*
1135 N. Highland Ave.
Hollywood, CA 90038

Diffusion material for photographic
use. Reflection material for light
gardens.

Santa Barbara Orchid Estate
1250 Orchid Dr.
Santa Barbara, CA 93111

Free catalog includes orchids to
grow outdoors in semi-tropical
areas.

Shaffer's Tropical Gardens
1220 41st Ave.
Santa Cruz, CA 95060

Specialists in phalaenopsis. Color
poster and catalog lists ($2).

Shoplite Co. Inc.
107 Harrison St.
Verona, NJ 07044

Indoor light growing fixtures and
supplies. Catalog ($.50).

Simanis Orchids
P.O. Box 8
J1 Pungkurargo ✕1
Lawang, East Java, Indonesia

Free list of rare species and
unusual primary hybrids of Asian
tropical orchids.

Singapore Orchids Pte. Ltd.
2 Swettenham Rd.
Singapore 10

Specialists in vanda hybrids.

SOS Photo-Cine Optics Inc.
315 W. 43rd St.
New York, NY 10036 *or*
7051 Santa Monica Blvd.
Hollywood, CA 90038

Products for reflecting and
diffusing light.

Fred A. Stewart Co.
1212 E. Las Tunas Dr.
San Gabriel, CA 91778

Color catalog ($1) of orchids,
advanced hybrids, some species,
is free to customers.

Texas Greenhouse Co.
2717 St. Louis Ave.
Fort Worth, TX 76110

Free catalog of greenhouses and
greenhouse control devices,
humidifiers.

T. Orchids
77/3 Jangwattana Rd. (Lim Klong
   Prapa)
Pak-kred
Nonthaburi, Thailand

Color catalog ($5) lists outstanding
Thai hybrids, especially
Ascocendas, and some species.

Tube Craft Inc.
1311 W. 80th St.
Cleveland, OH 44102

Free folder about light garden
stands and related supplies.

Vacherot and Lecoufle
B.P. 894470 Boissy
Saint-Léger, France

Free catalog of select phalaenopsis, cattleyas, odontoglossum hybrids.

Vegetable Factory Greenhouses
71 Vanderbilt Ave.
New York, NY 10017

Free catalog of acrylic glazed greenhouses. Guide to greenhouse heating.

Yamamoto Dendrobiums Hawaii
P.O. Box 235
Mountain View, HI 96771

Color catalog ($1) shows Dendrobium nobile hybrids.

Zuma Canyon Orchids, Inc.
5949 Bonsall Dr.
Malibu, CA 90265

Free catalog lists phalaenopsis and related hybrids in a wide color range.

Appendix

CHANGES IN NOMENCLATURE

ORCHIDS ARE named according to their flower structure, as is true for classification of other ornamental plants. The taxonomists in charge of correct nomenclature, like professionals in many fields, do not always agree. Some taxonomists prefer to use the slightest difference in structure to create a new species. Others prefer to view slight differences in color or form as natural variants in a single species. To be practical, one must also consider the actual name under which a given orchid has long been cultivated.

For example, *Brassavola digbyana* has been grown for more than a hundred years. Recently taxonomists decided that this species should be called *Rhyncholaelia digbyana*. Changes like this are frequently based on the discovery of a name that was applied to the species earlier than the current name. By international botanical law, the first correctly published scientific description for any given species establishes the accepted name. However, many early descriptions have been overlooked while a popular species is grown under a later name.

To complicate matters, the showy species are used as parents and offspring are internationally registered with their parentage, using the current nomenclature. For example, in the official *Sander's List of Orchid Hybrids* published by the Royal Horticultural Society in England, there is a note under the listing for *Brassavola digbyana*: "This is retained as the horticulturally recommended name for registration purposes, even though *Rhyncholaelia digbyana* is the botanically correct name for this species."

A similar note occurs with the delightfully fragrant-flowered *Epidendrum atropurpureum* where the species is reclassified botanically as *Encyclia atropurpurea*. Even more recently, the botanical name was switched to *Encyclia cordigera!* In this book I have used the horticulturally accepted names for species but with a note regarding botanically acceptable synonyms and recent reclassifications. The nomenclature I use will help you find orchids in catalogs, current literature, and hybridizing records.

ADVANCED ORCHID PHOTOGRAPHY

The basic information about photographing orchids (in Chapter 15) is enough to get you started. For an in-depth understanding of professional level orchid photography, especially lighting techniques, extreme close-ups, and field work in the tropics, consult *Garden Photography* by Charles Marden Fitch (Amphoto Publishing Co.) or *Handbook on Orchid Photography* (American Orchid Society).

OFFICIAL HYBRID REGISTRATION

If you create orchid hybrids or are the first to bloom a new hybrid, it is important to understand the international registration procedure. The Royal Horticultural Society in England is the international authority for orchid hybrids. If you are the *first* applicant to apply a proposed name in correct form, your application will be accepted and a fee of 5 pounds Sterling or the U.S. dollar equivalent (about $12) must be paid.

International rules give the registration privilege to the person who made the new hybrid. Commercial breeders will sometimes give their customers the privilege of registering a hybrid if the customer is the first to flower a plant from that cross. Of course, if someone else has made the same cross and already registered it with the international authority, no other names can be accepted. For example, a cross I made of *Phalaenopsis* Tyler Carlson with *Phal.* Terry Beth Ballard has been registered as *Phal.* Talisman Cove. All orchids resulting from a cross of these parents must be given the same name, *Phal.* Talisman Cove (grex epithet).

Correct nomenclature is vitally important for orchids. No orchid may receive an award until correctly named. Precise names are required for one to obtain a desired orchid from commercial sources, too. The official application forms for registration of orchid hybrids are available from:

> The Registrar of Orchid Hybrids
> The Royal Horticultural Society
> Vincent Square
> London, SW1P 2PE England

Potential registrants should obtain a copy of the *Handbook on Orchid Nomenclature and Registration,* which contains detailed information regarding acceptable names. Of special importance is the section "Grex Registration Procedure for Cultivated Orchid Hybrids."

If you are new to orchid hybrid registration, it is also important to check the hybrid parents in past volumes of *Sander's List of Orchid Hybrids,* available at most botanical gardens and horticultural libraries. Doing this important prechecking will save much time and postage since there is no point trying to register a cross that already has been officially named. Advice regarding registration can often be obtained from a commercial specialist where you buy orchids, or the American Orchid Society.

Application for Registration of an Orchid Hybrid

1. This form, duly completed, should be sent to the International Authority for the Registration of Orchid Hybrids, addressed to: "**The Registrar of Orchid Hybrids, The Royal Horticultural Society, Vincent Square, London, SW1P 2PE, England.**"
2. The form should be completed in duplicate. The Registrar will return the original to the applicant and file the duplicate for future reference. (Applicants who wish to retain written permission from Originators for their applications may obtain forms for this purpose from the Registrar.) The originator of a grex is the owner (or his assignee) of the seed-bearing parent plant at the time of pollination.
3. The registration fee is £5·00 sterling or the current equivalent in U.S. dollars. Payment should NOT accompany the application to which it relates. The Registrar will enclose a dated invoice for the registration fee in respect of each **accepted** application when returning the original of this form to the registrant; the invoice will be payable (a) by registrants in U.K. by the end of the month *following* the invoice date, and (b) by other registrants by the end of the *second* month following the invoice date.
4. Applications may be rejected if any part of the applicant's orchid registration account is outstanding six months or more after the invoice date. The Registrar reserves the right to regard as null and void any application which after registration is found to have contained inaccurate information.
5. Applicants are invited to give the varietal or cultivar epithets of the parents, awards, and any other information which is of interest although not published in the List of Orchid Hybrids and treated as confidential unless applicants authorise disclosure. Without such authority, only applicants' addresses will be disclosed.

Genus ....

Proposed Grex Epithet
{ 1st choice ....
{ 2nd choice ....

Parentage ♀ .... ♂ ....

Name and Address of Applicant ....

APPLICANT'S DECLARATION AS TO ORIGINATOR (to be completed in **ALL** cases)

(1) I am the Originator as defined in Note 2 above . . . . ☐
(2) The Originator is unknown to me FOR REASONS EXPLAINED OVERLEAF . . . ☐
(3) The Originator is (name and address).. ....

AND (a) has given permission for this application . . . . ☐
    (b) is deceased and has no surviving spouse, or is a firm gone out of business, or is an organisation no longer existing, for whom no assignee is known to me ☐
    (c) has not replied to my written request for permission as sent to him on ....(date), over six months ago . . . . ☐

Please tick ✓ and, if needed, complete whichever applies

Date of making cross (i.e. date of pollination)...................................... Date of first flowering..............................

Description of first flower(s) and/or colour photograph ....

....

.... (continue overleaf if necessary)

For any further comments on this hybrid please use **BACKS OF FORMS**   **DO NOT USE STICKERS OR SEPARATE SHEETS**

I certify that to the best of my knowledge and belief the particulars and declaration given above are correct. I do/do not authorise disclosure of parental varietal or cultivar epithets. I undertake to make payment in accordance with Note 3 above if this application is accepted. Bill fee direct to me unless otherwise instructed.

Signature of Applicant .... Date ....

————This part of the form is for the use of the Registrar————

The registration of the above-mentioned hybrid { has been accepted.
{ cannot be accepted.
{ has been postponed.

Reason for non-acceptance or postponement..............................

....

Signature .... Date ....

ORCHID PERIODICALS

Orchid periodicals contain the latest information on hybridizing trends, shows, propagation techniques, and commercial offerings. Although local groups may publish newsletters, small magazines, and show programs, the periodicals with international circulation and articles of broad interest are the most informative and best illustrated. Here are my favorites in English language orchid magazines.

American Orchid Society Bulletin (monthly)
84 Sherman St.
Cambridge, ME 02140

Australian Orchid Review (quarterly)
P.O. Box 60
Sydney Mail Exchange, Australia 2012

The Florida Orchidist (monthly)
133 South Miami Ave.
Miami, FL 33130

Hawaii Orchid Journal-Na Okika o Hawaii (quarterly)
1710 Pali Hwy.
Honolulu, HI 96813

The Orchid Digest (bimonthly)
1739 Foothill Blvd.
La Cañada, CA 91011

The Orchid Review (monthly)
5 Orchid Ave., Kingsteignton
Newton Abbot,
Devon TQ12 3HG England

South African Orchid Journal (quarterly)
c/o Editor Joyce Stewart
Dept. of Botany
University of Natal
Pietermaritzburg, South Africa

Glossary of Botanical Terms

Most of the botanical terms I use in this book are briefly explained in the text where they first occur, but for a convenient quick reference of the most unfamiliar words, consult this glossary.

Aerial roots	Those roots growing outside of the potting mix or hanging free in the air. Common in vandas and their relatives.
Agar	A medium derived from seaweed, used as the base for seed-sowing mixtures and to form a gelatinous base for culturing seedlings, meristems, and stem propagations.
Asexual	Not involving sex, without the exchange of male and female cells. Propagation by division and meristem is asexual.
Asymbiotic	Refers to the absence of a mutually helping or symbiotic relationship between germinating orchid seed and fungi. Orchid seed in the wild is invaded by a fungi which helps the seed to grow. Modern asymbiotic seed sowing on nutrient agar does not require the presence of fungi.
Backbulb	The older pseudobulbs located behind the growing lead. Backbulbs often have live dormant buds at the base which sprout when the backbulb is separated from the growing front portion or lead.
Bifoliate	Refers to orchids which normally have two leaves per growth, as in bifoliate *Cattleya skinneri*.
Botanical	A term used by orchidists to refer to species not widely grown for cut flowers, but appreciated by specialists in hobby collections.

Bract	A leaf-like sheath at the base of a flower stem, often seen in cymbidiums.
Clone	A sexually produced seed-grown individual and all subsequent asexual (vegetative) propagations. A *select clone* usually carries a fancy name in single quotes, such as *Cymbidium* Mary Pinchess 'Del Rey'.
Community pot	The transitional container used for seedlings between flask and individual pots. Community pots are usually shallow. They hold ten to thirty seedlings planted in a fine potting mix after the plants are removed from the flasks where they grew in agar.
Damping off	A rapid rotting of seedlings caused by botrytis and phythium fungi.
Diploid	A diploid orchid has the normal number of chromosomes.
Epiphyte	Refers to orchids adapted for life upon trees or similar supports. An *epiphytic* orchid is usually potted in a mix of bark, tree fern, or similar coarse nonsoil media.
Fasciation	An abnormality usually seen with stems or foliage that grows very thick.
Grex	A grex name is the label given to a cross between two different orchids. For example, the grex name for the cross of *Brassavola nodosa* X *Brassavola digbyana* is *Brassavola* Jimminey Cricket.
Keiki	Hawaiian term referring to small offshoots or plantlets produced on orchids. A form of vegetative or asexual propagation.
Lead	The active growing stem on an orchid, most often referring to sympodial genera such as *Cattleya, Cymbidium,* etc.

Meristem orchid

A select clone reproduced by tissue culture, hence called a mericlone.

Meristem propagation

A form of tissue culture in which growing cells are cultured on nutrient agar.

Monopodial

A form of plant growth in which a single terminal bud grows ahead each year, as seen in *Vanda, Phalaenopsis,* etc. Contrast with *sympodial* genera.

Offset

A plantlet that may form at the base of an orchid, on the stem, pseudobulb, or inflorescence. Offsets are used to propagate orchids by vegetative means.

Pseudobulb

A swollen water-storing stem especially common in epiphytic species such as Cattleyas. Orchids with pseudobulbs are *pseudobulbous.*

Raceme

A type of inflorescence on which individual flowers are arranged in spray fashion.

Rhizome

An above-ground stem connecting growths, easily seen in most sympodial orchids.

Peloric

A peloric flower has some abnormal regularity, such as seen in *Cattleya intermedia aquinii,* which has lip color flares on its side petals, thus giving a three-lip look to the bloom.

Sympodial

A growth habit in which the orchid sprouts a new bud each year, thus growing in the manner of Cattleyas, Paphiopedilums, etc.

Synonym

Abbreviated *syn.* or *Bot. syn.* (Botanical synonym), referring to the botanically correct name as contrasted with the widely accepted horticultural name. In common usage, the synonym is another often-used name for the orchid in question. *Vanda batemannii* is a synonym for *Vandopsis lissochiloides.* For ease in locating popular orchids, I have noted cases where more than one name may be used, as with *Encyclia* species, often referred to as *Epidendrum.*

Taxonomist

The scientific specialist concerned with plant names. Orchid taxonomists do not always agree on which name is correct for a given species, hence the regular shifting of names.

Tetraploid

Written as 4N in some catalogs. The 4 means that the plant cells have four times the normal number of chromosomes, compared to common species having a diploid number of chromosomes. Tetraploid orchids have larger flowers of heavier substance but are slower growing.

Tissue culture

A form of vegetative propagation commonly used for select commercially valuable clones. See "Meristem propagation."

Vandaceous

Refers to genera related to *Vanda* and having a monopodial type of growth.

Velamen

The thick, usually white layer of cells covering the roots of epiphytic orchids. Velamen turns gray to green when wet and absorbs moisture easily.

Bibliography

American Orchid Society. *Awards Quarterly.* Cambridge, Massachusetts.

American Orchid Society. *Bulletin.* Cambridge, Massachusetts.

American Orchid Society. *Handbook on Orchid Pests and Diseases.* Revised edition. Cambridge, Massachusetts, 1975.

American Orchid Society. *An Orchidist's Glossary.* Cambridge, Massachusetts, 1974.

Ames, Oakes, and Correll, Donovan Stewart. *Orchids of Guatemala.* Fieldiana: Botany Volume 26, No. 1, 1952. Chicago: Chicago Natural History Museum, Volume 26, No. 2, 1963.

Arditti, Joseph, ed. *Orchid Biology, Reviews and Perspectives.* Ithaca: Cornell University Press, 1977.

Davis, Reg S., and Steiner, Mona Lisa. *Philippine Orchids.* New York: The William-Frederick Press, 1952.

Fitch, Charles Marden. *The Complete Book of Houseplants.* New York: Hawthorn Books, Inc., 1972.

Fitch, Charles Marden. *The Complete Book of Houseplants Under Lights.* New York: Hawthorn Books, Inc., 1975.

Hawkes, Alex D. *Encyclopaedia of Cultivated Orchids.* London: Faber and Faber Ltd., 1965.

Honolulu Orchid Society and Pacific Orchid Society. *Na Okika o Hawaii-Hawaii Orchid Journal,* Honolulu, Hawaii.

International Orchid Commission. *Handbook on Orchid Nomenclature and Registration.* Second edition. London: International Orchid Commission, 1976.

Malaysian Orchid Society. *Malayan Orchid Review.* Volume 5 (1956–1960) and Volumes 6, 7, 8, 9. Singapore: Straits Times Press.

Millar, Andree. *Orchids of Papua, New Guinea.* Seattle: University of Washington Press, 1978.

The Orchid Digest Corporation. *The Orchid Digest.* La Cañada, California.

The Royal Horticultural Society. *Sander's List of Orchid Hybrids.* London, 1977. Addenda 1971–1975, 1964–1966, 1961–1963.

Sander, David F., and Wreford, Marjorie. *Sander's One-Table List of Orchid Hybrids,* 1946–1960, Volume 1, 2. Sussex: David Sander's Orchids, Ltd.

Schultes, Richard Evans, and Pease, Arthur Stanley. *Generic Names of Orchids.* New York: Academic Press, 1963.

van der Pijl, L., and Dodson, Calaway H. *Orchid Flowers, Their Pollination and Evolution.* Coral Gables: University of Miami Press, 1969.

Withner, Carl L., ed. *The Orchids, A Scientific Survey.* New York: The Ronald Press Co., 1959.

Withner, Carl L., ed. *The Orchids, Scientific Studies.* New York: John Wiley & Sons, 1974.

Index

Acineta, 117
Ada, 117
Aerangis, 17, 18, 45, 117–18
Aerangis calligerum, **118**
Aeranthes, 118–19
Aerial roots, 42–43
Aerides, 119–20, 203
Aerides odorata, 18
Aerides Pramote, 18, **43,** 120
Aeridocentrum, 119–20
Air circulation, 25–26
Air conditioning, greenhouse, 83
Aliceara Maury Island 'Vashon' **(color photo)**
American Orchid Society (AOS), 16, 196, 216, 241; judging by, 241–44
American Orchid Society *Bulletin,* 8, 241
American Orchid Society *Yearbook,* 241
Angraecum, 3, 18, 39, 120–21, 193
Angraecum compactum, 17, 120, **121**
Angraecum magdalenae, 17
Angraecum Ol Tukai, 120, **213,** 246
Angraecum philippinense, 17, 120, 121
Angraecum sesquipedale, 120
Angramellea, 155
Anguloa, 25, 121–22
Angulocaste Memoria Abbott Robinson, **122**
Anoectochilus, 24, 30, 122–24
Anoectochilus sikkimensis, **123**
Ansellia africana, 89, 124
Anthracnose fungus, 217, **217**
Ants, control of, 227
Aphids, control of, 227
Arachnis, 124–25
Arundina, 125, 178
Ascocenda, 14, 22, 113
Ascocenda Erika Reuter, **126**
Ascocenda Sauvanee 'Talisman Cove' **(color photo)**
Ascocenda Yip Sum Wah (*Vanda* Pukele X *Ascocentrum curvifolium*), 126
Ascocentrum, 13, 14, 30, 42, 110, 125–27
Ascocentrum ampullaceum, 126

Ascocentrum miniatum, 17
Ascofinetia Cherry Blossom, 126–27
Ascoglossum calopterum, 127
Asconopsis, 110
Aspasia, 21, 127–28
Aspasia lunata, 201
Aspasia principissa, 201
Aspoglossum, 21, 128

Backbulb growth, 185–86
Banrot (fungicide), 221
Bargains, 13
Baskets, 42–43
Beetles, control of, 228
Benches and racks, 86–87
Benomyl 50 (Benlate 50W), 222
Bifrenaria, 128–29
Bifrenaria harrisoniae, **129**
Black rot, 217
Bletilla, 129
Botanicals, defined, 11
Brassavola, 14, 18, 30, 89, 129–31, 203; basic characteristics of, 5; growth style, 3
Brassavola digbyana, **37,** 129, 130–31, 261
Brassavola Moonlight Perfume (*B. nodosa* X *B. glauca*), 131
Brassavola nodosa, 27, 75, 129, **130,** 214
Brassia, 14, 131–32
Brassia Edvah Loo 'Talisman Cove', **132**
Brassocattleya, 14, 241
Brassocattleya Hartland, 16
Brassolaeliocattleya (Blc.), 14; clone of (catalog example), 15–16
Blc. Herbert William Tickner 'Talisman Cove' **(color photo)**
Blc. Norman's Bay 'Hercules', FCC/RHS, JC/AOS (*Lc.* Ishtar X *Bc.* Hartland), how to understand catalog listing of, 15–16
Blc. Pride of Salem 'Talisman Cove', **240**
Blc. Tambourine, **211**
Broughtonia, 30, 203
Broughtonia sanguinea, 132–33
Brown spot, 218

Bud blast, 223–24
Bulbophyllum, 133–34
Bulbophyllum medusae, **133**
Bulbophyllum umbellatum, 17

Calanthe, 134–35
Calanthe vestita, 134, **135**
Captan (fungicide), 222
Catalogs: abbreviations in, 13; genus
    and species names, 13; how to
    understand a typical listing, 15–17;
    measuring systems, 11
Catasetum, 18, 135–37, 203, 231
Catasetum Francis Nelson **(color photo)**
Catasetum macrocarpum, 135
Catasetum pileatum, **224**
Catasetum pileatum (var. *aureum*
    'Orchidglade', AM/AOS X 'Icy
    Green'), 16–17
Catasetum Rebecca Northen, 136
Catasetum warscewiczii, 135
Caterpillars, control of, 228
Cattleya, 2, 13, 36, **38, 53,** 92–95, **187,**
    190, **198,** 203, **211, 212, 216,** 223;
    basic characteristics of, 5; crosses of,
    14; culture, 93; footcandle ranges, 29;
    growth style, 3; important parts of, **2;**
    light, 93; measuring system, 11;
    propagation, 94; selections, 94–95;
    stages of growth, **40;** temperature, 94;
    watering, 94
Cattleya aclandiae, 9, 67
Cattleya aurantiaca, 92, **202; (color
    photo)**
Cattleya bowringiana, 92
Cattleya citrina, 86
Cattleya dowiana aurea, **93**
Cattleya guttata, 92
Cattleya labiata, 92
Cattleya loddigesii, 92
Cattleya Louise Georgiana, **67**
Cattleya luteola, 9
Cattleya mossiae, 92
Cattleya Porcia 'Canizarro', **95; (color
    photo)**
Cattleya skinneri, 13
Cattleya Small World, **9**
Cattleya trianaei, 36
Cattleya warscewiczii, 36
Cattleyopsis, 137
Cercospora species bacteria, 218
Chysis, 138
Chysis Chelsonii, **138**
Cirrhopetalum, 134, 138–39
Cirrhopetalum guttulatum, 17
Clay pots, **37–40**
Clean*Air flasking station, **208**
Clone name, 15
Cloning, 196–97
Cochlioda, 14, 139–40
Cockroaches, control of, 228
Coconut fiber (potting media), 52–53,
    53
Coelogyne, 140–41
Coelogyne speciosa, **139**
Colletotrichum fungi, 217
Colmanara, **214**

Colmanara Moon Gold, **14**
Column, 3
Commercial sizes, 11
Compact *Paphiopedilum godefroyae,* **16**
Compact plants, 17–18
Comparettia, 141
Comparettia macroplectron, **140**
Containers and supports, 37–47; baskets,
    42–43; clay pots, 37–40; foam plastic
    containers, 41–42; hangers, 43–45;
    plastic pots, 40–41; tree fern slabs and
    poles, 47; wooden containers, 45;
    wooden slabs and branches, 45–46
Cork bark, 46
Coryanthes, 141
Cut flowers, orchids and, 234–39;
    conditioning, 239; cutting techniques,
    235; supplies for, 234
Cultivars, 13
Cuprinol (wood preservative), 45
Cycnoches, 18, 141–42, 203, 241
Cycnoches chlorochilon, 141, 142, 212;
    (color photo)
Cycnoches Cygnet, **142**
Cycnodes Ginger Snap, **165**
Cymbidium, 2, 21, 26, 71, 88, 95–99,
    190, 210, 234; basic characteristics of,
    5; culture, 97–98; footcandle ranges,
    29; growth style, 3, 4; light, 98;
    measuring system, 11; pollinating, **201;**
    propagation, 98; selections, 99;
    temperature, 97
Cymbidium Burgundian 'Sydney', **96**
Cymbidium finlaysonianum, 42, 97
Cymbidium Leodogran 'Cradlemont'
    (color photo)
Cymbidium Madrid 'Forest King,' **239**
Cymbidium Mary Pinchess 'Del Rey'
    (color photo)
Cymbidium mosaic virus, 219
Cymbidium Promenade, **96**
Cymbidium pseudobulbs, **192**
Cymbidium Red Imp 'Red Tower', **99**
Cymbidium Showgirl 'Malibu', 15
Cymbidium Showgirl 'Talisman Cove'
    (color photo)
Cymbidium Tiger Tail 'Talisman Cove',
    1
Cyrtopodium, 142–43

Decorating with orchids, 239–41
Dendrobium, 2, **6, 9,** 22, 30, 89, 100–3,
    197, 203, 216, 223, 225; basic
    characteristics of, 5; footcandle ranges,
    29; growth style, 3; plant groups, 100;
    selections, 101–3; water and fertilizer,
    101
Dendrobium Adrasta, **103**
Dendrobium aggregatum, 100, 101
Dendrobium canaliculatum, 100
Dendrobium cucumerinum, 100
Dendrobium discolor, 100
Dendrobium Golden Blossom, **102**
Dendrobium linguiforme, 17, 101
Dendrobium nobile, 21–22, 86, 100, 196,
    203, **215**

Dendrobium Otohime 'Talisman Cove' (color photo)
Dendrobium phalaenopsis, 100; **(color photo)**
Dendrobium superbum, 100, 101
Dendrochilum, 143
Diacrium, 143, 177
Disa, 143
Disa Vetchii, **144**
Diseases, 216–20
Doritaenopsis, 203
Doritaenopsis Purple Gem, **109, 195**
Doritis, 143–44
Dracula, 145, 161
Dracula chimaera, **145**
Dracuvallia, 145
Dwarf *Ascocenda* Sauvanee 'Talisman Cove', **12**
Dwarf *Phaliella* Speck O' Gold, 155

Eastonara Advancement, **150**
Encyclia, 30
Encyclia cordigera, 261
Epidendrum, 89, 145–47, 190, 203; basic characteristics of, 5
Epidendrum (Encyclia) atropurpureum, 18, 27, 30, 261
Epidendrum fragrans, 18
Epidendrum ibaguense, 47
Epidendrum pseudepidendrum, **147**
Epidendrum radicans, 30, **39,** 47; **(color photo)**
Epidendrum tampense, 18
Epiphronitis Veitchii, 179
Epiphytes, 67, 89–90; potting mixes for, 58–59
Epiphytic orchids, 3–4; establishing on trees, 89–90
Equitant hybrids of *Oncidium,* 168
Eria, 147–48
Ethylene air pollution, 223
Eulophia, 148
Eulophidium maculata, **202**
Eulophidium maculatum, 148
Eulophiella, 148–49
Eulophiella roemplerana, **149**
Eurychone rothschildiana, 149, **149**

Ferbam (fungicide), 222
Fertilizer, 53, 66–71; application of, 69; basic guidelines, 68–69; chemical types, 67–68; organic, 71; timed release chemicals, 70–71
Fir bark (potting media), **49**
First Class Certificate (FCC), 16, 167
Flower stem plantlets, 195–96
Fluorescent lamps, 32–33; combining with sun, 33
Foam plastic containers, 41–42
Fogging and misting, 24
Footcandle measurements, 29
Fox Tail Orchid; *see Rhynchostylis*
Fragrant species, 18
Fungicides and bactericides, 221–22
Fusarium wilt (*Fusarium oxysporum cattleyae*), 217–18

Gastrochilus, 17, 150
Genus and species names, **13**
Gloeosporium fungi, 217
Gold castings of orchids, 250
Gomesa, 150–51
Gongora, 26, 30, 151
Goodaleara (Gdlra.), 14
Goodyeara pubescens, 151
Grammangis, 151
Grammatophyllum, 151
Gravel, 57–58
Greenhouses, 6; air circulation, humidity and temperature, **23;** air conditioning, 83; basic styles of, 77–79; heat conservation, 82; humidity, 79–80; shading, 79; ventilation, 80–82
Grooming, 209–11

Habenaria, 152
Hangers, 43–45
Hanging containers, 73
Hardwood charcoal (potting media), 55
"Hardy Chinese Orchid" (*Ble. hyacinthina*), 129
Hardy epiphytic *Shomburgkia,* **4**
Health care: bud blast, 223–24; cutting off old flower spikes, 210–11; diseases and, 216–20; grooming, 209–11; insects and pests, 224–27; mice and rats, 229; pest control, 227–29; rots on new growth, 220–21, **221;** training stems, 215–16; when away from home, 229–32
Heat conservation, greenhouse, 82
Hexisea bidentata, 152, **152**
Holcoglossum falcatum, 17
Honey fungus, **225**
Humidifiers, 24; greenhouse, **80**
Humidity control, 23–24; *see also* Temperature and humidity
Huntleya, 153
Huntleya meleagris, **153**
Hybrid registration, 262
Hybrids, intergeneric, 13–15; *see also* names of hybrids
Hygrometers, 23

Indoor growing compartments, **75**
Insects and pests, 224–27
Intergeneric hybrids, 13–15
Ionopsis, 153
Isabelia virginalis, 154, **154**

Judges Certificate (JC), 16
Jumanthes, 155
Jumellea, 154–55

Kingiella philippinensis, 155
Kirchara, 147
Kirchara Kulowe 'Talisman Cove' (color photo)

Laelia, 14, 155–56; basic characteristics of, 5; dwarf types, 30
Laelia anceps, 30, 86
Laelia crispa, **156**
Laelia flava, 13
Laelia milleri, 30
Laelia pumila, 17

Laelia rubescens, 27
Laeliocattleya (*Lc.*)
   Bill P. Fitch, **233**
Lc. Chit Chat 'Tangerine' **(color photo)**
Lc. El Cerrito 'Talisman Cove' **(color photo)**
Lc. Gift of Spring, **235**
Lc. Gold Digger, **34**
Lc. Ishtar, 16
Lamp maintenance, 36
Lath houses, 88
Leaf spot (disease), 218
Lean-to greenhouse, **81**
Lepanthes, 156
Leptodes, 156–57
Leptodes bicolor, 17
Light and sunlight, 27–36; diffusing the
   sun, 30–31; fluorescent, 32–33;
   intensity, 28; lamp maintenance, 36;
   light gardens, 34–36; photography,
   248; practical applications, 29–30;
   supplemental sources, 75–76; timers
   (electric), 35–36
Lithophytes, growth style, 4
Lockhartia, 157
Ludisia discolor, 157
Ludisias ("Jewel Orchids"), 24
Lycaste, 157–58
Lycaste denningiana, **159**
Lycaste macrophylla 'Kiyoshi', **158**

Marie Selby Botanical Gardens, **70**
Masdevallia, 30, 159–61
Masdevallia caudata **(color photo)**
Masdevallia coccinea, 161
Masdevallia ignea (syn. *Masd.
   militaris*), 161
Masdevallia morenoi 'J & L', **160**
Masdevallia pachyantha, 159
Masdevallia veitchiana, 161
Masdevallia veitchiana 'Prince de
   Gaule', **161**
Maxillaria, 161–62
Maxillaria grandiflora 'Puyo', **162**
Mealybugs, 224; pest control of, 228
Meiracyllium trinasutum, 162
Meiracyllium wendlandi, 162
Mericlones, 10, 11, 197
Mice and rats, 229
Microclimates, 20
Miltassia Charles M. Fitch, **193**
Miltonia, 14, 52, 163, 190, **230,** 234
Miltonia Bremen 'Talisman Cove' **(color photo)**
Miltonia Limelight 'Imogene Smith', **164**
Miltonia rengelli, 234
Miltonia roezlii, 234
Miltonia vexillaria, **164,** 234
Miniature species, 17
Mirror panels, 76
Mites, control of, 228
Mixes, potting: for epiphytes, 58–59;
   ingredient ratios, 59; for terrestrials,
   58
Monopodial orchids, 3
Mormodes, 165
Mystacidium, 165

Nageliella angustifolia, 166
Nageliella purpurea, 166
Natriphene (fungicide-bactericide), 222
Neofinetia falcata, 17, 18, 166
Nomenclature, changes in, 261
Notylia, 166
"Nun Orchid" (*Phaius grandifolius*),
   170

Odontioda **(color photo)**
Odontoglossum, 14, 21, 52, **52,** 86,
   166–68; basic characteristics of, 5
Odontoglossum triumphans, **167**
Odontoglossum Yukon Harbor, **167**
Odontonia George Day, 168
Odontonia Tiger Cub, 168
Oncidesa, 151
Oncidium, 14, 25, 30, **63,** 89, 168–69,
   197, 203; basic characteristics of, 5;
   hybrids, 17
Oncidium henekeni, 17
Oncidium kramerianum, 210
Oncidium lanceanum, 18, **169**
Oncidium onustum, 17
Oncidium ornithorhynchum, 18
Oncidium splendidum, **62,** 75, **192**
Oncidium Star Wars 'Palolo', 13
Opsistylis, 174, 175
Orchids: basic structure of, 2–3;
   beginning a collection, 8–18; cost of,
   11–13; as cut flowers, 234–39;
   glossary, 265–68; growth styles, 3–4;
   introduction to, xi; keeping healthy,
   209–32; light and sunlight, 27–36; list
   of periodicals, 264; photography,
   245–49; popularity of, 6–7; potting,
   48–64; potting materials and methods,
   48–64; propagation, 185–208;
   societies, 241–44; source of supplies,
   254–60; temperature and humidity,
   19–26; watering and fertilizer, 65–71;
   window garden, 72–76; world
   conferences, 24–25
Orchid Biology (ed. Arditti), 197
Organic fertilizers, 71
Ornithocephalus, 17, 170
Osmocote 14-14-14 formula, 70
Osmunda (potting media), 50
Outdoor gardens, 84–91; benches and
   racks, 86–87; climate, 85–86;
   concerns, 90–91; epiphytes, 89–90;
   lath houses, 88; terrestrials, 88;
   weather watch, 86

Paphiopedilum, 2, 26, 30, **55, 57,** 76, 88,
   103–7, **188,** 190, 197, **206,** 234; basic
   characteristics of, 5; containers and
   composts, 104; footcandle ranges, 29;
   hybrids **(color photo);** light, 104;
   measuring system, 11; selections,
   105–6; temperature, 104
Paphiopedilum argus, 106
Paphiopedilum bellatulum, 17, 104, **105,**
   106
Paphiopedilum Clair de Lune, 104
Paphiopedilum concolor, 17, 106

Paphiopedilum Diane, **106**
Paphiopedilum elliottianum, 12
Paphiopedilum fairieanum, 106
Paphiopedilum glaucophyllum, 105
Paphiopedilum godefroyae, 17, 104
Paphiopedilum Maudiae, 104
Paphiopedilum niveum, 17, 104, 106
Paphiopedilum primulinum, 105
Paphiopedilum Transvaal, **105**
Paphiopedilum venustum, 106; **(color photo)**
Paphiopedilum volonteanum, 12
Paphiopedilum Winston Churchill, 106
Periodicals, list of, 264
Peristeria elata, 170
Perlite (potting media), 55
Pest control, 227–29
Petal-spotting, **218**
Phaiocalanthe, 134, 170
Phaius, 88, 170
Phalaenopsis, 2, 3, 22, 26, 39, 53, **55,** 76, 89, 107–12, **108**, 193, 195, 196, 197, **200, 203, 207,** 210, **215,** 218, 223, 225; basic characteristics, 5; **(color photo);** colors, 107–8; culture, 109–10; footcandle ranges, 29; growing tips, 110–11; hybrids with other genera, 110; measuring system, 11; special features, 107; terete species, 112
Phalaenopsis amabilis, 107, 110
Phalaenopsis cornu-cervi, 17, 111, **249**
Phalaenopsis equestris alba, 111
Phalaenopsis fuscata, 110
Phalaenopsis intermedia 'Portei', 111
Phalaenopsis Keith Shaffer, **109**
Phalaenopsis Little Sister, 111
Phalaenopsis lueddemanniana, 107, 111, **111,** 195
Phalaenopsis maculata, 111
Phalaenopsis Pin Up Girl 'Carmen Vazquez', **109**
Phalaenopsis schillerana, 36, 110
Phalaenopsis Talisman Cove, **54,** 262
Phalaenopsis Terry Beth Ballard, 262
Phalaenopsis Tyler Carlson, 111, 262
Phalaenopsis violacea, 110, 111
Phalaenopsis Violet Star, 111
Photography, 245–49; accessories, 247; backgrounds, 248–49; bellows, 247; cases, 247; close-ups, 245–46; daylight, 248; equipment, 245; extension tubes, 247; film choice, 249; lenses (close-focusing), 246; light at home, 248; professional level, 262; small flash units, 248
Phragmipedium, 170–71
Phragmipedium grande, **171**
Physan (fungicide-bactericide), 26, 222
Phytophthora cactorum fungi, 217
Plastic pots, 40–41
Pleione, 86, 172
Pleurothallis, 17, 30, 172, 180, 190
Pollination, 3, 197–203, **198, 199, 201**
Pollinia (flower pollen), **198, 199**
Polypropylene fabric, 31
Polyrrhiza, 30, 172

Polystachya, 172–73
Polystachya phalax 'Spring Hill', **173**
Potinara (*Pot.*), 14
Potinara Fortunes Peak, **218**
Potinara Magic Lamp **(color photo)**
Potinara Mariachi, buds of, **10**
Potinara Neopolitan, **28**
Potting, 48–64; care after, 64; drainage materials, **60;** media, 49–58; mixes, 58–59; preparing the medium, 59–60; repotting, 60–62
Pomenaea, 173
Promenaea Crawshayana, 173
Promenaea stapellioides, 173
Promenaea xanthina, 173
Propagation techniques, 185–208; backbulb growth, 185–86; cloning, 196–97; dividing plants, 186–92; flower stem plantlets, 195–96; by offsets, 193; seed production, 197–203; seed sowing, 204–5
Pseudobulbs, **63;** care of, 214–15
Pseudomonas cattleyae bacteria, 218
Ptychogaster fungi, 219
Pythium ultimum fungi, 217

Redwood bark (potting media), 49
Reflectors, 33
Renantanda Seminole, **116, 194**
Renanthera, 30, 110 , 173–74
Renanthopsis, **61**
Repotting, 60–62; dividing plants, 186–92
Rhynchocentrum, **44**
Rhynchocentrum Sagarik (*Rhy. coelestis* X *Ascocentrum curvifolium*), 174
Rhyncholaelia digbyana, 261
Rhynchorides Blue Princess, **119**
Rhynochostylis, 22, 42, 174–75
Rhynchostylis coelestis, 174–75
Rhynchostylis gigantea, 18, 174
Rhynchostylis gigantea 'Pride of Thailand', 13
Rodriguezia, 18, 153, 175
Rots on new growth, 220–21, **221**
Royal Horticultural Society (RHS), 16
Rust, 219

Saccolabium, 175–76
Saccolabium quisumbingii, 18, **176**
Sarcochilus, 176
Scale insects, 226, **226;** control of, 229
Schafferara Martha Schaffer, **127**
Schombocattleya Trudy Fennell, 177
Schombodiacrium Orchidglade, 178
Schomburgkia, 177–78; *see also* Laelia
Schomburgkia thomsoniana, **177**
Sclerotium rolfsii fungus, 219
Scuticaria, 178
Seed production, 197–203
Seed sowing, 204–5
Shade and shading: greenhouse, 79; window garden, 74–75
Shelves (window), 73
Shield (preparation), 222
Size of plants, 9–11; commercial, 11; compact and miniature species, 17

Snails and slugs, 224–25
Snow mold, 219; control of, 222
Sobralia, 178
Sophrolaelia Psyche 'Talisman Cove',
   179; **(color photo)**
Sophrolaeliocattleya Madge Fordyce
   'Red Orb' **(color photo)**
Sophronitis, 14, 17, 178–79
Southern blight, 219, 222
Southern blight stem rot, **220**
Spathoglottis, 179
Spathoglottis plicata, **180**
Species: compact and miniature, 17–18;
   names of, 13; rare, 12; *see also* names
   of species
Sphagnum moss (potting media), 52
Stanhopea, 18, 30, 179–80
Stelis, 17, 18, 30, 180–81
Subjective beauty, 12
Sun: combining with fluorescents, 33;
   diffusing, 30–31
Supplies, 251–60; shipments from
   abroad, 251–52; shipping methods,
   253–54; source list, 254–60
Sympodial orchids, 3

Temperature and humidity, 19–26; air
   circulation, 25–26; care after potting,
   64; classifications for orchids, 19–20;
   containers and supports, 37–47;
   greenhouse, 79–80; humidity control,
   23–24; microclimates, 20; prolonging
   bloom, 26; range, 20–22; for window
   garden, 72–73
Terete phalaenopsis, 112
Terrestrial orchids, 3–4; potting mixes
   for, 58
Thrips (insects), 227; control of, 229
Timed release chemicals, 70–71
Timers, electric, 35–36
Tobacco mosaic virus, 219
Tree fern (potting media), 50
Tree fern slabs and poles, 47
Trichocentrum, 18, 181

Trichoceros, 181
Trichocidium Elvena, **46, 51, 191**
Trichoglottis, 181
Trichopilia, 181
Trichopilia suavis, **182**
Truban (fungicide), 222
Tuberolabium kotoense, **176**

Vanda, 2, 3, 9, 14, 22, 30, 39, 42, 88,
   89, 110, 112–16, 193, 203, 211, 216,
   234; basic characteristics of, 5;
   flowers, 113; footcandle ranges, 29;
   growing techniques, 113, 114–15; heat
   and humidity, 113; hedge, 85; hybrids,
   91; light and fertilizer, 114; measuring
   system, 11; propagation, 115;
   selections, 115–16
Vandaceous types, 197
Vanda Chavananand **(color photo)**
Vanda coerulea, 113
Vanda cristata, 113
Vanda Jennie Hashimoto, **112**
Vanda sanderana, **114**
Vandopsis, 182
Vanilla, 183
Vanilla planifolia, **183**
Venetian blinds, adjustable, **31**
Ventilation, greenhouse, 80–82
Viral diseases, 219

Watering: general rules for, 65–66;
   outdoor gardens, 86
Weevil, **227**
Whiteflies, control of, 229
Window garden, 72–76, **74;** hanging
   containers, 73; humidity, 72–73;
   indoor compartment, **75;** lighting
   sources, 75–76; shade, 74–75; shelves,
   73
Wooden containers, 45
Wooden slabs and branches, 45–46

Zygopetalum, 18, 184
Zygopetalum crinitum, **184**